GUITAR WOMEN

GUITAR WOMEN

Conversations & Life Lessons with Six-String Heroines

SUE FOLEY

sh.
SUTHERLAND HOUSE

TORONTO, 2026

Sutherland House
416 Moore Ave., Suite 304
Toronto, ON M4G 1C9

First edition, May 2026

If you are interested in inviting one of our authors to a live event or media appearance, please contact sranasinghe@sutherlandhousebooks.com and visit our website at sutherlandhousebooks.com for more information about our authors and their schedules.

We acknowledge the support of the Government of Canada.

Manufactured in Turkey
Cover by Leah Ciani and Jordan Lunn
Cover image by Alan Messer
Book composed by Karl Hunt

Library and Archives Canada Cataloguing in Publication
Title: Guitar women : conversations & life lessons
with six-string heroines / Sue Foley.
Names: Foley, Sue, 1968- author, interviewer
Description: Includes bibliographical references.
Identifiers: Canadiana (print) 20260125555 | Canadiana (ebook) 20260129747 |
ISBN 9781998365302 (hardcover) | ISBN 9781998365319 (EPUB)
Subjects: LCSH: Women guitarists—Interviews. | LCSH: Guitarists—Biography. |
LCSH: Women guitarists—Biography. | LCGFT: Interviews.
Classification: LCC ML399 .F663 2026 | DDC 787.87092/52—dc23

ISBN 978-1-998365-30-2
eBook 978-1-998365-31-9

Contents

Introduction

Every generation has its myths about the guitar—who holds it, who defines it, what it means to play it. For centuries, it's been cast as a man's instrument, a symbol of rebellion and seduction. But the truth is more complicated, and far more beautiful. The guitar doesn't care who's holding it; it only responds to touch, to truth, and to devotion. For me, that devotion became a way of life, and eventually, a question that wouldn't let go. That's where this story begins.

When I began working on this book, my intention was to introduce the *guitar woman* to the world almost like an archetype—a singular figure with a clear set of attributes that could be easily defined and understood. After more than a hundred interviews with my fellow female players, I had to throw that idea out the window. The more women I spoke with, the more this "archetype" slipped through my fingers. What I found instead were entirely unique individuals, each with her own story, background, and way of seeing the world.

Some of the women I spoke with were tomboys; others were unabashedly feminine. Some were married; others were lifelong singles. Some came from affluence; others from poverty. They came from different genres of music, a wide range of cultures, and age groups.

What ties us together is our passion for the guitar, and that's the heartbeat of this story.

It all began with a conversation. In 2001, music journalist Don Wilcock was interviewing me about my latest album. During our talk, he mentioned a biography he had written on blues guitarist Buddy

Guy. Casually, I suggested he write a book about female guitarists. "You know," I said, "like Bonnie Raitt, Nancy Wilson, Ellen McIlwaine . . ." In less than a minute, I'd listed over a dozen women I'd admired for years. It was as if they'd been living in my subconscious all along.

For several days, that conversation lingered. When I searched for books about women guitarists, I realized there weren't any. At best, there were passing mentions, as if the subject were an afterthought. That angered and frustrated me, but it also lit a fire. If no one else had written it, maybe I was meant to. I figured I could just call up some players and talk about random stuff. I had no real agenda except to get deeper into the subject. Most of the guitar literature I'd read up until this time focused primarily on technique and gear. Very little spoke to the actual lives of players. I longed for that kind of story, and for connection.

At the time, I was thirty-three and mostly at home with my four-year-old son. I was a new mother, feeling out of my element. Until then, my life had revolved around music, and my guitar was everything to me. But suddenly, I was grounded—homebound with a young person to care for. I welcomed the change, but I also struggled with this new identity. Motherhood, like music, is all-consuming, but in a completely different way. I'd gone from focusing solely on my career to putting someone else first. I was thrilled to have my son, but I missed being part of the scene. Sometimes it felt like I couldn't have both.

That tension pushed me to seek insight from my sisters in the guitar world. I wanted to know how they managed this life. How did they juggle motherhood, relationships, creativity, health, and the physical toll of being a guitarist? What was it like coming up for them as girls in this male-dominated field? How were they handling aging in a business that worships youth?

Much of my career, I'd felt isolated, often the only woman on the bandstand, traveling with the guys, or hanging out backstage. Many of the women I spoke to echoed this feeling. It's funny to note that we were all on the scene, but we rarely encountered one another. We seemed to be orbiting around like little solo planets.

Over the next decade, I interviewed more than a hundred players, with genres from classical to gutbucket blues to heavy metal. I spoke with elders in the sunsets of their careers and thirteen-year-olds just starting out. Among them were multiple Grammy Award winners and players who rarely ever left their hometowns. I made calls between raising my son, playing shows, and keeping my career alive. Between 2001 and 2011, I collected a treasure trove of interviews, and then I hit a wall.

The sheer volume of material overwhelmed me. I drafted the book several times, but none of the versions felt right. I couldn't seem to shape it. I'd stop and start, over and over, until frustration set in. Part of me feared I was trying to tell too many stories, even my own, before I fully understood them. The *guitar woman* who I had been seeking to nail down began to slip from my grasp.

It was around that time that the scene for women guitarists began to open up in exciting new ways. I noticed more young women emerging as strong, confident players, and a growing body of writing on the subject. Artists like Brittany Howard; Rebecca and Megan Lovell of Larkin Poe; Samantha Fish; Molly Tuttle; and St. Vincent, along with publications such as *She Shreds* and *Guitar Girl Magazine*, were changing both the face and the narrative of women in guitar. I sometimes wondered if my interviews were becoming outdated or even obsolete. That doubt shook my confidence in the project.

As the years went by, a few of the women I'd spoken with passed away. I began to feel the weight of their words and the wisdom they'd shared. It haunted me, but it also kept a light burning. I felt a responsibility to honor their stories. Still, life moved on, and I turned my focus elsewhere.

Eventually, my love of research pulled me into academia, where I discovered how scholarship and storytelling could merge with my life as a musician. I earned my MA in music composition and began to find confidence as a writer. In 2020, *Guitar Player* magazine featured me, along with many of the women I'd interviewed, in a special issue dedicated to female guitarists. I reached out to Editor-in-Chief Christopher Scapelliti to see if they'd publish portions of my interviews. They agreed, and for a while, I wrote a column called *The Foley Files*. I also re-enrolled in school, this time pursuing a PhD.

I got accepted into the doctoral program at York University in Toronto, focusing on the female pioneers of the guitar. I did more research and created the 2024 album *One Guitar Woman* as part of my dissertation. That album explored the lives of women who paved the way for all of us—Memphis Minnie, Maybelle Carter, Sister Rosetta Tharpe, Elizabeth Cotten, and others. I studied their stories and learned their distinct playing styles. The project led to a Grammy nomination, several awards, and a one-woman show that's been deeply fulfilling.

While promoting *One Guitar Woman*, Canadian journalist Deirdre Kelly was hired to write a biography for my press kit. During our interview, I told her about this book idea I'd been chipping away at for years. She suggested I speak to her publisher, Ken Whyte, at Sutherland House. When I reached out, he was immediately interested. After sending Ken my work, we decided to focus the book on twenty-five interviews highlighting the trailblazing women who shaped the path for today's fertile scene. It was a number that felt digestible and meaningful, and it aligned perfectly with my previous work on the pioneers.

Many of these interviews were conducted nearly two decades ago. While the cultural landscape has continued to evolve, they remain grounded in the moment they were recorded. What appears here is a curated selection from a much larger archive, shaped by time, access, and the practical limits of a single volume. It is not intended as a definitive or complete record, but as part of an ongoing project that continues to evolve.

What you'll find in this book is a look into the unique lives of uncompromising individuals who see the world in their own way and choose to express that vision through the guitar. The guitar woman cannot be pinned down or easily defined, but she's real. She's powerful. She's soulful. And she runs deep.

I'm humbled to help share her story.

Sue Foley
October 18, 2025
Austin, Texas

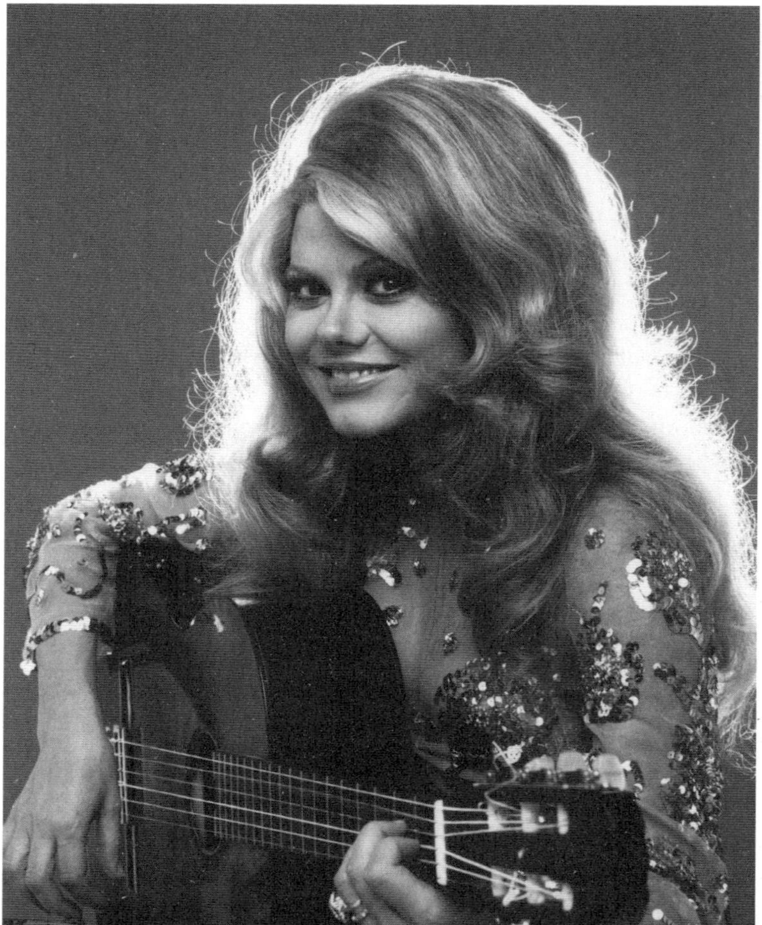

Charo

CHARO

I can't recall the first time I saw Charo, but I know I was very young. A mainstay on American variety shows from the mid-1960s to the 1980s, Charo was impossible to miss. And once she appeared, you couldn't look away. Her stage presence was captivating, and at times dizzying. She was a whirlwind of energy, enthusiasm, cheekiness, and magnetic charisma. Everyone loved Charo!

For a little girl lost in music and escapism, Charo was a dream come true. Her bouncy blonde hair, thick Spanish accent, and mastery of flamenco guitar seemed otherworldly. She could hold her own with top entertainers of the era, from Sammy Davis Jr. to Johnny Carson. But, it was when she picked up her guitar that she was transformed into a serious, creative, and profound artist. She was the first woman I saw who could truly play the guitar, and by play, I mean command the instrument, her fingers dancing up and down the neck, fretting and executing intricate lead runs. I projected all my aspirations onto Charo, and she responded beautifully, showing me that someone like me could aspire to be like her. Watching her sparked a lifelong fascination with Spanish nylon-string and flamenco guitar.

Born María Rosario Pilar Martínez Molina Baeza in Murcia, Spain, Charo learned the art of flamenco guitar from Romani musicians who camped on her grandparents' farm during the summers. Her journey was far from easy. After her father, a prominent lawyer, fled Spain under mysterious circumstances, Charo, her older sister, and their mother were left homeless and destitute. Yet despite these hardships, her prodigious talent earned her a place at Andrés Segovia's prestigious guitar school for underprivileged children, where she flourished as a classical guitar prodigy.

As a teenager, Charo became a recording artist and caught the attention of bandleader Xavier Cugat. Their marriage, despite a significant age gap, catapulted her career. She traveled to Las Vegas with Cugat's band, eventually becoming a headlining act in the city's top hotels and casinos. Around this time, her catchphrase "cuchi-cuchi" became a pop culture phenomenon, helping to cement her star status and unforgettable persona.

Charo later divorced Cugat and married Swedish businessman Kjell Rasten, with whom she had a son in the late 1970s. They relocated to Hawaii, where she produced and starred in the variety show *Tropical Heat*. By then, Charo was already a fixture on American television, gracing programs like *Sonny and Cher*, *The Love Boat*, and *The Carol Burnett Show*. In more recent years, she's appeared on *Dancing with the Stars*, *Jane the Virgin*, *Celebrity Wife Swap*, and was a beloved guest on *RuPaul's Drag Race*, where her signature blend of wit and resilience has endeared her to a new generation.

Today, her exact age remains a mystery; guesses about her birthdate range from 1941 to 1951, but her impact is beyond dispute. Twice named "Best Flamenco Guitarist" by *Guitar Player* magazine, she continues to command a devoted international following. In addition to her musical achievements, Charo is an outspoken animal rights activist, with her efforts contributing to the ban on bullfighting in Catalonia.

What strikes me most about Charo is her complexity. On stage, she embodies the exuberant entertainer, playful, extroverted, even self-deprecating in her portrayal of a "silly blonde" with her "cuchi-cuchi" persona. But behind the performance is a deeply intelligent, fiercely disciplined artist. Her guitar playing, shaped by thousands of solitary hours spent mastering classical and flamenco techniques, reveals a more introspective side. I've often wondered if her comedic act serves as a kind of Trojan horse, luring audiences in so she can reveal her truest self through music. If so, she's a master trickster, subverting expectations while showcasing her extraordinary artistry.

It's interesting to note how she bridges two worlds: the precise, structured discipline of classical guitar and the raw, improvisational spirit of flamenco. Most players specialize in one or the other; few move so fluidly between the two. Classical guitarists often struggle with improvisation, while flamenco artists rarely read music. Charo does both effortlessly.

She was my first female guitar hero, and, fittingly, the final interview I conducted for this book. Speaking with her was a dream come true.

CHARO

— *The Interview* —

[2020]

C: Okay, I'm ready. Tadah! Olah! Cómo estás?

SF: There she is!

C: Woohoo! Okay, well, listen. I am very happy to talk to you.

SF: How are you?

C: I am extremely, extremely happy to be alive, extremely grateful to God that he gives me both the energy and the ambition to keep it going every day. To me, it's a new day, and every day I'm hoping for the best. I have a choice. People all have a choice: either suffer and cry—which, many days, you will have it like that—or try to find something positive from that darkness and revive it. The one thing that's saving me is the music. Normally, you will find me in this studio—it's very cute—and find me playing guitar, playing a scale, or writing something. Instead of taking sleeping pills, my trick is *musica*. I get myself to play guitar or a scale and everything, and then I feel better and I go to my bedroom and I sleep. So, *musica* is a lifesaver.

SF: You're a huge influence on me. I usually play electric guitar. I saw you when I was young, and growing up it meant so much to me. My family all play guitar—my father and my three brothers—and I was the only girl who played guitar. I never saw another woman do it until you. It meant so much to me.

C: We women, until now, have been repressed of our potential. There was a time when my grandpa would say, "*a mujer y la sartén en la cocina a la que pertenecen*." In English: The woman and the pan, in the kitchen where they belong (*laughs*). Well, the new generation, they thought, "No way!" Give an education to a woman and she can do both things, be in the kitchen and cook for her family, but pursue her dreams. We were all born with the *consciente* to be a mother, so the best thing happening in the movement right now, is to see women running for politics, running for everything they want to do in their lives. And in your case, music!

I studied when I was very young, first with gypsies. My grandparents had a farm, and my grandma welcomed the gypsies. They'd come and they'd eat whatever food they could get. My grandma always gave them potatoes and bread. She was a very generous woman. She didn't know how to write or to read. Remember *Gone with the Wind*, when she says, "I swear I will never be hungry again?" My grandma said, "I swear that my grandchildren will go to a school. They will have an education. They will be independent." My grandmother was ahead of everything that is going on right now. She belongs in 2020. She worked very hard for our education.

So, in the summers, we grew up with the gypsies on the farm, and they teach me how to play flamenco. At the age of seven or eight, I was doing *bulerías* [flamenco rhythms], but I never was allowed to study with a pick. Then at the age nine going on ten, I went to Madrid, and over there I was lucky enough to learn classical. But the gypsies gave me the foundation for that freedom and beautiful modulation that you don't learn in school.

[The school] was promoted and paid for by Andrés Segovia, the greatest guitarist in Spain, but we never saw him on a daily basis. We were lucky if we could see him once every month. That was a miracle!

I remember he said, "Don't play by my technique, play from your heart." Right now, he would get very mad if I was in this position holding the guitar (*points to her crossed legs*). He would get pissed off. He wants you to sit down in a real chair and hold it like the men do it. But I find my way to look cute and play the guitar in Las Vegas. Because in Las Vegas you cannot sit down and play the way that they do where you can hardly see their face (*she pretends to hunch her body over a guitar*) holding and embracing the guitar. I find a way to play the guitar by sitting on a stool, where I can put the angle I hold it for a personal appearance—a spectacular way.

Anyway, one day a student caught me with a pick. I still have not forgotten that day. He was so mad. He said, "Get out of here. Shame on you. You are trespassing!" And now when I see the pick, I think, Oh no! I'm gonna get it again. When you stop learning with a pick and move to your fingers, you have the world in your hand. By doing it with my fingers and reach[ing] the speed, you can't have [that] with the pick. It takes practice, practice, practice. A lot of scales, day and night. And even when I'm traveling. When I'm in the hotels, I put a lot of napkins between the strings and the arm so I can practice without somebody in the next room knocking on the door, "What the hell are you doing?" It used to be like that (*laughs*). I would be practicing, and I would get calls to my room, "You're making too much noise." Because I'm a night person.

The way they teach me, you never see your thumb. God forbid. Because your thumb is giving you the strength to do like this (*mimes holding a guitar neck*). That's for rock and roll. You will never ever see me with a pick or doing this (*sticks out thumb*). It's passion and practice. Two Ps. No, it's passion and practice. And that is my secret, girl.

Segovia, his famous phrase, "If you don't practice for a week and you make a mistake, nobody is going to know. If you don't practice for two weeks nobody's going to know it, but if you don't practice for a whole month, the whole world will know it."

It's difficult for a girl. I don't know. You have babies? My life changed when I had a baby. I used to practice with my belly like a watermelon. When I had it like that, I could hardly reach the strings. And practice over and over. When you don't see, you concentrate more on what you hear. There was this composer, [Joaquín] Rodrigo. He was blind. He was not able to see the world like you and me, and that's why he was able to compose "Concierto de Aranjuez." Aranjuez, that is a small, little town outside Madrid that's famous for having a lot of roses. You open your window on your balcony and the aroma of roses comes to your room, and you feel like you are in the middle of a garden. "Concierto de Aranjuez" has been done by every guitar player. You've got to do it. It's our religion.

SF: Is that your favorite piece to play?

C: (*nods*) There was a time when I was younger—now I am changing my mind—that I said when I am dying, please play for me "Concierto de Aranjuez" because it's bigger than life. But now that I'm getting older, when I die, I want to play "Cuchi-Cuchi." Salsa salsa (*laughs*). But to be serious, the biggest masterpiece in my opinion is "Concierto de Aranjuez."

Spanish musicians, a century and a half ago, they don't have to pay bills. They don't have to pay taxes. Their music was very rich and spectacular because they did not have the tremendous stresses that now we are living. If you go back one hundred and fifty years ago, you went to see the incredible opera, that was the time when there were composers, when there was no stress, problems, depression. Those composers were always protected by rich people, or sometimes the king or the queen, and they made those incredible masterpieces that will live forever and ever.

I know when I'm finished talking to you, you're going to say, "Well, let's see if she's right." You're going to get home, you're going to call me—I'll give you my number—and you're going to say, "Charo, you were right!" You're going to sit down, have a glass of wine, and listen to the whole piece of "Concierto de Aranjuez," and then you're going to say, "That's beautiful." You're going to pick up your guitar, which I can see from here, and you're going to play

SF: I'd love that! So, how much do you practice right now, Charo?

C: More than when I was on the road. When you're on the road traveling, you get to thinking, *Okay, what kind of audience am I going to play for tonight? Are they classical? Are they conservative? Are they young and wild?* So you prepare the costume and the material for this audience. You don't stick to your routine. If you want to be a performer—even if you're already a great musician—be open-minded for the audience that is watching, and for your heart. Then you make them very happy, and you're also happy. When I'm on the road, I don't have the time to practice like I have it now. Instead of crying, being depressed, being worried, I practice more. Especially at night. And I am getting faster than I used to be maybe ten months ago.

SF: How do you practice? What do you do?

C: A scale. All the scales. Up and down, up and down in every fret. One and two and three and four and one and two and three and four. And then I try to time it in the down beat with the scale. Now, when I establish that rhythm, the scale that I'm going to play matches in the down beat, so the melody is going to marry in a perfect frame of the *bulerías*, which is the most difficult and number-one flamenco. When I teach children at the university between engagements, I don't give them the fun. Even if you don't like it: the scale. Discipline and scales.

Segovia congratulated me once, when I played "Romance of Love," because although I was like this (*sits up straight*) in a beautiful, beautiful dress and my hair like that, the way that I was playing, he said, "I am proud of you because you don't want to bore the audience. You want to play beautiful because it's a priority." I practiced and I was able to do it like this. Again, the two Ps, and maybe a little bit of talent (*laughs*).

But trust me, I'm proud to talk to you because you are a girl, and you're telling me all your family play music. Probably, they said, "What is she doing? Why does she want to play music?" I'm proud of you. Don't take anything for negative. Treat the guitar like it's a piece of jewelry, and the two Ps. Practice. Passion. The talent? If I have talent, thank God. But talent has to be helped by practice.

SF: Do you work on new songs too, or are you comfortable with the material you've been doing?

C: When you perform as much as I do, you have to know in your mind what is the most popular. I'm in Vegas, or today I'm in New York, or today I'm going to be in Miami. Because the personality of the audience you're going to get is telling you what you should play. Don't stick all the time with the same thing. Be yourself, but once in the while do something you know the audience is there to listen to. The one that I play if I want a huge applause, "La Malagueña" in flamenco. That's for when I am in trouble. When they're applauding but they aren't going "yeahh," that's when I turn around to my musicians and say, "Plan B!" (*starts singing the notes to "La Malagueña"*) But for me not to get bored playing the same "Malagueña," I sometimes surprise the musicians and make a different scale to challenge myself, and then for me it's very exciting. The melody is very pure, but sometimes I do a little something. But I've gotta tell you, "Malagueña" is a huge success. It's lifesaving. "Concierto de Aranjuez," they will love it. They will stop breathing when you perform it. You can hear a pin dropping.

SF: Do you perform "Concierto de Aranjuez"?

C: Yes, when I have the time—because the real *concierto* "Concierto de Aranjuez" is pushing fifteen minutes. But the middle part, that is spectacular. Listen to the middle part from Narciso Yepes. The guitar is singing from the heart. Also! Can you see me? (*holds out hands*) I have so much callous here, I can poke a needle and blood will not come out! And you will never hear me with a slicer. *Eeeee* (*pretends to run her finger down a guitar string*). You will never hear me doing that. No! Don't do that. Please! You hold it strong beneath the fingernail and tip.

SF: Are you talking about the sound going from string to string?

C: All of the slicer. You've got to practice your slicer between the fingernail and the tip. I don't know how you say in English. It slips smooth like a glove and people cannot hear the *eeeeee*. So, practice that.

SF: Ah, okay (*laughs*).

C: I have to go now because I have another Zoom about paella. A lot of people are wondering, "Oh, how can she make the paella?" I'm going to be changing into another costume. But you're beautiful. I can see. Beautiful! I can see clearly that the world is in your hands. You have already a good foundation: your family and how you start with rock and roll. So, you are not afraid of the pick.

And the PP: practice, passion. When you get mad at your boyfriend, when you have a bad day and want to cry and feel sorry, find a place to play where people can't bother you. Practice and create it—even if you practice for one person, practice for *you*! And play for you. Each person, from me to you. I connect it from my heart to the person. It's you. It's not for the theatre or people. Play for you. From heart to heart.

SF: Thank you.

C: This call is to be continued! I wish you the best, okay? Now I'm going to change, be chef cuchi-cuchi, and teach people how to cook paella, the recipe of my sister.

SF: One more question: does your sister play guitar?

C: My sister is the biggest singer in the world, but she don't play guitar. People don't know her. She's very famous in her art, in her own music, and she's a hell of a singer. I want to accompany her in some flamenco songs. She is definitely a unique flamenco singer, but she's shy. When I play my guitar, I hear from so far away her voice singing so beautiful. She closes her eyes and transports herself in a world of her imagination. But she is the best singer I ever hear. Definitely in the category of Whitney Houston and—oh, what is the name of the girl? I can't remember but she's a very good friend of mine, that did the *Grease*.

SF: Olivia!

C: Yes! Olivia Newton-John! Listen careful how she sings. She have a perfect pitch, and she sings soft like velvet. I'd be very honored to play the guitar for her. And we're going to get together and we want to change the world in a positive way. Talking about that, I love to talk to you and you're beautiful! Listen, follow my rule. The two Ps: passion and practice. We will be in contact again. Take care of yourself and (*blows kisses*) keep it going. Don't let anybody bother you with any negativity!

SF: Thank you!

C: You welcome! You're beautiful. Then I will teach you how to do paella with a recipe, okay? *Buenas tardes, amiga. Hasta pronto* (*blows kiss*).

SF: Bye! *Gracias!*

C: *Gracias!*

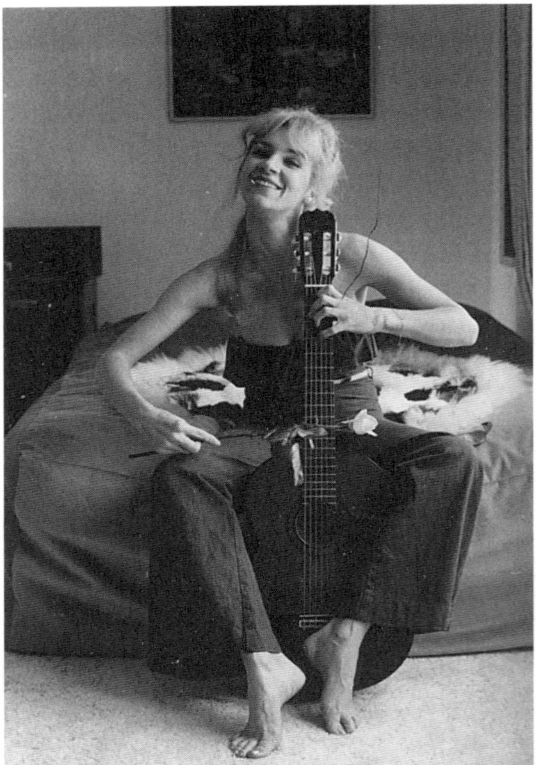

Liona Boyd

LIONA BOYD

The 1970s were the era of the guitar. Few sounds were more powerful than the scream of an electric guitar through a cranked amplifier. My brothers had them, Fender Strats and Gibson Les Pauls, which they turned up loud whenever my parents were out of earshot. My father, on the other hand, played acoustic guitars, using them for songs and storytelling, classic troubadour stuff.

In the world I knew, the guitar scene was dominated by men. My father's folk and country records, featuring George Jones, Hank Williams, and the Clancy Brothers, were ever-present around the house. But it was my brothers' music, and the posters on their bedroom walls, that shaped my view of the guitar. There were images of Led Zeppelin's Jimmy Page, Jimi Hendrix, Eric Clapton, and ZZ Top. These men weren't just holding guitars; they were living through them. The instrument was an extension of their bodies, a phallic symbol, a power tool, a scepter. It radiated energy and charisma. They were larger than life, the guitar gods.

Around the middle of that decade, I became aware of Liona Boyd. Her debut album, *The Guitar*, came out in 1974, and she quickly became a household name in Canada. Liona was a regular on Canadian TV specials and variety shows throughout the next two decades, and she made a striking impression. She would step onto the stage in long, romantic gowns, her flowing blonde hair draped gracefully over her shoulders. She was beautiful, ethereal, and untouchable, completely absorbed in her music. In her hands, the guitar became something else entirely, not a tool of rebellion or masculine power, but an instrument of love, beauty, and romance. It carried a different kind of strength, one of vulnerability, surrender, and seduction.

Liona Boyd's influence on me was profound. She was one of the first women I ever saw playing the guitar, and she did it without conforming to the rough, aggressive styles of the time. She played softly, fully embracing her femininity. She showed me that strength could look different, and she held a special place in my heart as part of my Canadian heritage.

Though Liona was born in London, she moved to Canada as a child and became a prominent figure in Canadian music. Known as the "First Lady of Guitar," she has released twenty-eight albums, won five JUNO Awards (Canada's equivalent of the Grammy), and received numerous honors, including five honorary doctorates, the Order of Canada, the Order of Ontario, and the Diamond Jubilee Medal. She has performed for royalty, presidents, prime ministers, and other world leaders, while also raising millions of dollars for charitable causes.

Liona's music, rooted in Latin compositions such as "La Malagueña," "Carretera Libertad," and "Torbellino," added to her allure for me. Her sound evoked adventure and escape, conjuring images of far-off, exotic places. Her life reflects that same nomadic spirit, constantly moving and reinventing herself. Over the years, she has shifted between coastal homes in Canada and the United States, laying down roots and pulling them up at will. When we spoke in 2006, she was finalizing her divorce from Florida real estate developer John B. Simon. She sounded resolute, even relieved, ready to reclaim her name and the freedom to play her guitar at 2:00 a.m. if she wanted to. Her private life has long fascinated Canadians, especially after her memoir revealed an eight-year affair with former Prime Minister Pierre Elliott Trudeau.

After a six-year hiatus from music due to musician's focal dystonia, Liona redefined her approach to the guitar, incorporating singing into her performances. She has since expanded beyond classical guitar, exploring folk and world music. Today, she maintains an active touring and recording schedule and stays connected with her fans through social media.

Liona Boyd taught me that you do not have to abandon your femininity to assert power in the world. Her life is a testament to the fact that rebellion, adventure, and ambition can take many forms, even ones as graceful and delicate as hers.

LIONA BOYD

— *The Interview* —

[2006]

SF: I've been wanting to talk to you ever since I started this project. I used to see you on TV all the time when I was growing up. When I'm doing these interviews, I'll often ask women what female guitar players they were seeing on the scene growing up. I was seeing you.

LB: Alice Artzt. That's all I saw as far as women. And Ida Presti.

SF: Ida Presti?

LB: I saw her in concert a couple of times. She was the most brilliant virtuoso guitar player. She was famous for having the most amazing, amazing technique. And she was really the one that started that playing on right side of the nail. It wasn't [Presti's partner Alexandre] Lagoya.

She died tragically in Rochester, New York. She taught Alice Artzt. Then I took master classes with Alice Artzt. I don't know if you know her. She doesn't play anymore.

We were really different personalities, like opposite, and yet we've been great friends all these years. She always used to say to me, "Liona, I'm sure you're just going to get married and have kids." She still sends me emails all the time. She never became hugely famous around the world, yet she played everywhere. She did concerts in every little [American] embassy from Africa to wherever. She was very intellectual and preferred slightly more skilled contemporary pieces than me. I was into the mushy, romantic, Spanish stuff. But she was a good role model. She was the only woman that I used to see. Sometimes I would go and stay with her when I was in New York.

And there was another woman guitarist who's quite well known, called Sharon Isbin. We were the three best-known guitar ladies. Sharon was just getting started then. We went to visit Sharon at her apartment. I remember we took a picture; I wish we still had it. I don't know what happened to it. We did connect way back; it must have been in the late '70s early '80s in New York.

Alice would come to Toronto [to] give classes, when I was like eighteen, nineteen. She signed with two of the little labels that were always going bankrupt, poor thing, and never really made it internationally. Then I signed with London Records and then CBS, so I somehow had a lot of international things happening. Sharon started coming on the scene later than me, but she's particularly known for concertos and seems to do really well both teaching and touring. So, my hat's off to her. I know how hard it is.

SF: You've had an amazing international career, though.

LB: Yes, I've been very lucky.

SF: One thing about Ida Presti before we move on, when I talked to Sharon, she said that Ida was actually the better guitar player in the duo with Lagoya. People used to say that she was the more natural guitar player.

LB: Yeah, I can believe that. She started when she was very, very young, which always gives somebody a slightly more natural technique than you and I who started when we were thirteen. I don't know what age she started, five or six. But listen, they were a great duo because Lagoya arranged a lot of the music. She was an amazing player, and the guitar world really had a big loss when she died.

SF: Do you spend a lot of time practicing?

LB: Oh, every day.

SF: Have you ever had any physical problems from playing guitar so much, like physical problems, or, you just were taught well?

LB: No, I took a year off and then started touring again. I had tendonitis in my left hand when I started playing again. It was really painful. I would wake up in the morning and couldn't feel either of my hands. They'd be numb. It was from pressing too hard on the bar chords. I think I was pinching a nerve, too. Being a guitar player, if you get tense, it's not good for the hands. I had taken my year sabbatical and then suddenly [was] thrust in front of thousands of people.

SF: Do you do anything special to keep yourself calm under all these traveling conditions?

LB: I do deep breathing, yoga breaths. I've always believed in exercise. I walk twice around my island every day, that's good exercise, [both] in general, [and] because I'm getting older. I used to get away with doing absolutely nothing. The only exercise I got for years was running to catch planes in airports or lifting my guitar case; that was about it. I eat very well; I'm a vegetarian.

SF: When you were growing up, besides those few women you mentioned, you must have felt like an anomaly.

LB: It's a man's world.

SF: And how did you get comfortable in this male world of guitar? Did you find you ever had to assert yourself?

LB: No, I just took it for granted that there weren't too many women and that I can't really dwell on it too much. All the businesspeople I was meeting at record companies were mostly men; there were very few women that I dealt with.

I went up and did my thing, made my records with different producers and different artists. I knew it was an advantage at certain times:

I probably got on more magazine covers, whatever. And I was a bit of a pioneer in some things, like that calendar I did, it got too much flak from the record company. They wouldn't release my next record. It's so ridiculous. Now when I see how they market classical musicians and every Latin artist has calendars like you wouldn't believe, but I guess I was just ahead of my time.

SF: It also struck me that you're very feminine. Most of the women I have talked to are very, not to say masculine, but tomboyish, or that side of their personality is very developed.

LB: That's true.

SF: And you still have maintained this very feminine aura, which is unique.

LB: That's what people tell me. They say it should have toughened me up, this guitar world. But my basic personality is always the same. I'm not that strong, tough woman. I'm a romantic.

SF: But there must be something very tough inside you to have given you this drive.

LB: Well, not always, it's very hard. I wish I had had a really tough manager who could have done international things, but so much of the weight was on my own shoulders, even now. I have a good manager/agent for Canada, but he is only involved with the concerts. He does my bookings, but everything else I'm handling myself. I have to make a decision when I'll tour, what pieces I'll do. I'm my own record company, which has the advantage that you can do what you want, but the disadvantage that you have to pay for everything.

I'm working on a new album; I don't know when it will come out exactly or how to promote it. *Camino Latino* came out in the States, but because I didn't have a band, I wasn't able to tour and promote it. It is mentally frustrating for me that this album hasn't got pushed anywhere because it's just not practical. As you know, when you travel with seven people, the costs are crazy.

I guess I was spoiled all those years, going solo. And that's really what I'm doing, still will be again, not with a whole big group—which is problematic. I just don't want to have to go through that, of putting a band together here in Miami. Believe me, I thought of that when I first came here; that was my intention. [But the] ethical economics of it don't really make sense. I get better as I do a tour, [so to] get everything ready and just do like two three shows doesn't really make sense. That's why TV is really good. There's time for other things in life. Finally, I'm getting to smell the roses a little bit before they lop them over the top of the casket.

SF: I was reading your convocation speech that you wrote when you received your honorary law degree. You have such a natural way of seeing things: follow your dreams and be passionate. It seems to me you've just stuck to what you've believed in from the start.

LB: Yes. Actually, I hope to continue being somewhat of a role model in that. I've gone out after my dreams, and it was never easy doing that. It's easier just to follow in somebody else's footsteps.

SF: Are you staying in Miami?

LB: Yeah, I love it here. I used to hate Florida. Now, Miami is like a Latin American city. I speak Spanish and I love being in that Latin environment. Not just for the weather. It's just great. You can sleep in your underwear all day. You don't even have to bother getting dressed. The weather is perfect all year, except the summer.

SF: I know about your affinity for Latin culture. You've got Spanish heritage?

LB: I lived in Mexico, and that's probably where it started. There's a Spanish connection with my father's family, but I've always loved the language and the music.

SF: Why does the whole Latin thing resonate so heavily for you? It seems to be more of an influence than your English heritage.

LB: If I could explain that—I don't know; it's just something. I love the language; I love the rhythm; I love the like ambient music too. I have several friends from Peru. I have friends from all over Latin America.

I think it must be in a past life, I can't explain it, but when I think back, that was always the music that I loved the most, the Spanish and the Latin. I played Bach and all the early music. But this just had more passion, more emotion, and it just drew me. It touched my soul more than the more restrained, less emotional music.

And I know my audience particularly likes it. The album that seems to outsell everything these days is called *The Spanish Album* [1998]. That's a very boring title, [but] that one outsells everything on Amazon, outsells everything on my site, so it's obviously not just me who is attracted to Spanish music. It's just exotic. There's a romance to it.

I've never been a flamenco player, never really got my left side really happening that well. I mean, I fake my way through "Granada" and "La Malaguena," pseudo-flamenco pieces, but it's really not true flamenco. That's why when *Camino Latino* came out [in 2005], I said it's not flamenco, so I sort of coined the term nuevo-flamenco Latino, which is really what it is. It has Latin influences, but it is not pure Latin. It's my interpretation of Latin.

SF: And it has some pop influences, too.

LB: Oh, absolutely.

SF: When you're composing your own stuff, do you write it all out?

LB: There's different ways; sometimes it's not one set way. Sometimes I'll painstakingly write it all out; other times I'll just tape it and write it out later, just basically the chords. It's a pain in the neck to sit down and write everything, and then I'm not always good at writing all the rhythms, then I'll have someone else help me write it out exactly correctly. I wasn't even encouraged to write my own music, almost discouraged, at university level, [by] my own teachers.

SF: I thought it was funny in your book how you kept getting that reference from teachers saying, "Well, you're going to be a teacher," and you're like, "No, I want to be a concert performer."

LB: And that's true. I ran into that quite a lot and still do sometimes. But I can't take it so seriously. It's ridiculous.

SF: Do you think it's just because you're a woman?

LB: Yeah, exactly. Without the long blonde hair or something, maybe they would have taken me seriously. But they didn't. I didn't have the image that they would have taken seriously.

SF: Right, but it seems like you have a lot of drive.

LB: I still do.

SF: And a lot of courage.

LB: You don't know half of it. I came to Miami knowing nobody. I started a whole new life and it was hard. Believe me, sometimes I've got to be crying, thinking, *Aye, what have I done?* It's not always quite as easy as it looks. And the business kind of drives you crazy. It eats up so much time. I continue to get swamped with fan mail from all over. That's my biggest challenge, finding enough time for my music every day. Playing gets shipped to the end of the day, and that's what we really live for. Then I'm like tired, and its midnight, and I want to play, and I think, *ugh*.

When you're younger, the days seem so much longer. Now it's very difficult to get in as much music, but I make a point of doing that now. I've got kind of system that I do my exercise, I go on my walks, I sit down and do the guitar before the phone starts ringing, then come 9:00 I'm sunk, the phone's going, and I've got a lot of business stuff to do. And trying to have a social life, too. It's hard to pack everything in.

SF: Have you been a loner a lot of your life?

LB: Yeah, in a way. It probably suits me better living alone right now, because at least I can play guitar at 2:00 in the morning if I want. I don't have a husband saying, "Why aren't you in bed?" So yeah, I'm actually enjoying that aspect of it.

SF: You mentioned your marriage breaking up, and your husband saying that you were married to your guitar.

LB: Right, it was my decision, but anyway, I don't want to get too personal here. Basically, what I'm trying to say is everything always comes secondary to my music. It's always number one in my life.

SF: And it's always been that way?

LB: It still is. For a lot of artists, it's just that way. People that aren't musicians don't really understand that, and my husband was jealous of my guitar. But what can you do? It's like an extension of me. I'm sure you feel the same way.

SF: I couldn't possibly give it up, not for anybody.

LB: And if somebody asked you to, you'd grow to resent that.

SF: Definitely. I think you've been a very influential person for other women in the guitar world.

LB: Why, thank you, that's one of my life missions.

SF: You were definitely in my psyche my whole life. You influenced me because of what you did. You had a high profile. You were out there.

LB: Why, thank you—that's really meaningful to me. Sometimes I think that it's so fulfilling that I had touched people in that way, so my music has reached out, and I don't even know unless people call me or tell me that. Who knows?

SF: From what I read in your first book, it sounded like you had a great upbringing and great parents.

LB: Yeah. My mother helped me a lot. They were really encouraging in many ways, [but] very often I heard, "Aw, forget it, you'll never do that. You'll never succeed, like what are you trying for?" They didn't understand I'm the one that was always ambitious, and both my mother and my father would always say, "Why don't you just have a nice calm life?" My mother would step up to help me, but she always thought I was a bit crazy.

So it wasn't like they were, "Yeah, go for it." They were always pulling me back, like, "Don't do the popular music" and "stay classical." I remember reading an interview with Nana Mouskouri and her parents wanted her to be an opera singer, the same sort of thing. When I look back, I pushed ahead anyway. And my parents did not always, I mean when I did the *Persona* tour [in 1986, a rock hybrid album] they were horrified.

SF: I got a different impression, you guys seem like a close family, because you traveled together and stuff.

LB: Yeah, some ways, but some [other] ways we're very different. I have been very lucky that my mother, certainly in my early career was very supportive, traveled with me, did everything to try and help—all the time saying, "You shouldn't be doing this; it's too much." But I pushed myself.

SF: And did they ever change? Like, after the fifth JUNO or whatever?

LB: No. They're still saying, "Come live in Canada. What are you doing down there? You'll never do it."

SF: What do you think is the biggest misconception people have about you?

LB: Maybe people think because I have this image of being sort of ethereal and distant, or being up on the stage, that I'm not approachable. But I'm just a real person, you know. I haven't in any way changed since I was a kid really. I'm not a diva; I'm not a prima-donna. I never have been. So maybe some people might have that impression. What the heck? Now anybody can reach me, but I don't want to encourage anybody else to reach me.

SF: You're a very beautiful woman and you've been beautiful your whole life. Do you ever think that was kind of a setback in a way?

LB: Yeah, it was.

SF: In the way people perceived you?

LB: Exactly, a lot of times people didn't take me seriously, or they thought I was cashing in on my looks or that I was taking advantage of pretty blonde hair or something. Heck, I probably did cash in on my looks—you know, I sat on the white horse [on the cover of *The Best of Liona Boyd*]. But that's what I love about the Latin world, because it's all so natural there. Women are supposed to be beautiful and sexy. My mother says, "Why are you worrying about this? Just be natural and don't worry about image," but to me that's all part of it. That's what gives me pleasure.

SF: It's definitely part of who you are.

LB: Somehow, they think that I'm vain. I'm really not. I'm my own worst critic, believe me. I'm really not obsessed with looks or anything like that, but I think it's part of the whole thing when you're on a stage. You have to make an effort to look nice. And in the Latin world they totally understand that—I mean the women go overboard, I wouldn't go to the efforts they do.

They somehow celebrate it more; you're supposed to be sexy at night if you're a Latin performer, and it doesn't matter if you're young or old. If you got it, flaunt it, that type of philosophy. Whereas being Canadian . . .

SF: You're supposed to play it down.

LB: Down, yeah, it's like the British heritage.

SF: Do you ever wonder why more women don't pursue the guitar over other instruments?

LB: I know why they don't: because it's very difficult. They can't find the time. Most women are not as obsessive as men. Don't you find that? You've got to be a little obsessed to play guitar. You've got to have a lot of drive, and a lot women would rather be possibly the girlfriends. They just don't push themselves quite as much as men.

You see the difference in the male brain and the female brain, men are able [to] focus much more and really push through on something, whereas women often get distracted. Just a different type of brain we have. So that's probably it. And also a lot of women maybe start out with ideas of doing concerts or doing recording and they get distracted with boyfriends and families and kids—and you can't blame them. I mean, there is no other reason why women shouldn't be just as plentiful as men in the guitar world or in any musical instrument.

SF: Guitar is still kind of macho, too.

LB: Yeah, there is standard I guess that women more or less play piano or sing. Guitar is still a man's world in many ways. Maybe they perfected it. The guitar is like a feminine type of instrument, maybe it draws men more to it than women. It's even shaped like a woman. Women, it's not that they don't love the guitar, but we don't have that same obsessive personality—not that I'm really obsessive. I spend hours talking to my girlfriends and all kinds of other things. In life I'm not as obsessed as I used to be, but when I think back to my other career, I was slightly obsessive. You can tell from my book that I never lacked for boyfriends.

But I'm trying to juggle about four down here as well.

SF: Oh boy.

LB: Trying to do guitar, exercise, and to eat. I mean this is like a feat for me; there's just so many interesting people to meet and shows and concerts and producers and musical events. I shouldn't complain; I mean, I'm very lucky to have my freedom back again.

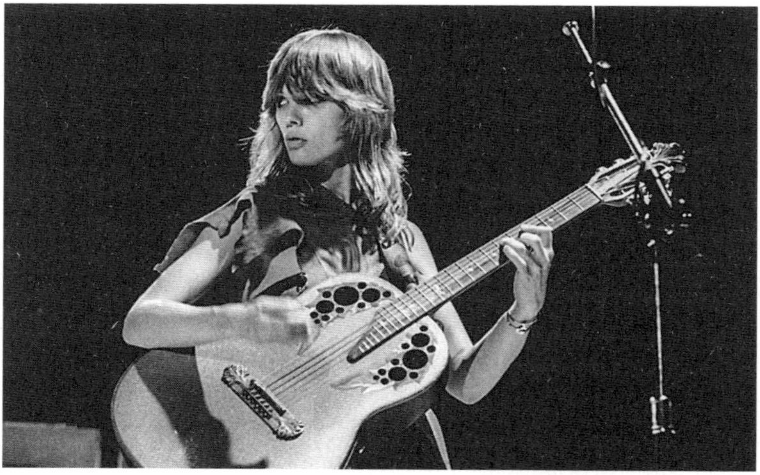

Nancy Wilson

NANCY WILSON

I was nine years old when Heart's *Little Queen* came out in 1977. I can still recall the thrill of holding the LP, and staring at the cover in awe. The band members looked like gypsies, but it was Ann and Nancy Wilson who drew me in, standing front and center, captivating and mysterious. I especially identified with Nancy, the fair-haired beauty who played the guitar.

Ann and Nancy Wilson were trailblazers in the male-dominated world of rock music. They didn't just hold their own among the guitar gods of the 1970s; they commanded the stage with both ferocity and grace. My older brothers were massive Led Zeppelin fans, and Heart felt like a natural counterpart. Ann's voice, a powerhouse instrument of its own, rivaled the technicality and intensity of Robert Plant's, if not surpassed him. Nancy, while not a virtuoso shredder like Jimmy Page, wielded her guitar with a commanding presence, exuding authority and confidence. Together, they redefined what it meant to play rock music as women, showing that femininity could be a source of strength and that their skills could cut through the noise of a testosterone-heavy genre.

Born and raised in Seattle, Washington, Ann and Nancy Wilson grew up in a musical household. Their father was a Marine Corps officer, which meant frequent relocations during their childhood, but music remained a constant. Nancy started her journey with a ukulele at six before graduating to the guitar. Ann, a few years older, naturally gravitated toward singing. By their early teens, the sisters had already formed their first band, Viewpoints.

It wasn't long before their musical ambitions began to take shape. Heart's story actually began in Canada. During the Vietnam War, Ann Wilson followed her boyfriend to Vancouver, where he was evading the draft. Nancy soon joined her, and together they started performing on the Canadian nightclub circuit. Covering hard rock bands like Led Zeppelin, Heart quickly built a loyal following. But it was their decision to write and perform original songs that truly set them apart. Their first two albums, including *Dreamboat Annie,* were recorded while they were still living in Vancouver. They eventually left town after an acrimonious split with Mushroom Records, which was run out of a studio of the same name.

Heart's music defied easy categorization. They blended the bombast of hard rock with the introspection of folk and even touches of classical, thanks to Nancy's versatility on the guitar. While Ann's voice soared with raw power, Nancy's playing provided the perfect counterbalance: intricate, lyrical, and deeply musical. Together, they created a dynamic that few bands could rival.

Dreamboat Annie was a revelation. The album produced the hits "Magic Man" and "Crazy on You," establishing Heart as a force to be reckoned with. Over the next decade, they released a string of successful albums, including *Little Queen* (1977), which featured the iconic single "Barracuda." Written out of frustration with sexist treatment in the music industry and aimed squarely at their former label, Mushroom, "Barracuda" became a defiant feminist anthem.

The 1970s and 1980s saw Heart reach staggering heights of success, selling out arenas and releasing "Straight On," "Even It Up," and "Alone." Despite their fame, the Wilson sisters faced significant challenges as women in the music industry. Sexism was rampant, and they often had to fight to be taken seriously. Instead of backing down, they leaned into their artistry, letting their talent speak louder than any stereotype.

Nancy's ability to navigate the rough-and-tumble world of rock and roll without losing her femininity resonated with me. She exuded a kind of quiet confidence that didn't rely on aggression or bravado. During an interview, she spoke of the "poetry" that drives female guitarists, a concept that stuck with me. It shifted my perspective, showing me that true power lies not in dominating the instrument but in becoming one with it, letting it sing with ease and joy.

Heart's success wasn't just a testament to their talent but also to their resilience. Along the way, the Wilson sisters have weathered both personal and professional storms, from grueling tour schedules and shifting musical landscapes to the relentless pressures of fame. Their bond was tested when a family incident led to a very public falling out in 2016, and the two didn't perform together for several years. Yet, true to form, they eventually reconciled and returned to the stage. Through it all, Heart has endured, continuing to inspire generations of musicians and fans with their strength, artistry, and sisterhood.

Today, Nancy Wilson is widely regarded as one of the most influential female guitarists in history. Her innovative approach to the guitar and Heart's massive commercial success have earned her a place among the greats. Ann, with her unparalleled voice, remains one of rock's most iconic vocalists. Together, they have left their mark on music history.

What strikes me about the Wilson sisters is how they have remained true to who they are. Their sense of self and the way they fearlessly established themselves in the world of rock was no doubt made easier by the love and support of a close-knit family. Their parents' simple wisdom continues to resonate: "Above all else," they said, "don't let fame or money change who you are."

NANCY WILSON

— *The Interview* —

[2007]

SF: Did you think twenty or thirty years ago you'd still be doing this? Like this?

NW: Twenty or thirty years ago, I was thinking we might be able to make a couple of records and do a couple of tours, and then I'd probably go ahead and become some kind of teacher or veterinarian or something like that. But it's actually the longevity part of it that's really stuck. We've been on the rollercoaster ride for twenty or thirty years, too. I mean, it hasn't stuck the whole time. But every time we face a drop, like a downtime, Ann and I are pretty dogged in our determination to keep the inspiration, and our career of being able to play music, going. We just basically worked our butts off to make our various comebacks.

SF: Have you gone to YouTube and looked at all your stuff from way back?

NW: Oh, no. I haven't, actually.

SF: It was really cool because I saw so many different incarnations.

NW: Oh, it's crazy when you look back at a longer life. I'm fifty-three right now [in 2007], and so when you see yourself, like say you look at your journals from your teens and your twenties or your thirties or forties, it's like—wow. How many lifetimes do people have? How many hairstyles and costumes? It's pretty cool because you collect your soul as you go. Your soul expands with each incarnation of yourself that you live through, and all the mistakes you make along the way, and all the things that you collect. That all goes into your playing as you grow. But yeah, you look at yourself in your twenties and go, what was I thinking?

SF: You guys had so much charm back then. There was nothing like what you were doing.

NW: We're still a very unusual rock band. We've never fit any mold at all. There were the '80s when everybody tried to fit the '80s mold, and we sort of fit that for a few hit songs, you know. But thank goodness the Seattle explosion happened when it did, because we were getting pretty sick of the hairspray and corsets by then, and the music was overproduced—the big glossy power ballad thing. I think everybody else was sick of it too, because look what happened. That was one of the most interesting times in music I've ever seen because there were people who had huge No. 1 smash hit singles, and then by about 1991 or 1992, the next minute, the next week, they were dropped from their label. Because Nirvana, and Soundgarden, and Alice in Chains, and Pearl Jam—there was a collective consciousness working there. I think it's getting kind of similar to that right now in music, because everything is so plastic—just handed to you for what's a hit and what's not a hit. That's part of the reason stuff like U2 is so huge, because that's where you can get to the authentic stuff, where real people live.

SF: When you guys were coming up, you were very organic. You guys look like you've come totally full circle now. It's your presentation and just the way you look.

NW: Yeah, I know. It's funny. You sort of go on these wild rides and journeys, but usually who you were to begin with is how you end up, if you're lucky.

SF: If you're lucky. If you don't get swallowed up.

NW: Yeah, if you don't get swallowed up and the world doesn't take you and change who you are. That was what our parents told us starting out: "Whatever happens out there in Tinsel Town, girls, you just stay who you are. Stay yourselves because you are beautiful people. You're really talented. There are so many pitfalls, and if you get rich and if you get famous, there's gonna be a lot of fair-weather friends, and a lot of heartbreak to live through." And of course, they were absolutely right. I guess also having each other, because me and Ann are really, really close. She's one of the funniest people I've ever met, and so we have our humor. We ground each other and we survive together, steering a pretty big ship all these years called Heart. Leading at the helm and being the leaders, making decisions with only a few major accidents along the way. We've done pretty good.

SF: I think it would be a really big comfort to have her.

NW: Yeah, because we were really soulmates. We really can talk about anything and we can laugh about everything.

SF: When you were starting, you stood out.

NW: It's always been a rare thing. I always felt that there's the percentage of great people or great artists that you can trust your life with. Talent, great talent. It's really narrowed down when you have the big collective of all these people out there and there's a few that are gonna rise and float to the top. The cream is gonna survive. But by the time that happens, a lot of them fall by the wayside or they drop like flies. We feel really lucky and privileged to still be able to be doing what we love, and playing live is just a thrill. It's just—well, you know what it's like when you're on stage. You get that conversation going with the audience and you can really transcend your day.

SF: When I watch you perform, you really look like you're enjoying it. Like you're enjoying the art of performing. Not just playing, but you're really alive. Are you a shy person in general?

NW: I started out really shy, but I've grown into more of an approachable person because I'm a team player and a problem-solver and a peace-maker inside the group and inside the family. Ann is actually, believe it or not, the shyer of us. She can go out there and just blast away on stage and be the center of the universe, but then in day-to-day sort of situations it's harder for people that don't know her that well to get in and find her or feel accepted or like they even know her very well. She's pretty guarded. I'm the demure one. I think because I shut up more on stage.

SF: Why were you drawn to become the guitarist?

NW: I think I was born to play guitar, coming from our family who's very musical. We always had pianos around, and ukuleles and a lot of music playing and singing going on—even in the larger family with grandparents, aunts, and uncles. My uncle taught me the ukulele when I was about six or seven, and we used to play lots of funny old English/ Irish pub songs and stuff as a group. We had a great, great family. A solid family, a funny family, and a musical family. So, we've carried that along.

I was a natural on the ukulele. It was so portable, and, for a kid, so easy to learn. Then we saw the Beatles on *The Ed Sullivan Show* and it was like, "Oh my God! We have to have a band. We have to get guitars now!" We got our guitars and we started learning every Beatles song, the guitar chords out of the *Mel Bay's Guitar Chords* book. We just started immediately to try to have a band like the Beatles. By the time I was ten or eleven, we had a band and we played around, little school things and a lot of living rooms and churches. Ann was our manager. Ann thought she had to write a letter to Brian Epstein, the Beatles' manager, to get permission to play Beatles songs live. We were pretty naïve, but we were really into it.

It was really great to be able to get involved in the late '60s with the whole cultural revolution that was happening then, with the hippie thing. You could crash a party and play guitars until dawn, and just learn every song in the book or every song on the radio. We still do that in the band. We sit around on the bus sometimes, or in a hotel room and we just pull out our guitars and sing every song we know until it gets light. It's a hootenanny kinda vibe, the way we started, and it was for our families too, even before then. So, that's what we still crave, to be able to sit around and play with other people. Or when we get on the stage with our band, it's just the best fun we could have in the world.

SF: That's amazing. So many people get jaded, especially about the business.

NW: The business part of it's not the funnest part. The imaging and the business of paying your mortgage or paying for things like the lights, electricity, and water. That stuff is not the feeling part. And there have been a lot of times that we didn't know if we could make it, a few different times where we were scraping the bottom of that barrel.

SF: How did you learn how to deal with the business? Because this is a mean business.

NW: It is a really mean business. It's really cutthroat. I think that we had a little sense of self. I mean, as women and coming from the era that we came from, there was not such a pressure on being so sexualized. We were more about being flower children. We're out of the Led Zeppelin idea of sexuality really, because we were kind of androgynous at the time.

We thought there was a bunch of old fogies, a bunch of old suits, a bunch of leeches running the business. Kinda true back then. They were like, "Hey babe, how ya doing?" We were insulted. That's why we got into so many problems right away, legal problems. We tried to leave our first record company because there was somebody involved that really insulted our delicate little artistic integrity in a sexual way. So we left, and then we could have potentially been barred from recording another album for two years because of it. We worked it out and were able to keep going. But it was really disappointing, because we were on such an inspired high. When our first album did well, we were flying. We were soaring and that was a reality check. That was really a contrast.

SF: When you went into litigation, you couldn't bring up any of those facts?

NW: We couldn't finish the album we were working on. We had to make a settlement that the previous record company could finish for us, so we had to compromise. They put other players on it and they put some live music from a club gig that we had on there, which was the *Magazine* album. They used the title for the one we were trying to make. We paid a big price for being super idealists at the beginning. But we just kept going. Lesson learned. We were always on the road, always writing, always in the studio trying to stay current with our music and not listen to everyone else's opinion about what we should be doing or what we should look like or sound like. We were still really brave coming out of our era, real individual with it. It wasn't until the '80s really, with MTV, when the image thing got so heavy-handed and the corporate guys with all the big money were really controlling everything. There wasn't as much give and take between the artists and the corporate world anymore. Like, now they don't develop artists anymore. They just use them like disposable junk food

SF: I hope you're right and there is a turnaround coming.

NW: Oh, I think there is. In my longer experience at this thing, you see that happening. You see everything get really disappointing for a while and plastic and fake and then something usually explodes and it changes again. Then it gets kind of healthy. It's sort of like: you prune the tree and it helps the tree grow better. It's one of those times when there's a groundswell of better things coming because the human spirit is strong. There are all these new things that are really popular underground. That's really a good sign.

SF: Do you think it's a positive thing that so many artists are starting their own labels?

NW: I do, because something's gotta give. There's no room for the creative spirit much in the old-school version of the music industry anymore, and there are no real record stores left. So, it's the whole new digital ride and everything has to shift again. I think that's gonna help people have a direct vote on what they want and what it is that they love. I think that's really good. It's just a change-up. Everything's gotta change up again.

SF: I know. Where did you live when the band started?

NW: We lived in Vancouver. Ann is a landed immigrant, so she has dual citizenship, but we started up there because all the major labels turned us down at least once.

SF: There are so many people who always tell me, "Oh, Heart is Canadian."

NW: Yeah, we sort of are. We consider ourselves part-Canadian because we really did live there and work there during the Vietnam War. Ann's boyfriend, who managed and did the sound for the band, was a draft evader up in Vancouver, and his brother was a guitar player. The band came up there and formed around her there, and I finally joined later. They'd been up there working the cabarets for quite a while.

SF: And what were those gigs like?

NW: Those gigs were long. When you played clubs then, you played four sets. Each set was about forty-five minutes and then the last set was like thirty. It was a lot of work, but we really cut our teeth on the live stage that way. We played a lot of originals for a club band, but we mostly also played stuff like Elton John and Zeppelin, Deep Purple and Pink Floyd. All kinds of hit-radio rock and roll.

SF: Is that where you started to get a name as a touring act? In Canada?

NW: Yeah, they'd done a lot of touring all through Canada, and I did some with them, too. I was playing clubs for a few months with the band, not even quite a year I don't think, before we got the small record label deal with [Vancouver label] Mushroom to make *Dreamboat Annie*. We were doing clubs and recording and writing all at the same time. We never slept, but it worked. When you're that young, you can do stuff like that. After that, we took it region by region through the States. We drove to every major radio station and got to know the DJs.

SF: Now, in those early days when you were just joining the band, did you have anybody who helped you with the guitar? Did you ever have any mentors or musical guides to teach you?

NW: As a player, I was always such a Jimmy Page and Paul Simon fanatic, kind of a crossbreed.

SF: Paul Simon for the fingerpicking?

NW: For the acoustic more. A little bit of the Joni Mitchell in there, and a lot of Crosby, Stills, Nash & Young in there. A lot of those guys were my heroes. Even with Ann as a singer, she emulated more of the guy singers, like Elton John and Robert Plant, than she ever did, say Aretha or Grace Slick. It was really fun to be in a rock band. I had been in little mini rock bands with Ann before, but this was the real thing. I'd been playing a lot of coffee houses by myself by then in college as an acoustic solo performer, but [the rock band] was really fun. You know, it was scary. It was so loud.

SF: Did you start playing electric guitar right away?

NW: I had an electric guitar that I liked to play, but I was mainly an acoustic player first. And then in the band, I got a chance to step up and do a few leads here and there. The guys in the band taught me how to play a little more lead here and how to be a good support player.

SF: One of the best lessons to learn.

NW: I know. A lot of it's what *not* to play, right? It's when to shut up.

SF: There was an article out a few years ago and the title was, "Where Are the Female Guitar Heroes?" There's no woman Hendrix. There's no woman Page. But women have been playing the whole time. It's just that maybe we might be a little different in the way we express, because we're different creatures.

NW: Yeah, there are a lot of flashy guy lead players like Hendrix and Page. They come from a male spirit, and when girls go up and try to whack off, it's just not quite the same. A lot of girls can do that. I've seen a lot of girls able to play, technically, anything a guy can play. But there's a different kind of soul, and I think a lot of it's just the basic instinct of women. It's more nurturing. And there's a lot less "proving it" and it's not a posture. It's not a saber rattle. It's more of a poetic thing that happens with women players just by nature. It's ridiculous to try and compare. It's apples and oranges. Technically, women can do anything that men can do, but what they create more naturally is usually less of a flashy thing and more of a poetry thing.

SF: Do you have a lot of young women coming up to you still? Asking for advice?

NW: It's so cool. The last few years on the road, in the summertime, it's amazing to see who comes out to these Heart shows. You have all of the people our age—older than our age—and their kids, or teenagers and college kids, and a lot of really young kids are showing up lately. You see these little guys watching the band doing like air drums and stuff. You see air-guitar players and little girls that are front row, and whenever I see kids right in the front row like that, I know that they're little players and I always give them a guitar pick. There's one kid named Corey who I've come to know. She's in the fan club and she's come back and met us, and she's a really good little player. I think she's around eleven, and she sent me a DVD of her playing at the talent show at her little school and she learned a song that I do live, which is Tom Petty's "You Wreck Me" from *Wildflowers*. It was fantastic. She's great, a little genius. And I remember being all about that myself as a little kid, so it's really wonderful to see it being passed along.

SF: Do you ever give them advice on the music business?

NW: I try to say what our parents told us, which was, "Don't let anybody tell you what to look like, what to sound like, or how to act. Just be natural and be yourself. Even if it means you have to give up a lot of big money to stay who you are. Don't take the money. Keep the joy."

Keep your joy: That's easy to say, but sometimes being a holdout is gonna be easier in the long run—especially these days.

SF: Yeah. I mean, gratuitous sex is—

NW: Yeah, everybody's a pole dancer, man.

SF: How did that happen? Was that video?

NW: Good question. How did that happen? From the '60s or '70s up until somewhere in the '80s, sex was okay. You weren't going to be risking your life just to have promiscuous sex with somebody. It's different now. I think it's an overcompensation factor for the fear level that comes with sex. It's an interesting theory, anyway. I don't know. I'm just always trying to figure out how it got this way. It's more about the fantasy, and the sexual posturing than it is about the real thing.

SF: And putting plastic in your body—being plastic.

NW: Being plastic. Barbie dolls. There are so many of these Hollywood people. I don't look at those magazines all the time, but when I do it's like, how can you ever distinguish them from each other? How can you tell which person is which?

SF: That's a good question. You look great though. In every picture I've seen, you look fantastic.

NW: Well, thanks. You know, I'm a naturalist. I've never altered myself, but I take a lot of vitamins. I drink a lot of water and I do yoga and exercise. I like to cook and eat good food. Like, healthy food. But I also like to enjoy some wine, and I like to enjoy some beer, and stay up too late sometimes. But being a mom now, you have to really be wise about when you have your fun. You have to leave a buffer around your fun because if you have to get up and go to school or do something with the kids, you don't wanna be a derelict. You wanna be healthy in general, and just have your fun wisely.

SF: You waited a long time to have your kids. Was that conscious?

NW: Yeah. I was so busy for so long. The '80s really ramped up and in the '90s I started giving it a try, but it took a while to get it going for me. But I love it. I love being a parent. I felt really lucky to have [my husband] on my side because Ann's doing it as a single mom. She's doing a great job, but it's a tough scene even when you do have a partner. She's doing an awesome job without the partner part of it.

SF: Do you think this is keeping you young?

NW: Oh, I definitely think it keeps you young. You get to see life again through their eyes, and you remember all the amazing discoveries of what it's like to be little. Even in the relatively ideal setup I have, when I do go on the road in the summertime it's really heartbreaking to leave home, even for a week or two. Two weeks is all I can hack. I can't take it after that, even though grandma comes and stays and helps. They have a great support group, and dad's with them, and I talk to them on the phone all the time, but it's just not the same. There's the hunger of being together and seeing everything happen. You just don't wanna miss it.

SF: How do you keep it together?

NW: Well, it is tough to keep things together, but humor is my main weapon of choice. Because it gets really tense and it gets really stressful. It gets really rough and painful, deeply heartbreaking at times—and lonely.

It's hard to have confidence when you work your butt off and the album sort of disappears and nothing happens. There are really a lot of disappointments to ride through. Like for instance, one time Ann and I put out an album that we worked really hard on, [1993's] *Desire Walks On*, and as soon as it came out it kinda fizzled out. We had worked really hard. We traveled, worked, and went to studios. We were involved in every level of writing, recording, producing, mixing, photo shoots. You know, people probably don't realize there's so much to it. It doesn't come out of the air. And then we went back to Seattle.

It was like, *Oh man, this is really a bummer. This really makes us sad. This is really a drag. Let's be sad. Let's just go for it. Let's fly straight into the face of sadness.* And so we did. We went and got *Terms of Endearment* and *The Color Purple* and a big box of Kleenex and we just watched two of the saddest movies we could think of and just cried our eyes out together. And that was that. Then we had to laugh at ourselves. We got that done and then, *Okay, so what's next for our band?* We can do that together.

We come from a military, a Marine Corps family, so we have a real attitude of, "Just pull up your socks and keep marching, soldier." That's always been part of our little arsenal of keeping it together. You gotta have ammunition and you gotta have a defense mechanism, and humor is a really good one. So is a community of friends. Your band, family, people that can catch you when you fall, and you catch them. People you can trust, and where the love is reciprocal.

SF: You're lucky you've been grounded.

NW: It's really a lucky thing. It's not always a charmed life, but definitely a lucky one. Good timing and good people involved, and passionate and talented people. A lot of times I think Ann's voice is some kind of gift that comes out of the sky. You don't just learn that in some class. That's a gift. And so when you have something that's undeniably great on your side to begin with in your band then you're doing pretty good no matter what phase is happening to you. You can rely on that talent and you can always fall back on talent. You can always sing different types of songs and play different kinds of songs, or go back to your roots, or do something completely wacky and redefine, regroup, and resume. There's just no easy way. But in general, life isn't easy. People die on you, and things just get really terrible sometimes. Your heart's gonna get broken along the way. There are no guarantees. There's no fast path.

SF: So many people I've talked to pointed directly to you, when I ask them if there are any women who have influenced their playing. Your name comes up all the time.

NW: Thank you very much. It's really good to know that after all this time, having worked hard doing it, that it means something to people.

SF: I thought, I wonder if she realizes how influential she's been? But I thought, chances are she's looking forward not backward. You're looking into the sun, not behind at your shadow.

NW: Being an influence does mean looking forward, because it does bring it forward. The best part of you does move forward into the next chapter of women in music, and just in music in general. But I couldn't be more pleased, because that's what I always was hoping, that I could imprint something that was in some way elevating and inspiring to people that heard our music—my music. It's like the people that inspired me and elevated me to do it in the first place. I know it sounds corny, but that's the shit, man.

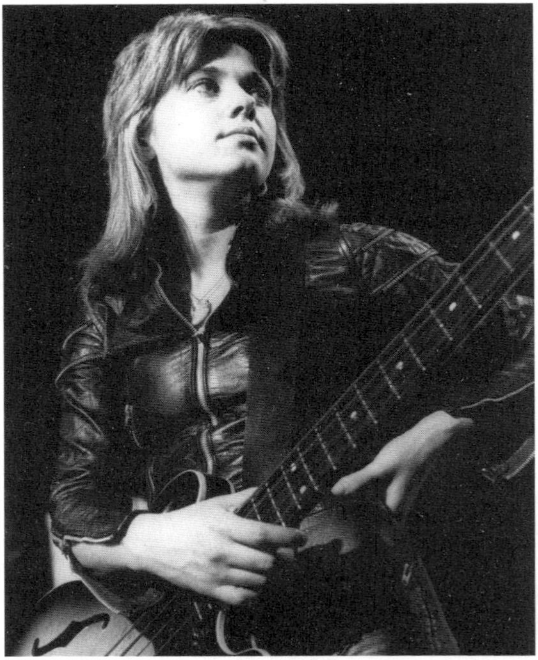

Suzi Quatro

SUZI QUATRO

Before Joan Jett, Chrissie Hynde, and countless other women strapped on electric guitars and black leather there was Suzi Quatro. Like millions of fans in the 1970s, I first encountered Suzi through her character, Leather Tuscadero, on the sitcom *Happy Days*. She entered my consciousness like a freight train at full speed. I didn't even know I'd been waiting for her, but when she appeared, it all made sense. Suzi didn't look like the other women I saw in the music world. She was one of the boys, a down-to-earth, tough girl who could handle herself in a man's world. The ethereal and feminine qualities of Nancy Wilson and Liona Boyd seemed out of reach for me, as did the cheekiness of Charo. It wasn't until I saw Suzi Quatro that I felt a life playing the guitar could actually be mine.

Self-creation and originality are central themes in this story, but Suzi didn't just invent a personal identity; she forged an archetype: the rock chick. She inspired a generation of women to claim their space in the music industry, showing that they could be tough, sexual, accomplished, and ambitious while still bringing a distinctly feminine edge to the picture.

The whole idea of self-creation solidified for me when I got my first guitar at age thirteen. I stood in front of the mirror a lot in those days, self-conscious about how I looked. I was awkward, uneasy with my changing body, and uncertain of my place in the world. Those feelings of insecurity and doubt shifted when I held my guitar and assumed "the stance."

You know the stance. Chrissie Hynde had it. Joan Jett had it. A woman holding her guitar low around her hips, staring straight ahead, daring the world with a silent "fuck you." Suzi Quatro created that stance.

I was starstruck and a little nervous when I got the chance to speak with Suzi, but I was relieved to learn that she was as down-to-earth and cool as her stage persona. That Detroit-tough, no-nonsense attitude that you feel just seeing a photo of her rang through everything she shared—her stories, beliefs, and philosophies. Hearing her talk that way reminded me that authenticity, not image, is what makes an artist unforgettable.

Suzi has achieved one of the hardest things in life, particularly in the entertainment world: she's managed to stay grounded. On stage she's a rocker, but offstage she keeps her ego in check. "I wasn't a wild one off stage. I was a wild one on stage." She has balanced a high-profile career while raising her kids, and she's now settling into life as a grandmother. Despite her upbringing in the rough streets of Detroit, she nurtures a softer, spiritual side.

Suzi Quatro was born in 1950. She grew up in a musical family, with her father, Art Quatro, leading a jazz band. Encouraged by her parents, Suzi and her siblings were raised playing instruments, and she took an early interest in piano and percussion. By the time she was fourteen, she had joined her sister Patti in a rock band called the Pleasure Seekers. Initially the band's percussionist, Suzi quickly gravitated to the bass guitar and lead vocals, roles that allowed her fiery energy to take center stage.

The Pleasure Seekers toured extensively for seven years, pioneering a scene where women in rock were a novelty. Suzi's fierce determination was evident from the start. On one occasion, she famously used her bass to hit a man who climbed onto the stage uninvited. These early years taught her how to navigate and fight for respect in a male-dominated is repeated a lot in this book, maybe just say "fight for respect in the industry."

In 1971, British music producer Mickie Most spotted Suzi's talent and brought her to England to launch her solo career. It was there that the Suzi Quatro we know today—the black-leather-wearing, tough-as-nails rock goddess—was born. Her debut single, "Can the Can," topped charts internationally in 1973, establishing her as a force to be reckoned with.

Over the decades, Suzi has sold more than 55 million records, with hits like "48 Crash," "Devil Gate Drive," and "Stumblin' In" cementing her legacy as a pioneer of glam rock. She also gained fame for her acting, including her time on *Happy Days* between 1977 and 1979. She starred in the West End musical *Annie Get Your Gun*, hosted her own talk show *Gas Street*, and became a popular radio broadcaster. In 2007, she published her autobiography *Unzipped*, a candid exploration of her life and career.

Reading her story, it's clear that Suzi's path was never just about luck or timing. It was about persistence, vision, and sheer will. She credits her longevity in the music industry to staying true to herself and maintaining a disciplined work ethic. That authenticity has resonated with generations of fans and inspired countless women to pick up guitars and defy expectations.

Today, Suzi continues to perform and record, proving that her fire hasn't dimmed. She's a grandmother now, but the leather pants and her Fender Precision bass are still part of her identity. Suzi Quatro didn't just play rock and roll; she embodied it. In doing so, she gave generations of women permission to stand tall, plug in, and turn up loud.

SUZI QUATRO

— *The Interview* —

[2006]

SF: It's really astonishing how many times your name has come up as an early influence for so many musicians. You must know that you have had that kind of impact.

SQ: Well, yeah, because I didn't have a role model, basically. There wasn't anybody for me to model myself on, so I created the serious rock and roll musician model.

SF: You created the rock chick?

SQ: Nobody had it before that. I was aware that I was holding out actually, not succumbing to becoming like the other girls. I was thinking, *Oh, my God. What if I don't make it?* I was a little bit nervous, but I just had to stick to what I was. Luckily enough, that made it.

SF: What was the scene like when you first started playing in Detroit in the '60s?

SQ: It was very Motown. We were weaned on that, and also there was a real vibrant rock and roll movement, which spawned people like my first group the Pleasure Seekers. Let's see: Ted Nugent, Grand Funk Railroad, Iggy Pop before he became Iggy Pop, MC5—I could go on and on.

SF: Alice Cooper?

SQ: Yes, he was a very good friend.

SF: How come the bass?

SQ: It was given to me. We started the first band after seeing the Beatles, and everyone quickly said, "I'm playing the drums." Or, "I'm playing the guitar." I think it was my sister, Patti, who said, "You've got the bass."

I asked my dad, "Do you have a bass?" and he said, "Yes. You can borrow one." Destiny rules, you know. Everybody has a destiny. So, all the other girls had cheap copies of instruments, and I got given a 1957 original Fender Precision. So, I think it was in God's plan right from day one that I was going to be a bass player.

SF: Did you practice a lot when you started playing?

SQ: I practiced until my fingers bled. The Fender Precision is one of the widest necks and hardest basses to master. I'm small, as you know. I've got small hands. They are really strong fingers—very thick, strong fingers—but small hands. I had to really stretch. Luckily, I knew piano, so my hands were stretched anyway. But until you get the feel for it, they're really hard on your fingers.

SF: Did you have some early bass influences?

SQ: Yeah, [James] Jamerson from Motown.

SF: What about Carol Kaye?

SQ: Yes. She was really, really good. But because I grew up in Detroit, I was more into that early Motown sound rather than the later Motown sound. But Carol Kaye is superb. A really, really, shit-hot bass player. Absolutely. But I've got to say that Jamerson was the one I was weaned on. I used to put his records on and copy his bass lines to learn his style.

I had a game I used to play. Put on "How Sweet It Is" by Marvin Gaye. Play it for fifteen seconds, take it off, and hum the bass line. Put it on again, and you get the shock of your life. It's none of the notes you thought you heard! He is the master of the spaces. I'd be learning it, and I'd say, "What?!" There's no note there and there should be, but that's what gave him his feel. So, like I said, I studied him, and I'm very much like him.

SF: Bass is a hard instrument and probably the most important instrument in the band in so many ways.

SQ: Yeah, I didn't even think about it—hence my personality, I guess. I just strapped it on and away I went. I didn't even think about it being heavy. And you know, I've got a ridiculously strong back and big muscles under my arms. I'm embarrassed sometimes to flex them.

And if you haven't got the bass and the drums, you've got fucking nothing. It's your engine. That's what I've always felt about it. You take the bass and the drums away from Motown for instance, forget it.

SF: Do you get asked much about your bass playing?

SQ: All the time. People know now that I'm a serious bass player. I've been doing a fifteen- to twenty-minute bass solo every night since I was seventeen or eighteen years old. Every time I think, *I'll just take that out of the show*. But I get compliment after compliment. It's become an integral part of my show. I do it with the drums and it's orchestrated, and it goes through every style. It's quite flashy and I guess it's just the token watch-how-I-can-play-this-thing that they like to see. Every now and again I think, *Oh God, how long can I keep doing this? Maybe they're getting bored*. But they don't want it out.

SF: Do you do any slapping and stuff, too?

SQ: I do all that. I do everything.

SF: Are you living in Europe all the time now?

SQ: Yeah. I moved here in 1971. My first husband was English, and the guy that had signed me was from here and we just ended up setting up home here. I go back to America five or six times a year. I wouldn't mind having a place there. I want to get back there and tour again anyway. It's been too long.

SF: Do you miss coming over? Or do you miss things about American culture?

SQ: I miss my home, you know. I've been planning a trip to Detroit. I want to go there soon, just to reconnect with my childhood. But yeah, I do miss America. I always have.

SF: You've got a great international career, and you built that up very young, right?

SQ: I did. I got in this business for a lifetime. I started branching out quite early on. First of all, *Happy Days*, and then I did musicals. I did everything. I am a rock and roller—that's my heart and soul—but I also wanted to be an entertainer. I wanted to try all the other things it offered me. And I do love it. I love communicating with people.

SF: How did you get your image? Was it from Elvis?

SQ: I had three sisters and one brother, but the girls were feminine.

SF: And you were a tomboy.

SQ: Yeah, I went the opposite way. I remember distinctly when I was eight years old *The Ed Sullivan Show* was on, and Elvis came out and he did "Don't Be Cruel." My sister, Arlene, who is nine years older than me, was screaming next to me. So, I'm watching him, and I was mesmerized. I've got to say, I was hypnotized by this guy. And I'm looking at Arlene thinking, *why is she screaming*? Then, he did that thing in "All Shook Up" where he goes, "Uuumm." I felt a sexual thrill and I couldn't name it. I didn't know what it was. I just knew I'd never felt anything like that before. Then my dad came in and switched off the TV and said it was disgusting. I always say that was the moment Suzi Quatro was born.

I had made up my mind at the age of eight that I was going to be him, and it never occurred to me that he was a guy. Then when I saw the [1968] comeback concert with the leather, the whole thing made sense to me. He was responsible for the image I created. I always wore blue jeans and leather jackets anyway, but when my first recording came out and it was time to dress as Suzi Quatro, my manager asked, "What do you want to wear?" I said I wanted to wear leather, and we had a big argument. He said it had been done by everybody, and I said, "It's never been done by a girl." Then he asked, "What about a jumpsuit?" And that was it. I kinda always knew what I was. Let's put it this way: I knew what I *wasn't*. I didn't fit into any existing mold and that was scary.

SF: Was that hard as a kid?

SQ: It was hard all through my life. I never knew where I belonged until I got on stage. The first gig that we ever did with the band, I remember standing up there and thinking, *I'm home. At last I'm home.*

SF: Like that sexual thrill you felt when you saw Elvis, did you want to do that to people?

SQ: That's exactly what I thought. I thought, *someday I want to do that to somebody else.* And according to a lot of the people I've talked to, I did do that. So, I'm really pleased.

SF: I was a very big *Happy Days* watcher, too.

SQ: I was just watching it tonight. I have a granddaughter now. She's five. I put on *Happy Days* the other day and she's in love with it now. She wanted me to put on another one again today. It's a great show.

SF: It is a great show. I've seen every episode, so I've seen you many times in it. Like I said, when I talked to people and your name would keep coming up, I think it was just that image.

SQ: That's right. I mean, I shocked a lot of people. When I appeared on the screen, everybody was like, *Oh, my God.* They hadn't seen that before, and I was doing it with a band of heavy guys and holding my own. In fact, being in charge. Nobody had seen that, and I like to think that I gave women a voice in rock and roll.

SF: What do you think of things now? Do you think we've regressed?

SQ: There are some good bands coming up. What I don't like is—and I have a real aversion to it—is women who pick up instruments and don't play them properly and use them for props. That really pisses me off.

SF: Yes, me too.

SQ: I think, *what the hell did I bother for? You're going to sit there and pretend to play that. If you can't play it, don't fuckin' pick it up!*

SF: They all want to be associated with the instrument, but they don't put in the time to learn it and really do it.

SQ: It's insulting.

SF: Did you ever think there was a stigma attached to the lack of female players? Why don't we see more women really playing these instruments?

SQ: You said it earlier on. It's a very hard instrument to play, especially the bass. Guitar is a lot more delicate. I've been playing all my life, and I had to rehearse long hours. I had to carry that thing all around the place, and it weighs nearly as much as I do.

SF: When you were coming up, were there any other female musicians who influenced you?

SQ: No.

SF: None?

SQ: None.

SF: How about now?

SQ: No, because I'm already the style that I am.

SF: Are there any that inspire you?

SQ: I can't think of any that I've seen and gone, "Wow!" I'm sure there are some, but a lot of girls will use the guitar to chug along and be up front. I mean, Bonnie Raitt is a serious slide player. She's excellent.

The girl from Fanny was very good, June Millington. There have been a few girls through the years, but few and far between.

SF: You did an episode of *This Is Your Life* and Chrissie Hynde came on.

SQ: That's right.

SF: Are you friendly with her?

SQ: I've known her for a long time. In fact, when she was still a journalist, she came to interview me here in England for the *New Musical Express*. I always remember that she was telling me that I was her influence and she was going to do what I did. I was thinking, *yeah, yeah, yeah, here's another girl with a dream*. Eventually, she had her No. 1 hit "Brass in Pocket" and I sent her a little telegram. It said, "Dear Chrissie, I thought you were a dreamer. Now you're a winner." I'm a big fan of the Pretenders. I think Chrissie is great. She has a wonderful voice and writes great songs.

SF: Yeah, and she has that stance like you, with the leather and blue jeans and stuff. Where else would she have gotten that?

SQ: Exactly. I remember doing my first photo session in the jumpsuit. I was in charge and my hands were on my hips. I just took the stance naturally. That was my stance. I remember the photographer, he said, "Okay, give me a Suzi Quatro look." I did this look, and I don't know where it came from, but it became the Suzi Quatro look. Don't ask me where it came from, because I have no idea.

SF: It's attitude.

SQ: Yeah.

SF: Tough.

SQ: Detroit tough. Yeah.

SF: What do you think is the most important thing you've learned after sustaining such a long career in the music business?

SQ: Well, you've got to keep normal at all times, and I am very normal. I'm totally grounded. You've got to leave your ego on the stage where it belongs, and you must never lose your dream. I'm always hungry. I always want more and that's a good thing, because it keeps you creative. You've just got to follow your heart. It doesn't even have to be making you money. It just has to be what makes you happy.

SF: In those early photo shoots, you're always hanging out with these really bad-ass looking guys. Were you sort of living clean throughout your career?

SQ: Yeah, I wasn't a wild one offstage. I was a wild one on stage.

SF: And that's how you achieved your balance?

SQ: I have Suzi Quatro, and I have little Suzi from Detroit. They're both me, but they are two different people.

SF: That's excellent advice. So many people get caught up.

SQ: They get caught up in the image. You mustn't do that. I have an "ego room" at home where I have everything that I've ever done. I call it the ego room so that it stays in a room.

SF: You're still a tomboy?

SQ: Yeah, I am. My granddaughter said to me today, "You never wear skirts, Grandma." I always will be a tomboy, I guess. Even if I do have to put on a slinky little black number to go out to a special, I still stride. It's hilarious to watch.

SF: There's a lot of spiritual stuff associated with you and your website right now. How did that come about? Was it gradual?

SQ: It was. I went through a very bad year in 1991, when I was going to divorce my ex-husband. My twenty-year-long marriage, my guitar player who I had my two kids with and wrote "Free the Butterfly" with. That was my freedom song. I got divorced, and my mother died. My mother-in-law died, then my father-in-law died, and then my brother-in-law died. It was like getting punched nonstop. I spent a year alone, and when I came out of that and was ready to take on the world again, it was a very spiritual journey, so I decided to try to help other people through that hard time.

SF: And how do you do that?

SQ: Just by talking it through. The main lesson is that you're not alone. Everybody likes to think that this never happened to anybody. That's not true. There is a joy in sharing a bad story. You're actually taking joy in the sadness of it, if that makes sense.

SF: How did you raise your kids out there? Did you keep them on the road with you?

SQ: I took them on the road. They went everywhere. When they got to proper school age, of course, we had to do our tours a little bit better. I never went away for more than two weeks at a time, and we tried to keep that to a minimum. I hated that. That really, really gutted me. I couldn't stand it. I had a live-in nanny because I didn't have a choice. I hated that too, but I couldn't do everything. I like to think I'm Superwoman, but I'm not.

SF: How many people work for you? Do you keep a team?

SQ: I keep it very small. I don't have a manager. I always looked after myself. I've got a very good lawyer. I've got a theatrical agent and a rock and roll agent, and my husband is a promoter and he books me a lot. I don't have an entourage.

SF: I'm a guitar player, and you're etched in my consciousness in so many ways. It's inspiring to know you're still here. You're still vibrant and looking in new directions. I think for anybody in this business, that's as good as it gets.

SQ: That *is* as good as it gets. You're absolutely right. I never want to be bitter. It's not in my psyche. I'm an optimist.

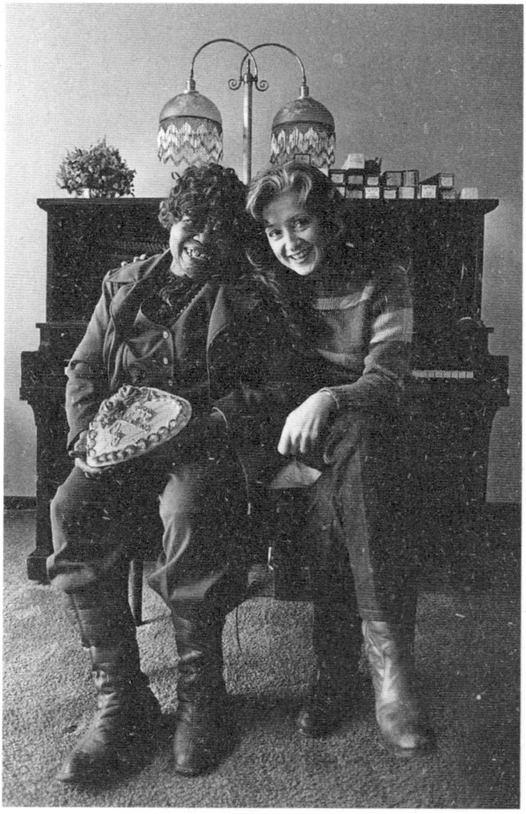

Bonnie Raitt with Sippie Wallace

BONNIE RAITT

I was in my early twenties, on the verge of recording my first album, when Bonnie Raitt was lighting up the Billboard charts and collecting her first Grammys. As a young blues-playing female guitarist, I thought I was unique, until I realized Bonnie had been doing it for decades.

Bonnie Raitt's commercial success in 1989 redefined perceptions of what a Grammy Award–winning pop artist could be. Suddenly, that person could be a middle-aged, down-to-earth, socially and politically outspoken, guitar-playing redhead. It felt like a victory for all of us. Bonnie struck a remarkable balance between singer-songwriter and instrumentalist. She didn't shred the guitar in the traditional sense; instead, she used it to accentuate her singing and songwriting. Her approach was understated yet powerful, with tone, phrasing, and technique that seamlessly complemented her remarkable vocals and heartfelt songs. She hit the sweet spot.

When Bonnie finally broke through, it seemed like we started to see guitar-playing women everywhere. In the blues scene alone, artists like Debbie Davies, Joanna Connor, Deborah Coleman, Carolyn Wonderland, Susan Tedeschi, and others, including myself, were emerging. Meanwhile, singer-songwriters like Lucinda Williams, Tracy Chapman, and Patty Griffin were gaining prominence. In a sense, we were all living in Bonnie's formidable shadow. Watching her rise gave me something I hadn't seen before: a woman at the top of the charts who played slide guitar with grit and grace, and who did it entirely on her own terms.

When I spoke with Bonnie, I shared my thoughts on her influence and what I called a "paradigm shift" for women guitarists that her success had sparked. She responded with humility and confidence. She acknowledged her role as a trailblazer but attributed her impact to timing, a fitting coincidence given that her breakout album was titled *Nick of Time*.

Bonnie's career was shaped by legendary mentors and collaborators. She formed lasting bonds with strong, outspoken female blues and R&B icons like Ruth Brown and Sippie Wallace. Growing up in Los Angeles, she was immersed in a vibrant music scene filled with liberated, unapologetic second-wave feminist musicians such as Linda Ronstadt, Emmylou Harris, and Phoebe Snow. With these influences and her own undeniable talent, Bonnie broke through at the perfect moment.

Born in 1949, Bonnie grew up in a musical household. Her father, John Raitt, was a Broadway star, and her mother, Marjorie Haydock, was a pianist. At age eight, Bonnie received a guitar as a Christmas present, setting her on a lifelong musical journey.

In the 1960s, Bonnie left Los Angeles to attend Radcliffe College in Cambridge, Massachusetts, where she studied social relations and African studies. Between classes, she honed her guitar skills and played coffeehouse gigs. After three years, she left college to pursue music full-time. She wasn't just studying music; she was living it. Even then, she carried the conviction of someone who knew her purpose, even if the world hadn't caught up to her yet.

It wasn't long before she was performing alongside blues legends like Mississippi Fred McDowell, Son House, Muddy Waters, and John Lee Hooker. She released her debut self-titled album in 1971 and recorded six more albums over the next seven years. Her career reached new heights in 1990 when she won three Grammy Awards for *Nick of Time*.

Beyond her music, Bonnie has been a tireless advocate for social and environmental causes. She co-founded organizations such as MUSE (Musicians United for Safe Energy), the Rhythm and Blues Foundation, and the Bonnie Raitt Guitar Project. She has also lent her voice to Artists United Against Apartheid and has worked for environmental protection and the rights of women and Indigenous peoples. Today, she serves on advisory and honorary boards for organizations including Little Kids Rock, the Rainforest Action Network, the Music Maker Relief Foundation, and the Arhoolie Foundation.

In 2022, Bonnie released her twenty-first studio album, *Just Like That,* which earned widespread critical acclaim. The album's title track won the Grammy Award for Song of the Year in 2023, a remarkable achievement for an artist at this stage in her career. The album showcased her deep storytelling, poignant lyrics, and continued relevance in the music world.

Adding to her storied legacy, in December 2023, Bonnie Raitt became a Kennedy Center Honoree. This prestigious recognition celebrated her unparalleled contributions to American culture through her music and activism. The ceremony highlighted her profound impact on generations of musicians and audiences, solidifying her place among the most influential artists of our time.

Bonnie often says her charitable work feels like raising children, since she never had any of her own. In many ways, her advocacy may prove to be her greatest legacy. Yet it's her music—the voice, the slide guitar, the honesty—that continues to remind us of what authenticity sounds like.

Bonnie Raitt's career embodies a perfect balance between power and vulnerability. She made it feel natural, and even inevitable, for a woman to play lead guitar while captivating audiences. Her influence is profound, yet she achieved it with such grace that it almost feels effortless.

BONNIE RAITT

— *The Interview* —

[2009]

SF: When you broke through in the early '90s, I had just come to Austin and I saw very few female guitar players. But after you broke through, it seemed like there was a paradigm change. It was just like *bam!* We were all there all the time, but all of a sudden we were being seen. I've always attributed that to your success.

BR: Well, that's really sweet. It makes me really happy if that wider attention blew open the doors a bit, inspired more women to take up the guitar, especially playing lead electric. I'm glad it's made a difference, but I've actually never focused as much on my guitar playing as I think others have. I've been much more into finding songs I love and then figuring out the coolest way to accompany myself on the guitar. There are so many players much more dedicated than me, who've spent years honing their chops and sound, stretching out and trying different tunings, guitars, new gear.

I think I was just in the right place at the right time in the early '70s, and playing blues guitar, especially slide, set me apart from other women out there. I also think it's what helped keep my career going this long. I'm really proud I've been an inspiration to younger women, especially to get better on their instruments. I can tell from the letters and CDs I get from women, and they're rockin' on the guitar!

SF: With all the interviews I've done, your name has come up more than anybody as an influence. It's been you and Joni Mitchell and Nancy Wilson.

BR: Well, we all know how reviewers need to compare us to someone. When I started out, they said, "Oh, she's somewhere between Janis Joplin and Judy Collins." But the blues guitar caught their attention. We all listened to Etta, Aretha, and the same soul, folk, and pop singers. I never thought much about gender or guitar or what kind of music—just whether it got me. And I loved the Stones as much as I loved Joni Mitchell, Robert Johnson, and James Taylor. I wanted to play it all.

SF: When you were coming up as a guitar player, as a young woman, did you feel isolated in what you were doing? There were only one or two others who were doing the blues stuff, playing guitar.

BR: I didn't really feel different, because it seemed like everybody I knew wanted to play the guitar when I was a kid. The folk revival had spread all across the country, and so many of us idolized Joan Baez, Odetta, Bob Dylan, Pete Seeger, and Peter, Paul and Mary. We just wanted to play those songs. I wanted to change the world singing protest songs. My heroes were those who were leading the rallies and just breaking my heart, spurring my mind with their music. There was a whole social context to the '60s that made us all feel connected.

I got turned on to the blues from a record called *Blues at Newport '63* when I was fourteen, and that's when I veered off into those styles of guitar. I taught myself nearly every song on that album, and those early artists were so influential. John Hammond, Mississippi John Hurt, Brownie McGhee, John Lee Hooker—they were all there. Then I got Chicago blues from the Stones and Brits turning us on to it. And we got to the source with Muddy, Wolf, and all the others. Once you get that bug, that's pretty much it for life.

At the time, it never occurred to me to notice whether it was a man or woman playing guitar. I just fell in love with the music, and of course, when I found out how badass Memphis Minnie and Sister Rosetta Tharpe were on the guitar, that really turned my head. In the folk scene, I also want to mention two women not too many people know about now, but Barbara Dane and Judy Roderick were really great blues singer-guitarists on the folk scene in the '60s, and we should acknowledge them.

There were some others around the time I was starting out, too. Rory Block has been incredible since the beginning—still such a killer blues guitarist and singer. Ellen McIlwaine—another redheaded folkie who played slide. In England, Jo Ann Kelly was a very well-respected blues woman who died way too soon. And, of course, Joni Mitchell, Joan Armatrading, and Phoebe Snow were recognized right away as brilliant guitarists.

There were rockers, too. June Millington from Fanny has been my good friend, great player. Terry Garthwaite with Joy of Cooking, Lita Ford with the Runaways, Nancy Wilson with Heart, Wendy Melvoin with Prince, and Jennifer Batten in Michael Jackson's band. So many more since then. And hey, now Beyoncé's band is all women who can really play. Who'd have thought that back in the '70s?

I do think playing blues guitar, especially slide, "like a man," or whatever the reviewers would say about my early gigs, definitely helped get my foot in the door and keep it there. I realized when I first started getting those early comments that it must have been unusual, so I was just glad to have something that set me apart from the pack. But I didn't feel isolated. I just felt proud.

SF: You have two brothers, you said?

BR: One older, who just passed, and one younger.

SF: Any sisters?

BR: No.

SF: I was gonna ask you if you were a tomboy.

BR: I was absolutely a tomboy. I still feel like I am in some ways.

SF: Do you think you have to be to do what you do?

BR: Not really. But I think you gotta like being around guys, or you're going to mind being out on the road. There are more mixed bands now, especially in the alternative scene. But a lot of the crews are still mostly guys. It helps to at least not be offended by a rowdier kind of scene. But you just learn to hang with people you dig on the road. You make it work or you pick another band. I just think blues, metal, and rock tend a bit more to that sex-and-drug party scene. But hey, that's part of the appeal! At least when you're young. It's a lot less cool these days to be as wild as we were, though.

I love being on the bus. Always have, probably always will. It's been forty years now hanging with mostly guys in close quarters. I must like it, or I'd have given it up by now.

SF: Did you ever feel like you needed to be as boisterous or more boisterous than the guys?

BR: Yeah, a bit. I think to prove that I could be tough, hang with my brothers and the older guys. I just wasn't into the girly, *Oh, you're sooo strong* thing. I picked up on the double standard early on and didn't dig it. I thought it was unfair and stupid to think we couldn't be just as good at everything as they were: throwing a baseball, running as fast. Being a second-class citizen and making yourself pretty and sweet—real compliant—to get yourself a husband and be happy. Didn't buy it.

But I wasn't a hell-raiser. I was a good student, majored in social relations in college. And then when I met Dick Waterman, who managed Son House, Mississippi Fred McDowell, Buddy Guy, Junior Wells, and some other blues legends, my whole life changed.

I took on a "blues mama" persona early on because I always wanted to be older. I couldn't stand my voice. It was way too high and fruity. I wanted to drink and smoke and sound as much like an old blues woman as I could by the time I was twenty-five. And I did a pretty good job of trying. But after a while, I grew up, dropped the need to prove I was cool. By your late twenties, hopefully, you're growing more into accepting who you really are. That didn't really sink in for me until much later, but I was very lucky to have gotten so much validation and peer respect from my early records, and that helped my self-esteem a lot.

But I don't think you have to be overtly macho or tough to make it in the man's world. It just happened to be the way I thought was cooler. At least back then, I think tomboys fit in easier in that blues/rock scene. I don't think you have to be like that now. You can be anything you want. But look around. Tough is still cool, for guys or women. From Eve to Beyoncé to Avril Lavigne to Chrissie Hynde, Sheryl [Crow], Melissa [Etheridge], and all the female rockers. They're tough because they want to be. It's standing up to those old stereotypes of the docile, compliant, and sex-toy babe. There's that part of the business too, but it's the opposite of what our tribe is about.

SF: I was similar in the way I felt like I had to be tough, just being around the guys all the time.

BR: Yeah, you're like a little sister. That's what I was. I had crushes on my brothers' friends, and I'm sure you did if you have three older brothers. But you know, to this day I can't hang with the girly-girl thing. Fashion and nails and shopping aren't where I live. Women are much more than that, and we've come a long way in understanding what really makes us powerful and really beautiful. I have a lot more female friends now, and I'm glad.

SF: Now these bluesmen, like Muddy and Mississippi Fred, were they your mentors?

BR: Yeah. And also my Cambridge buddy, Chris Smither, and Spider John Koerner, John Hammond, and Sippie Wallace, of course. Those guys were also big influences on me, especially as a blues player, and as personal friends as well.

SF: I was gonna ask if you had any female mentors.

BR: Well, Sippie was the only blues woman I knew well. We hooked up in '72, after I cut a couple of her songs. There was a great sisterhood in my twenties with Maria Muldaur, Emmylou Harris, Linda Ronstadt, and some others out in Los Angeles. That whole scene was very close and special, and it included Jackson Browne, Little Feat, Tom Waits, the Eagles, and others. We mentored each other, really. Later in the '90s, I became close friends with Ruth Brown and Mavis Staples, who'd been huge influences on me.

SF: What did you learn off your older women blues mentors?

BR: I sure learned about resilience and what not to put up with in the business and in your love life. From Sippie, I got an incredible education on how it was on the road back in the '20s. What it was like being a woman, and a Black woman at that. And I marveled at the humor and dignity she showed having to rely on others to help her after her stroke and being widowed so many years. Those are big lessons for a young woman, as I was. And the incredible joy she got from both her blues and gospel music and her abiding faith.

SF: What was Sippie doing when you met her?

BR: She'd had a stroke and was only playing in church. She was first rediscovered in the mid-'60s by a young guy named Ron Harwood, who'd done a lot of research and found out she was in fact alive and living in Detroit. He brought her out of retirement and recorded an album with the Jim Kweskin and the Jug Band, [a band] with Maria Muldaur. They went to Europe and she had a little bit of resurgence there.

Then she had a stroke, and after that she was just singing gospel in church. I heard an album of hers that I found in London in a record store in '68, and that's when I thought she might still be around. Then I found out she was still alive and we ended up meeting at the Ann Arbor Blues Festival in 1972. We formed a friendship and toured together for fifteen years until she passed away.

It was one of the greatest gifts of my life. She was the funniest, saltiest, wisest, sweetest, most talented musician I've ever known, and a great songwriter who could wail on that piano. Her body of work is just incredible.

From Ruth Brown, I learned so much about persevering in the face of adversity. Like Sippie, she had to learn to do without a man. Although she would have loved to be in a great relationship, it just wasn't to be. But she had her family, her fans, her music, and her incredible pride. She had experienced the heights of stardom in the '50s, only to be shot down and shunted off as musical tastes changed, and her boys needed to be raised. Mistreatment by men, by record companies, you name it. She was wearing it and still didn't let it get her down.

SF: Did that get you interested in the Rhythm and Blues Foundation?

BR: Ruth's case and several other of those early R&B legends were the inspiration for the founding of the organization. In 1988, Howell Begle, the Washington, D.C., lawyer who represented many of them, appealed to Atlantic Records to address their lack of proper accounting and royalty payments. The way older contracts were fashioned, most artists who recorded before 1970 still owed money to their labels and had yet to receive any royalties—although they'd sold millions of records. This was an industry-wide problem, and we formed the R&B Foundation to address it.

SF: Has your career always been the number one thing in your life as far as relationships go?

BR: I'd say it's been a priority, but it's also been possible to have relationships going on while I'm working. I can't imagine one without the other, really. I didn't sell a lot of records, so I had to make my living on the road. I also grew up with a dad who made his life and living in music, and you have to go where the audiences are. Thankfully, I love what I do and love the road but it takes a toll on your personal life. You have to find someone really adaptable and understanding, or it just won't work. In some ways, those absences can make the heart grow fonder!

SF: Were you surprised when your career just broke wide open?

BR: Oh, yeah. It was incredible. I had changed my lifestyle and made a better record I think, but the music scene was changing and by '89 when *Nick of Time* came out. For me, Tracy Chapman's success was a big sign that things were getting back to having room on the radio for a funkier sound.

SF: Do you see changes happening again now?

BR: There's always been great music all along. It's just a matter of finding it and getting it out there. I think satellite radio and the internet have made a huge difference, but in general, the music business is really messed up these days.

We've got to figure out how to get music out to people in a way that's fair to everyone. I feel terrible for friends of mine I've worked with for thirty years in publicity and promotion, newspapers, promoters. They're all out of a job, and that was before this latest recession. Luckily, you and I can take our guitars and go play live. There's a whole industry of people in management, recording, light, sound, and gear equipment who are being pushed out of a living. We're going to have to really work to find a way out of this that includes everyone.

SF: Are you talking about the downloading and stuff?

BR: Yeah, that and the fact that record companies and CDs are becoming more and more obsolete. If people keep thinking that music should be free, most of the people I know aren't gonna be able to make a living. So many clubs and venues are closing, radio playlists are getting tighter, but I think the recession is just making it harder for everyone in all businesses to make a living. Thank God people still want to be entertained in hard times.

Before they started laying everybody off, there were a lot more women in promotion and different aspects of business, in journalism and radio and executive positions. There are more female drummers, bass players, and there are a heck of lot more women guitar players, but whether we're ever gonna see somebody that plays as well as Stevie Ray Vaughan, I have no idea. It's been forty years and I haven't heard her yet.

SF: It's one of the questions I ask in this book: Why haven't we seen a chick really break out on guitar?

BR: It's not even the breakout. I just have never heard anybody that blew me away like that. You know, it's an interesting question, and I just have no idea. It's not a contest, really, and I don't feel it's sexism, but it's something we all have wondered about for a long time.

SF: I don't know either, and sometimes I think a lot of women just haven't adopted that pose, for whatever reason.

BR: I've really thought about it. It's certainly not genetic and it's not hormonal. Maybe it's role models and the fact that there haven't been female lead guitarists to emulate. There'll be somebody that is so blown away by Hendrix or Stevie Ray that they'll just be fourteen and sit in their room until their fingers bleed and they'll come out sounding like the next Jeff Beck and we'll all be blown away.

SF: I have a feeling it's coming. Just a matter of time.

BR: You know, one thing I will say, that in terms of women in this business, I think you still have to look cool. You don't have to be a total fox if you play your ass off, but you can't be an absolute dog either. I think it's probably the case with men too, if you think about it. You have to have some kind of look to make it all the way.

SF: Sometimes, I think maybe women just automatically adopt more of a supportive role as far as playing goes.

BR: It's just role models. I mean, I'm not that famous, because if I was really as big a deal as Britney Spears, then there'd be a lot more girls playing lead guitar. It feels a little bit more about sex and dancing than it is about instruments.

SF: I think video has dictated a lot of that.

BR: I think most women artists care more about the actual song and arrangement and the performance of it than they do about who's playing lead guitar. I mean, Sheryl Crow doesn't solo, and does it ever bug you that she's not taking the lead? I don't even really think about it too much, but it's just odd that there aren't more [women] to be talking about by now. Every time somebody says, "Wait until you hear this person," I listen and I go, "Yeah. It's pretty good, but it ain't Stevie Ray."

SF: You've said your guitar is an extension of your voice. I've heard other women say that, too.

BR: Especially with slide, because it does actually vibrate. It even sounds like a voice, a crying voice.

SF: And you have a very recognizable sound.

BR: I just do it according to what I think sounds good. I was never that into playing lead solos. I couldn't really do that anyway, until I got a bass player or a band to have something to play over. Then I got into soloing and I really dug it. When you get your sound and the right song and other players with you, that's when the good stuff happens.

Lowell George and Ry Cooder are my great inspirations for slide. For country blues, I love Mississippi Fred McDowell, Son House, Robert Johnson, Muddy Waters. We all grew up listening to the same bunch of blues records. I just developed a certain style and then Lowell helped me get more sustain by sharing what he used. He gave me an MXR compressor and that made a lot of difference. It's like getting to surf on a bigger wave—lots of power and control.

SF: Do you still bring your old guitar with you? Or does that stay at home?

BR: Oh, yeah. I play it every show, and my Guild for the acoustic stuff.

SF: The same guitar for how long?

BR: Well, a Guild F-50 since the late '60s; then I got a newer one in the mid-'70s. The brown Strat I bought in '69 and have played it nearly every show since then. Especially when I could afford a band after my third album came out in '73.

SF: How has your focus in your career and life changed since your early twenties?

BR: Success made a big difference. I mean, success is relative. I've heard that people are really struggling in an effort to get a record deal. I was very lucky that right out of the box, in what would have been my senior year, I started playing with my heroes and got offered a record deal on my own terms at Warner Bros. Through all these years, my fans have stayed loyal, and I never had to think about changing jobs. That kind of longevity is how I really define success for myself. My only real rough spot was in the mid-'80s, when I was floundering a bit personally. Still, I was lucky that it wasn't a career-busting crisis.

SF: How old were you when you quit drinking?

BR: Thirty-seven. I was going to work with Prince, and if we ended up making a video together, I didn't want to be fat. So, I initially quit to help get in shape, and by the fifth day of hanging out with the musicians at my local recovery group, I realized, *Hey, this sounds a lot like me; I've got a lot to learn here.* Like everything else in life, you learn from those around you. Sobriety really changed my life. I felt and looked and played much better than before, and it just stuck. I was lucky I didn't have a steep bottom to hit—run over anyone, or go to jail. Angels watching over again.

SF: Do you think you would have had that success had you not stopped?

BR: Hard to say. Sure wouldn't have happened if I'd gotten worse. I think a lot of things came into play around that time, and if you take any one of them out, it's hard to say if the stars would have so aligned.

Having said that, the question is achieving balance, and I'd say that's what I'm working on now. Having done the creation, promotion, touring cycle for nineteen albums and nearly forty years now, and having gone through a lot of family illness and death the last decade, I think I'll be taking some time to kick back and hopefully let some new shoots come up in new directions. Besides, the music business has a lot to sort out. You want to make sure you have your ducks in a row before putting out more music in this climate.

SF: Do you find it's hard to stay healthy on the road? You probably have it down by now.

BR: Well, I have it better anyway. Having the bus drive at night instead of all day—so we have some time to exercise, get outside, and have a life—has made a big difference. And being sober, of course, makes the focus much more on staying healthy anyway. But I have to work at it.

I eat organic and do yoga, walk, and ride with the other band guys on the bikes we carry in the bus. That helps. As you get older especially, it's important to build up your stamina to have a better time on stage. Huffing and puffing while trying to sing and play some badass music doesn't really cut it. Hey, at some point, vanity meets gravity, so it's a good motivation.

SF: I was listening to an NPR interview and you said that your volunteering is like your children, and then you've got your band and then you've got the Rhythm and Blues Foundation and all these people you have to look after, and that has taken the place of having children in a way because it's so much.

BR: Helping get more respect and reward for that older generation of R&B and blues artists—as well as the other causes I'm really involved in—has been a lot of my mission this time around. Hey, maybe if I'd been able to have a wife, I could have fit it all in! I think all of us would love to have a wife.

SF: I see a lot more young women at my shows, and because I really felt alone when I was coming up, when I started working on the book and I talked to all these other artists and they felt the same way. You know, it's like we were all living these little parallel lives and we didn't even know about each other.

BR: We're so lucky. I mean, I don't think I'd have this long a career if I didn't play guitar.

SF: I'd be in a straitjacket.

BR: We can be proud we're part of this breakthrough generation. And I think it's great that you're writing this book, so we'll be able to mark how it's going down—influence the next ones.

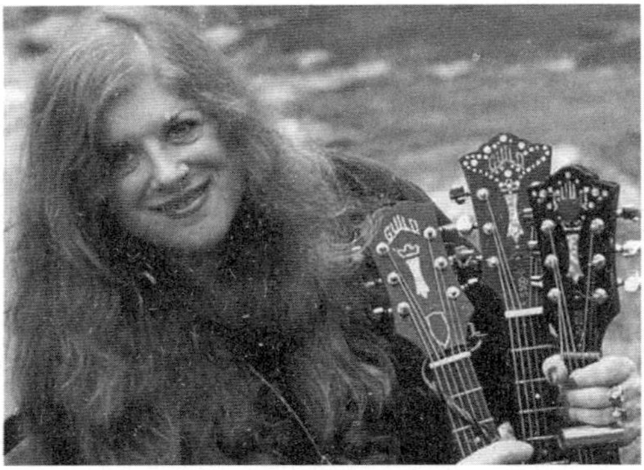

Ellen McIlwaine

ELLEN McILWAINE

When I was a teenager just starting out, Ellen McIlwaine was already lighting up the international blues scene with her fiery slide guitar and unmistakable voice. Originally from the United States, born in Nashville, Ellen eventually made Canada her adoptive home, where she was embraced as one of their own. She was legendary for her association with Jimi Hendrix in the 1960s and for forging a career at the intersection of blues-rock and the women's movement. Ellen was among the first women to play a bold, aggressive style of slide guitar, delivering her music with fiery passion. With her mane of flaming red hair, high-heeled strut, and five-octave vocal range, she was a force of nature and a true original.

As a young musician entering the scene, I was aware of Ellen's legacy, but it wasn't until years later that I officially met her. During our first interview, I found her to be soft-spoken, articulate, and generous in sharing her hard-earned wisdom. She warned me about the challenges of the music industry and the dangers of being a "female" guitarist, or simply a woman daring to stand out. It was clear she had endured a lot, carrying deep scars from her battles in a male-dominated world.

Born in 1945 to missionary parents, Ellen's early years were nomadic. Her family moved frequently, and she spent much of her childhood in Japan. This time abroad shaped her musical and cultural worldview, exposing her to a diverse array of influences from Egypt, Pakistan,

Lebanon, and Jamaica. Though she often spoke of feeling out of place, her global upbringing fueled a creative vision that would later set her apart.

After returning to the United States in her teens, Ellen picked up the guitar and began performing in coffeehouses, bars, and restaurants. By 1966, she had moved to Greenwich Village, immersing herself in the vibrant folk and blues scene. There, she hung out and jammed with legends such as Jimi Hendrix, Mississippi John Hurt, and Odetta, the latter becoming a lifelong friend. Two years later, she moved with her band Fear Itself to Woodstock, New York, before launching her solo career.

Ellen signed with Polydor Records in the early 1970s and gained a cult following with albums such as *Honky Tonk Angel* and *We the People*. By the late 1970s, she was exploring electric lead guitar, collaborating with Cream bassist Jack Bruce and drummer Paul Wertico on her 1982 album *Everybody Needs It*. Her music transcended the blues label, blending Indian and Pakistani influences with her own distinctive slide-guitar style. She described her work as "world music" long before the term became mainstream.

In 1987, Ellen became a Canadian citizen, settling in Calgary in 1992, where she continued to tour and record. She composed live scores for plays and contributed to film soundtracks. In 2019, she received the Lifetime Achievement Blues with a Feeling Award at the Maple Blues Awards in Toronto.

Ellen's journey wasn't without struggle. She battled addiction for decades, using alcohol to cope with anger and sadness. Sobriety eventually became a cornerstone of her identity, and she proudly lived drug- and alcohol-free for nearly forty years.

A pivotal moment in my own career came when I organized a tour through Western Canada featuring a lineup of female guitarists. Ellen joined us and closed each show. Watching her perform was transformative. Her slide guitar style was unmatched—technically intricate yet emotionally transcendent. Amplifying her acoustic guitar, she wove Indian classical scales and semitones into her playing, creating music that defied categorization. I remember standing side stage, mesmerized, watching her hands glide across the strings as if conjuring sound out of thin air. Paired with her vocal range and raw intensity, her performances were spellbinding, stealing the show night after night.

Ellen McIlwaine's legacy extends far beyond her genre. Dubbed the "Goddess of Slide," she was the subject of a 2024 documentary celebrating her life and music. Though often categorized as a blues artist, Ellen continuously pushed boundaries, incorporating global influences to create something entirely her own.

She spent her later years living in Calgary, where, in addition to her musical work, she drove a school bus—a humbling role for such a unique and groundbreaking artist. Ellen passed away in 2021, leaving behind a towering legacy of innovation, resilience, and artistry. She was ahead of her time, breaking barriers for women in music during the 1960s and 1970s. Often isolated and without support, she faced backlash from societal norms, yet she stayed true to her muse, paving the way for generations of female musicians to follow.

ELLEN McILWAINE

— *The Interview* —

[2002]

SF: When I started this project, your name came up immediately. Do you realize how much of an influence you've had on women guitar players? I see you in the same light as Memphis Minnie, a real trailblazer doing something that was really gutsy a long time ago. Do you ever wonder how far the reaches of your music career have gone?

EM: My perspective isn't in that way. It's like, *God, I went through hell for a long time.* I played alone for a long time. Slide guitar exclusively. Being a female guitar player doesn't have any restrictions, but other people who use that term seem to think it does.

SF: It appears your influences are really varied.

EM: Slide is a really individual thing. If you listen to all the slide players, we're all different. I didn't learn the way someone else does it, and so I was really a pariah for a long time in the business. I didn't fit in the box or play nice little songs. They're comfortable with that, but they're not comfortable when you play bass lines and blast them out.

I had one album [in 1978]—they called it *Ellen McIlwaine*—but I wasn't allowed to play the guitar on it. I wasn't told that until we started recording. We should've had a great record, but it was so controlled. It was the producer's idea of what would sell. I was even told how to sing. There's very little of me in it. It was the first and last bad press I ever got. I can remember spending nights holding my acoustic guitar. Sitting in a chair and crying. Rocking back and forth. That happened in 1978. It was a disastrous experience for me. After that, I put a band together to tour that album, and I had a weird-looking black guitar, which is still one of my favorites to this day. Then I started playing electric guitar. Of course, I wasn't in a position to play lead yet, really, but I was starting to do it. I was determined to do it.

SF: So up until you got that guitar you were just playing acoustic?

EM: Through an amp with a wah-wah pedal. Breaking all the rules. Not paying attention to this is how you do it.

SF: Not being the nice girl, a soft player.

EM: No. That just wasn't interesting. I have to play. You know how it is. You have to play what comes out of you. In order to do that, you can't try to put the brakes on.

SF: And why should you?

EM: Women do. We're concerned about how we look. *Am I attractive to men? Do I sound okay? Am I not too threatening?* I think because all this is swirling around in our heads, we play music like we're driving around with the emergency brake on. We don't need to do that. We're constantly judging ourselves. Doing whatever women do. Getting surgery, going on diets, and doing all this stuff. I think we should just play the music.

SF: It would be nice if people didn't judge you by all that.

EM: I think if more of us said, "That's nice, but get over it," they wouldn't be able to. It's discouraging. I just did a workshop at Selkirk College in Nelson, [B.C.], and there were both men and women there. The men were players and the women were singers—mostly. One woman said,

"I want to do this. How can I get myself to do that?" I didn't know what to tell her. First, I learned from a flamenco guitar player, so I learned to use my right hand—the whole thing. That's why I use finger picks and fling my hand around instead of just holding a little flat thing. There are guys who do that and they do it well, but that's not my style. My style is flinging my whole right hand at the guitar.

SF: Where were you when you took up flamenco?

EM: In Georgia, after I came back from Japan.

SF: Are you a U.S. citizen?

EM: I am, but I was raised in Japan until I graduated from high school. I was adopted, so I really don't know who I am descended from, but I was born in Nashville, and it was funny because people would look at me—even when I got my nose pierced—and they'd say, "Oh, you play country music?" And I would say "No, no, no." Then I got the birth certificate, and my mother was from just outside of Memphis. So there's a genetic excuse for the way I play.

SF: Did you study flamenco in Japan?

EM: No, I studied piano. My parents bought a piano. I never had lessons or anything. When we moved to the States there was no more piano, so I borrowed a guitar from somebody and I liked that, so I bought a little nylon string. The first guitar player that was an influence on me was a flamenco player called Jeff Espina in Atlanta. He showed me how to play all those rhythmic patterns that flamenco guitar players use. Then a year after that, I started playing and I earned my living playing guitar. Patrick Sky came to Atlanta and saw me and said, "Come to New York and I'll introduce you to my manager, but you've got to get a steel-string guitar." So, we put steel strings on my nylon string and the neck just bowed. Then he got me this guitar, that I still have today, for fifty bucks from Guild [Guitars]. I love this guitar almost as much as I love myself. It's been with me through everything.

SF: Are there any women on the scene today or in the past that you've been influenced by—who you thought dispelled the myths?

EM: There was nobody there but me. Memphis Minnie wasn't somebody that anybody talked about. Those women who played blues—like in the '40s—kind of got buried and passed over. I hadn't heard of them until much later. There was nobody else around. I was on the scene for maybe five years, then Bonnie Raitt appeared. After that, there was a gap. There were always acoustic players.

I consider Joni Mitchell to be a great guitar player. I am a big fan of hers. She's right out there, too. She explores everything. She's not worried with how she looks. She's playing, and I think that's what we have to do. I think that's what men do naturally because they don't have all those constraints. If there's anything we can give each other, it's just, "Let's go for it!"

SF: When you describe just rocking back and forth in that chair and holding your guitar and crying, I can relate.

EM: I went on the road with a band to support that [self-titled 1978] album, and it was all guys, of course. The guitar player that I had—he had a double neck so he could play bass and lead. I played rhythm. No one's ever failed me with saying I was a bad rhythm player, but they sure don't want you to step out and play the lead. At this period of time, we'd have rehearsal and they would reach over and turn the pegs on [my] guitar. I was in open tunings, and only I knew what they were. I can't tell you how bad that felt. It feels like the constant message was, "You know nothing. What are you trying to do?"

SF: How old were you at that time?

EM: I must have been in my early thirties.

SF: Did it take you a long time to learn to assert yourself in situations like that?

EM: Well, I just told them to fuck off. That was my lowest time for self-esteem. I see my life as before I quit drinking and after I quit drinking: 1982 was when I quit drinking; 1978 to '82 was the bottom for me. Today, if anybody said, "You're not playing," I would just say, "Then you'll have to find somebody else to make your fucking record, then." Pardon my language.

I'm okay today. I haven't had a drink or a drug in twenty years, and I know what's going down and I know who the hell I am. I stick to my guns. For a while, I thought maybe they were right. But the fact that I held my guitar and cried let me know that I knew they were wrong. Inside of me, that was wrong. It might work for somebody else, but it was wrong for me. After that disastrous tour, they said they wanted to do another album, but I said, "Absolutely not."

Then I moved back to Atlanta and let me tell you, I love the way they play down there, but at that time there was nothing in the South for me. So I moved to the Northeast. We made an album with Jack Bruce. We recorded the whole thing on an eight-track. Then we won the Independent Record Award for the No. 1 rock album in 1982. It was a great record.

If people have a problem with my gender, it's their problem. It took a lot of years of suffering. It was always their problem, but I didn't know how to handle it. Today, the best way I know to handle stuff like this is I carry around this list, and when people ask me, or say that there are no other female guitar players, I say, "Have you heard of all these women?"

SF: When I started researching this project, I could find no literature on female guitar players.

EM: Do you know who Camille Paglia is?

SF: No.

EM: She's this person who rags against women and considers herself to be totally liberated. She actually said that there were no women guitar players out there because women just didn't have the ego for it. I wanted to pick her up by her nostrils and show her some ego for it. I couldn't believe she actually said that, and they printed it and nobody wrote letters and said, "Excuse me?" I was so grossed out. Because no one's ever heard of us, they pretend we're not here.

SF: Do you still think it's an uphill battle?

EM: Yes.

SF: Do you still think you have to prove yourself onstage?

EM: No. I figure if I'm playing for an audience, all I have to do is play the music. I don't even talk. I play music that I love and let the music speak for itself.

SF: How come you're in Canada?

EM: Because it's easier up here to lead a band. It's easier up here to get hired as the lead guitar player in a band and take your band on the road. There are lots of guys who are willing and able to play with you, and they are willing for you to be the employer and lead the group.

SF: Do you think it's more difficult in the States?

EM: I think the musicians are okay, but not the clubs. When I still lived in Connecticut, the food concessions guy booked the band at the University of Mass[achusetts]. I called him and I said, "I'll send you a tape." I called him back later to see if we could be booked, and he said, "No. This is a rock and roll room. We don't think a chick can handle it." What are you going to do?

SF: How do you feel about the business after being in it so long?

EM: I'm very fortunate that when I came up in the '70s, radio was wide open. The DJs listened to everything, and they played what they wanted. I got a real strong underground following. Today, I have them and their children and other younger people. When you moved to Texas, I was scared for you.

SF: Really?

EM: Yes. I thought they'd eat you alive. How come you're not all over the place? Why aren't you touring with the Rolling Stones? You have to remember that it's not because you're not talented or that you couldn't do the gig. Just look who's running the show. I had to get out of the constant wondering, *God damn it, why is it like this?*

SF: Did you go through a period of anger?

EM: When I was drinking, I was stuck in that loop of anger. When I stopped, it took me about four to five years before I got over it and I just started to say, "What am I going to do today? What am I going to do right now?" I'm financing my own gigs and I'm getting out of the bars. I'll put ads in the paper and promote myself. We have to pay attention to the business part. We have to take more control of our careers. Not all of us are in the position to do that, but we really have to try.

SF: This is a really tough racket. It's hard enough just to pay your bills on time for those of us with the artistic mindset.

EM: But if you have to borrow money from somewhere to promote yourself, do it. Believe in yourself. There's no reason why we can't.

SF: Were you more of a tomboy?

EM: No, I don't think so. My mother was very independent and strong, a great role model. I was brought up to believe that male and female were equal.

SF: Do you think that there's a stigma attached to the guitar where it's more associated with masculine than feminine?

EM: I do, and I think it's very odd. I have a friend who's a nurse, and he gets called a male nurse all the time and I get called a female guitar player. I think they are sexually identified roles. People don't do that on purpose. There's just so many more guy guitar players. That's what people relate to.

SF: Do you think it makes people uncomfortable to see a woman really play hard?

EM: (*sweating and making faces*) I think it's fear. I think people would rather see Sally Field tell someone to fuck off than say, Anjelica Huston. Because if Anjelica Huston told someone to fuck off, they know she'd make you do it. They're more comfortable if you're little and nonthreatening. But if you're big and scary? I think it's the same in Hollywood. Women get past thirty and there are fewer and fewer roles and jobs for them, so they are starting to form their own companies.

SF: So you're saying it's the time to take things into our own hands?

EM: Otherwise, things won't change.

SF: Do you think it's just a matter of there not being a lot of women out there on the scene that we don't see more women guitar players?

EM: It doesn't get us dates. I think a lot of men go into playing music because it's a way to get chicks. I never noticed that playing music was a way to get guys.

SF: I think more women will go into softer instruments, be a singer-songwriter.

EM: But that's the getting-guys thing. It doesn't seem very exciting to me. It's not exciting, but at least you're on the stage and you're nonthreatening, and maybe after your set some guys will come and try to buy you a drink.

I did [the] Music West [conference] out in Vancouver, and a guy got up and asked me, "Do you know your guitar sounds like feedback?" I said, "Actually, I work really hard to get my tone just the way it is." I wish I'd thought to say, "I dare you to come back tonight and ask Rick Derringer the same question." So, that's one extreme. But what happens now is men who are thirty and under will come up and they'll say, "What kind of amp is that? Or what kind of foot pedal? Did you play with Hendrix?" I think it's just this whole generation of guys whose mothers worked. They don't see anything different about it.

SF: You don't see it on popular music channels. You just see women being complacent eye candy.

EM: That's who's running the business.

SF: You mean the men behind those women?

EM: Who's hiring them? Who's financing the shows? That's what it is. That's why Madonna makes more money. Still, the highest-paying job for women is prostitution and modeling. Not being the CEO of anything. With that headspace happening, that's like saying "fuck" a lot instead of learning adjectives. It's easier—the lowest common denominator.

SF: Do you live by yourself?

EM: Yes.

SF: Were you ever married?

EM: No. I was in love with this guy in college and I would've gotten married—had two boys and two girls and this wholesome life—but he said I was too young. It didn't work out, and I'm glad—because today the world has another female guitar player. I think what happens a lot is women have a couple of kids and they get distracted and it's hard to keep your career going. Joanna Connor has a couple of kids and her mom keeps them while she's on the road.

I think at one point in my life, I would've had a baby just to have a baby, because I was lonely. But that's not a good reason. My finances are all over the place. I couldn't have a child on my paycheck, so in the end I'm married to music and my career. I've had several relationships, but in the beginning the guy would say, "When are you going to stop playing and stay home?" If you want to get rid of me, that's a good place to start. I developed to be kind of promiscuous. Maybe they were my boyfriend for a night or a week. Five years of one-night stands, but there was no commitment because music was my commitment. They were okay with that.

SF: You still feel that way?

EM: No. I look at relationships differently now than I did when I was younger. I would look at a man today as a companion more, not *is he cute and do I want to do him*? I would look at him as, *does he like to do the same stuff I do and is he fun to be with*? But I'm happy the way I am. I'm not one of those people who needs a relationship. I really don't care. If I have one, that's great. It's like icing on the cake. But if I don't, I've still got the cake.

SF: Do you notice a difference between how men and women play the guitar?

EM: I don't think that how we play the instrument is different. What we're trying to project is different. I don't think we're intent on jumping around and looking mean, and most good male guitar players don't do that either. Our attitude is different when we play with other people because we interact differently. We are less likely to jump all over the people we are playing with. Why would we do that? Most of us anyhow. I think most of us hang back.

SF: In the blues scene, I've been witness to and involved in the whole "cutting contest" thing. I almost hate jamming with people, because I feel like, *oh God, here we go.*

EM: Mostly, I get drowned out. I think it's just a big attitude. But you have to look at blues, too. Who plays blues today is not the same as who played it fifty years ago.

SF: One of the things I found interesting seeing you live was the Middle Eastern type music you were playing.

EM: It sounds a little like a veena. That's an Indian cross between a sitar and a guitar. Its influence is Middle Eastern.

SF: Did you study this stuff formally?

EM: Probably because I grew up in Japan and I was exposed to all the different cultures. My geometry teacher was from India. We had two hundred students in our school and twenty-eight nationalities. We were exposed to each other's cultures. Then when I came to the States in the '70s, Ravi Shankar was touring. If you look at one of the early records that I did called *We the People* [1973], there is a raga-type tune and that's when I started doing that. Back then, people just said, "What is that? That's really weird." But it's part of the whole thing called "world music." I've always done it. I've always been fascinated by minor keys and those strange scales from Middle Eastern music.

SF: Do you play it by ear?

EM: Yeah.

SF: Because there are half tones and stuff like that.

EM: I just love it. I listen to Nusrat Fateh Ali Khan from Pakistan, and whatever else I can get my hands on.

SF: Have you ever been over there to play?

EM: No. I'm not sure how I would be received. I'd have to be prepared. I know there's restrictions on women and restrictions on everything, and right now it's not a good climate for people in the arts or people who are open-minded.

I love people. Every kind of people in the world has wonderful contributions to make, and I think religious fanaticism, or any kind of dogma, destroys a lot of it. People should just share music, dance, food, and art, because we have so much to give each other. How many times have you looked at another culture and seen how they think? You could wonder, *I never would have thought of that.* We just have so much to add to each other.

SF: But the climate is very bad for that right now.

EM: It's very bad. But it's all religious fanaticism. It's not the people.

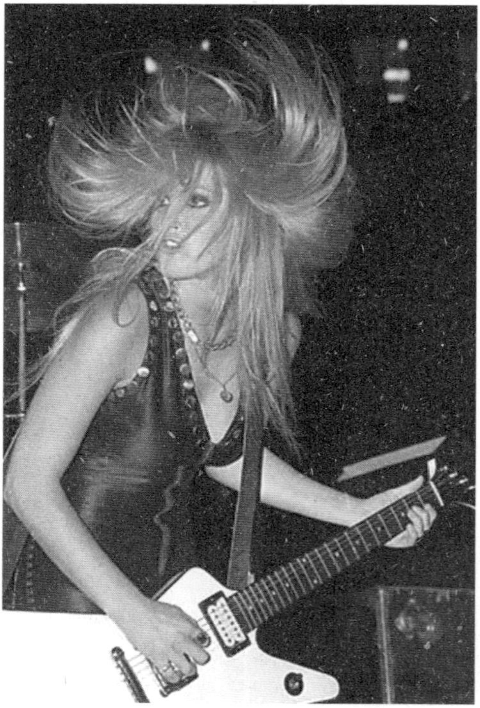

Lita Ford

LITA FORD

The first time I saw Lita Ford, it was the 1980s, when heavy metal ruled the airwaves and, with the rise of music videos, image was everything. Lita stormed into that world like a fireball, dressed in tight leather and spandex, radiating unshakable confidence. She was overtly sexual yet entirely in command, wielding her guitar like a weapon. No woman had ever broken through in heavy metal the way she did. Lita didn't just join the scene; she crashed the party.

Born in London in 1958 and raised in Los Angeles, Lita picked up the guitar at age eleven and never looked back. I had the chance to speak with Lita in 2009, when she was living on a private island in the Caribbean with her then-husband, Jim Gillette, and their two sons. It was just before she released her album *Wicked Wonderland* that September. But before I could even hear her voice, Gillette, who was also her manager at the time, answered the phone to screen the call. It was a small moment, but one that would take on a different meaning years later.

During our conversation, Lita spoke about her lifelong commitment to heavy metal and her dedication to being a great player. Unlike many musicians who rely on formal training, Lita taught herself to play by ear, after just two weeks of lessons. At seventeen, she joined the Runaways, the all-teenage punk band that also featured Joan Jett. They were controversial, ahead of their time, and despite never achieving huge commercial success, they made history. The Runaways kicked open the doors for all-female bands, even if they were often marketed as jailbait. The music industry and audiences objectified them, dismissing their talent and reducing them to a spectacle. But Lita, and Joan Jett, were the real deal, and they both went on to carve out monumental careers.

After the Runaways disbanded in 1979, Lita built a solo career in the '80s heavy metal scene, a genre notorious for being misogynistic. Her breakthrough came in 1988 with the album *Lita*, which featured the hits "Kiss Me Deadly" and "Close My Eyes Forever," a duet with Ozzy Osbourne. The album went platinum, proving that a woman could not only front a metal act on guitar, but could also dominate it. She followed up with albums like *Stiletto* (1990) and *Dangerous Curves* (1991), further cementing her status as a metal powerhouse.

Lita's career has always been about mastery, not just of the instrument but of herself. She built her identity around precision, control, and the refusal to compromise. Every note she played came from sheer willpower and instinct. Her performances were bold, stripped down, and fiercely physical, reminding anyone watching that the guitar doesn't need a dude to pull and stretch the strings to their limits. A woman will do just fine in this case. She walked straight into the world of heavy metal and made damn sure she wasn't ignored.

Despite proving herself over and over again, one of the biggest challenges she faced was simply getting people to believe what they were seeing. Audiences just weren't used to a woman playing like that, so they assumed the guy on stage was doing the heavy lifting. Lita battled these perceptions her entire career.

During our short interview, something stood out to me. Whenever a question touched on her career decisions, she often deferred to her husband, Jim. When we discussed my possibly hearing an advance track from *Wicked Wonderland*, she responded, "Maybe he can send you a piece of the song to listen to. He's in control of all that." Something about that stuck with me. Maybe it was the word "control," or just her overall tone of voice.

As it turned out, my instincts weren't wrong. A few years later, Lita and Jim Gillette had a very public divorce and an ugly custody battle over their two sons. The details were messy, painful, and heartbreaking. She later revealed in the press that she had only a forty-five-minute window to escape the marriage. The same woman who had fought so courageously for her place in rock and roll now had to fight for her freedom in a very different way.

In 2012, Lita made a triumphant return with the aptly titled *Living Like a Runaway*, an album that reflected her personal struggles and resilience. She has continued to tour and release music, reaffirming her legacy as a pioneer in heavy metal. I was honored to cross paths with her while putting the finishing touches on this book. I caught her set live at the Notodden Blues Festival in Norway, and I can attest that she's as badass as ever. Dressed in red leather, she tore through her set, playing straight through a pair of Marshall stacks and leading her band like the seasoned pro she is. I was blown away. Later, I met her briefly for a quick photo op. She looked incredible—fit, confident, standing tall, and completely in command.

Decades after she first picked up a guitar, no one has truly followed in her footsteps. While there are many talented female metal players today, none have achieved the same level of fame or cultural impact as Lita Ford. This may be due, in part, to the changing landscape of rock itself. The heyday of heavy metal belonged to the 1980s, when Lita was making her earliest records and defining what it meant for a woman to lead in that world.

Being ahead of your time is a double-edged sword. You fight the hardest battles and might never fully reap the rewards. You make the path easier for those who come after, but the glory may belong to someone else. "I just hope I have made a path for other women to come," she told me.

She has. But so far, no one has walked it quite like Lita Ford.

LITA FORD

— *The Interview* —

[2009]

SF: I'd like to talk about how you started playing.

LF: I started when I was eleven. Now my son is eleven and he is starting to play, which is pretty cool, following mommy's footsteps. I just picked it up and started playing, it was like a gift from God or something.

SF: Did anybody else in your family play?

LF: No. Everybody used to just tell me to shut up (*laughs*).

SF: Was there something about the instrument that you saw that inspired you to pick it up?

LF: Ritchie Blackmore was my inspiration. He really did a lot for me as far as inspiring me to pick up the guitar and play. I idolized Ritchie and I thought his playing was tremendous.

SF: Were you always into heavy metal and hard rock?

LF: There was a time where I listened to the Monkees a lot, and from there I got heavier and heavier. Even now, I don't listen to death metal, but I still do like heavy metal music.

SF: When you first started playing, did you take lessons? Was it difficult to learn guitar or did you just pick it up and play?

LF: I took two lessons and I really felt like I wasn't learning much. The guy who was teaching me would show me something, but I would say, "I already know that." And then he would show me something else, and I would say, "I already know that too." Then he went on and showed me different chord patterns. He did help me and got me going, but I only studied with him for two weeks and that was it.

SF: How did you learn? On your own? Did you use instructional books?

LF: I learned it by ear. If you showed me a chord sheet or a music sheet, I wouldn't be able to tell you what the notes were by looking. I really learnt totally by ear.

SF: Did that make it difficult later on to explain things to other musicians?

LF: People thought it was weird that I could play so well at such a young age. I really didn't get it—why they thought it was weird. To me it was normal and natural. I couldn't figure out why they weren't doing it. I figured if I could do it, why couldn't they? It was like a gift from God.

SF: Did you have any female influences?

LF: Janis Joplin—I think she was awesome. She didn't play guitar, but vocally she was an influence. I didn't sing at first; I had to train myself to sing. And then singing and playing together was a whole different beast in itself. Johnny Winter was a big inspiration, because he used to walk around on stage; he would play and sing and never once would he look at his guitar neck. He just knew right where he was. I would practice on playing and singing at the same time without looking. I went so far as to have a guitar made for me with no dots on the frets and no names or pictures on the fretboard. It was a plain black neck with no dots, so I really couldn't find my way if I looked at it. I wanted to be able to play without seeing where I was, to just feel it. There is a feel to it, and I wanted to master it. I just wanted to be able to wail and not have to look to see where I was at.

SF: I am a little younger than you, but when I was starting there were so few women out there doing it. And I can only imagine there were far fewer when you were starting out.

LF: I always have felt like I was before my time. When I first started a band, I put together a three-piece band with just guitar, drums, and bass, no other guitar player. I really threw myself into the fire. I forced myself into learning how to sing and play at the same time. Later on, I added a keyboard player and a guitar player, which lightened the load. But I was already where I wanted to be by the time I did that.

SF: Was this pre-Runaways?

LF: Yes. I rented a warehouse and I locked myself in there. We would sing and play and scream our heads off if we wanted to, and I would do whatever I had to do to learn how to play without looking at the guitar. I never wanted to use effects, either. We went to see some band once and I was in the girls' bathroom between shows, and I could hear one of the girls talking to another girl in the bathroom, and they said, "Oh yeah, all she did was step on a box, she didn't even play the guitar." I figured, *okay, no boxes.* So I would plug straight into the amp and not use any boxes or effects. Slowly, now after so many years, I have added a digital delay and a wah-wah and that's all I use.

SF: What kind of amp are you using?

LF: Marshalls, of course.

SF: And guitars?

LF: I'm using my old B.C. Rich.

SF: Are you still playing with the double neck?

LF: Yeah, that's my baby.

SF: That's another first; I have never seen another woman do that.

LF: That's another thing that I thought would be different. I really jumped into the fire full force.

SF: When you left the Runaways did you know what you were going to do?

LF: I had a dream, and I followed the path to the dream—and it worked. It came true. I saw a vision and I wanted to do that and make that vision come to life.

SF: What was that vision?

LF: The vision was to be on stage playing guitar in front of a lot of people. At that time, I was just a little kid. When the Runaways came out, I was the oldest one in the band; I was seventeen. The rest were like fifteen and sixteen. Joan is the closest to me in age; we are just a few days apart. Other than that, it was tough—in a man's world too. Being underage we could only play certain clubs. We couldn't play [at] places that served alcohol.

SF: How old were you when you got out of the Runaways?

LF: The Runaways lasted for five years until we broke up.

SF: So by then you were in your twenties. When did Lita Ford, rock artist, arrive? How long did it take you to make the transition from being in a band to being a rock goddess?

LF: I was pretty much already there by the time the Runaways ended. I was figuring out guitar parts and I had riffs for new songs. I already had it in me, and everything fell into place. It was unbelievable. It was really magic. At least now I know that if I die soon, I will die a living legend. Hopefully what I did will help, and has helped, other women rock. I hope I have made a path for other women to come.

SF: Do you notice more women shredders now?

LF: Yeah, I have, and not even women, but men as well will come up to me and say, "Dude, if it wasn't for you, I wouldn't be playing guitar right now." That is worth its weight in gold to hear people say that.

SF: It kind of shocks me that there haven't been any other women shredders or guitar players that have come up and taking your place.

LF: When I left, I left a pair of boots and nobody has yet to come and fill them. They are still sitting there where I left them.

SF: Why do you think that is?

LF: Everybody has their own style and their own taste in music, and they play what they want to play and sing, and that could be part of it. But really, I don't know; I can't answer that. I am sure there are some wonderful young girl guitar players out there, but we just don't know about them yet. They will surface eventually. Maybe me playing guitar will help kick-start their careers.

SF: Do you think you came before people were ready?

LF: Yes, and the Runaways did too. The Runaways were before their time. But I'm not dead yet, so let's hope it opens up the path for a lot of other women. I would love to see it.

SF: I was curious about the fact that you are such a sexy person and performer, and you were very overt about your sexuality—and I'm not saying there's anything wrong with that. I just wonder if you ever thought or ever experienced double standards in the way people interpreted that.

LF: To my knowledge, no, I don't think so.

SF: What's the biggest misconception people have about Lita Ford?

LF: The biggest misconception people have about me would be: "Did she really play the guitar on that? That's not her playing the guitar; that's the other guy." A lot of times I would be on stage and I would be playing the solo but I would see the spotlight go on the other guitar player. It's like, *wait a minute; it's me.* People can't swallow [it], they can't grasp the idea that a female is doing that. Even today people ask me, "Who played the guitar solo on 'Close My Eyes Forever?'" I mean, I did, and it's not even really that difficult a solo. But that is by far the biggest misconception.

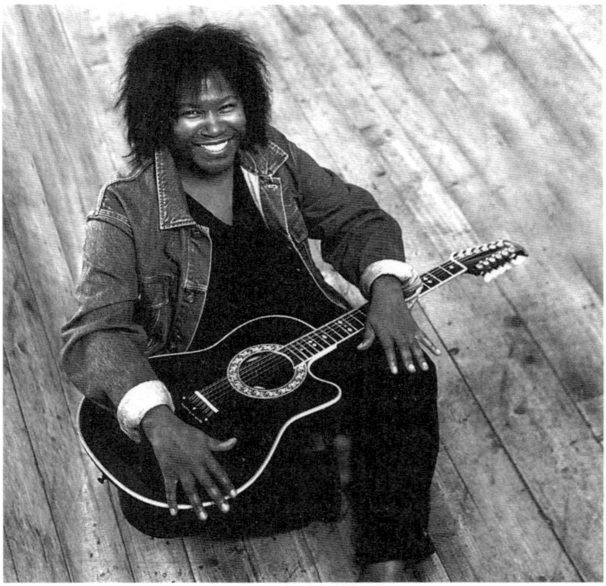

Joan Armatrading

JOAN ARMATRADING

In 2007, Joan Armatrading released *Into the Blues*, featuring her on lead guitar. By that time, I was a few years into conducting interviews, and when I learned that, in addition to being a world-class songwriter, Joan was also an accomplished guitarist, I jumped at the chance to speak with her. Like so many others, I first came to know Joan through her songs—timeless pieces that have left an indelible mark on the history of music and in the hearts of her devoted fans.

For me personally, it was *Me Myself I*. When I was twelve, I played that album incessantly, belting out the chorus with Joan: "I came into this world alone / me, myself, and I." It resonated deeply. While I hadn't yet reached the stage of full-on rebellion, I could sense it coming, and the song's message was empowering—you must love yourself and be content in your own company. Being alone was not just acceptable; it was power.

When we spoke, Joan brushed off her abilities as an instrumentalist, modestly explaining that she had been playing guitar her entire career and had simply evolved into playing leads. The word "evolve" seems to encapsulate Joan and her philosophy—she is constantly moving forward, acquiring new skills, and conquering new creative challenges along her journey.

Joan is the first Black British female singer-songwriter to achieve international success, and among the earliest British women writing and performing their own material to reach a global audience. Although she considers the United Kingdom her home, she was born in St. Kitts and moved with her family to Birmingham, England, when she was seven. Her first introduction to music was her mother's piano, but she was always drawn to her father's guitar. Frustratingly, it was strictly off-limits. When she later spotted an old guitar in a pawnshop window for three pounds, she convinced her parents to buy it. She taught herself to play and immediately began writing songs.

By the age of twenty-two, Joan released her critically acclaimed debut album, *Whatever's for Us* (1972). Two years later, she signed with A&M Records, launching a string of hits that included "Love and Affection," "Willow," and "Drop the Pilot."

At the time of our conversation, Joan was actively involved with Women of the Year, a U.K. organization dedicated to supporting and celebrating women. She spoke passionately about empowering young women to embrace their abilities with confidence and assertiveness.

Joan's achievements extend far beyond her music. Honored with the Most Excellent Order of the British Empire (MBE) in 2001 and the Keys to Sydney, she has also composed for theater and released her twenty-first studio album, *How Did This Happen and What Does It Now Mean* (2024). She holds honorary degrees from the University of Birmingham and the Royal Scottish Academy of Music and Drama. At fifty-eight, she ran her first marathon, raising €76,000 for charity, and remains a devoted ambassador for causes such as The Prince's Trust. She was among the dozens of artists who performed at Wembley Stadium in 1988 to celebrate Nelson Mandela's seventieth birthday, and in 2001 she was commissioned to compose a song in his honor. Joan's connection to causes she believes in is as genuine and heartfelt as her music.

During our interview, Joan shared much wisdom, her words carrying the same honesty, humility, and emotional clarity that define her songs. She is at home in her own company, thriving in solitude, and she has channeled that self-possession into a lifelong pursuit of learning and growth. In recent years, she has slowed her touring schedule but remains resolute in her belief that she will never retire. As a long-time subscriber to her newsletter, I can attest that she is always delving into new creative challenges and pursuits.

Joan Armatrading stands as an inspiring example of someone who knew her calling and followed it with quiet determination, evolving and excelling every step of the way.

JOAN ARMATRADING

— *The Interview* —

[2008]

SF: Are you at home right now?

JA: I'm at home, but currently I'm president of Women of the Year Awards, so I have a lot to do for that, lots of meetings and stuff.

SF: What does your role involve?

JA: It's a big job. The founder of the organization, Tony Lothian, just died. She founded it in 1955 and her premise was that it would be for women of achievement. So, as the president, it's my job to make sure that I try to keep her vision—but I also have my own vision. My job is to take the organization forward, keep it current, and think of the future.

SF: Is this job as much a focus as your music career?

JA: I don't know if it's as much of a deal as my music, because music is a very powerful focus. But it certainly is very important. You find yourself getting very, very emotionally attached to these women because of what they've done. Tina Turner was given the award because she was in that abusive relationship and had the courage to walk out of it. The inspiration she's given to ordinary women who are in situations like that is immeasurable.

SF: I've been a fan since "Me Myself I." I was about twelve when that song was a hit. I was out on the road this summer with a couple of other women guitar players and one of the women was playing your latest CD over and over. Before then, I hadn't even realized you play the guitar.

JA: That's very nice of you. I think a lot of people don't realize that I play guitar. They might hear the guitar in my records, but they just assume it's somebody else. When I did the [1995] record *What's Inside*, there's a really bluesy song in there. It has a great guitar solo and everything. The record company did a focus group on it and they asked, "Who's playing the guitar?" They mentioned just about every guitarist you could think of, but only one person thought it could be me.

People just think of me writing and singing. Some people don't even think of me as a writer. They just think of me as a singer. I started on the acoustic guitar, but at some point on all my records I'm playing electric guitar. That's not what people are looking at or listening to, though. I always have another guitarist when I'm on stage for a long period of time, and sometimes when I play a solo, I can see everybody looking at the other guitarist. People just don't notice that I also play a lot of the guitar.

SF: Do you think that's because you're female, or is it because everyone sees you as the singer-songwriter?

JA: I think it's probably a combination. Also, I'm not a very showy person. When the guitarist is playing, he tends to do all the poses. When I'm playing, I'm quite quiet. I saw Madonna just now on a big concert. She was playing one of her songs on the electric guitar and it was only like three chords, but I tell you, she threw in every shape possible. It looked absolutely fantastic. I thought, that's exactly what I should be doing. But I can't, because it's not me.

SF: Did you have early guitar influences?

JA: Not really. I always say that I was born to be involved in music. I was born to write songs. I didn't wake up one morning and wonder if I could write a song. I just woke up one morning and I wrote a song.

SF: How old were you when you wrote your first song?

JA: I used to write limericks, funny stories, and poems and stuff. Then when I was about thirteen or fourteen, my mom bought the piano. As soon as that piano arrived, I started writing songs. With the piano, it's much easier to find the melody than on the guitar. It's relatively easy to find chord shapes and make things up, so I didn't have any lessons. My dad had a guitar, but he wouldn't let me touch it. He would hide it and he didn't really like playing around me. I was really, really interested in it.

SF: Were you the only child that was interested in playing music?

JA: Certainly, at that time. I saw a guitar in a pawn shop. It cost three pounds, so I asked my mom if I could have it. She didn't have the money, but she had two old prams. She told me if they would swap the guitar for these two prams, I could have it. That's how I got my first guitar, which I still have.

I didn't start with books; I just did the same as I did on the piano—just started to work out where the chords were and do everything by ear. Obviously, later I graduated to books, but the initial thing was just me strumming and making it up.

I also knew from other songs that you had bass, strumming guitar, and piano. So, when I started the acoustic guitar, I tried to play all of those things at once. I think that's why my acoustic guitar playing is so written—because I'm trying to do it all. When I was working for the first time with other musicians, I would always do all my demos myself. I was getting in everyone's way, because I was playing the guitar parts, the bass parts, and trying to cover everything. I had to learn how to stop playing all the bits and let the person who's supposed to play those parts play those parts.

SF: I guess you're doing that again right now because you're producing your own records and playing all the instruments.

JA: But I've always arranged my songs. I've always known what I wanted to hear. Because for me, writing isn't just writing. It's arranging. When I write my stuff, I know where all the parts go. I know where the chorus is, where the middle eight is, where the bridge is and how it all fits together. I know the type of instrumentation I want, and I generally know what I want people to play.

SF: Were you always able to express that to a producer, especially in your younger years?

JA: Yes, because it's music. If it was something else, I would have had more difficulty. But this came quite naturally to me.

SF: I know a lot of young artists get in with big producers and get very intimidated. They end up letting the producer take all the control. You never did that?

JA: No. I'm a very strong person and what was really fortunate was that my first producer, Gus Dudgeon, was the best anybody could have as a first producer. He could recognize that I knew what I wanted. Even on my very first record, I'm playing quite a few instruments: the guitar, the piano, the squeezebox. I'm not sure if it would have been another story if I'd had a different producer. But as things worked out, I was very fortunate to have somebody like him.

SF: Were you a shy kid?

JA: I think I'm probably the shyest person I've ever known. When I went to my first record company, I remember I used to say, "They knew I could sing, but they didn't know I could talk."

SF: You told the *Guardian* in 2005: "I found my sound early on and I stuck to it." That quote really struck me, because sometimes it takes an artist twenty years to grow into their sound. That's also my own experience. But you managed to do that right away.

JA: I think that's because I was so into writing. That's what's important to me. Even though I want people to know that I'm a guitarist, I want them to get connected to the songs. I don't want somebody to say, "Well, she's a fantastic guitar player but I'm not so keen about the song. She should get somebody else to write." I am not going to be happy with that. I am happy when they say, "'Love and Affection' has the best opening line to any song." Or they say, "'The Weakness in Me' describes where I'm at, or what I'm going through."

SF: If you were going to give advice to young musicians, is that what you would say to them? To compose for themselves?

JA: Even people who can write can't write everything. Some people can only write the lyrics, some people can only write the chorus, and some people can only contribute the riff. Some people need to work with a team to write. I would never say to somebody that the only way to get your sound is to write, but I would encourage people to write, because it's a nice way of discovering certain things, whether it's to do with the instrument or how you put words and music together. But not everybody is going to be able to do it well. You just have to recognize that, and then do the thing that you do well.

When I was on tour just now, we went around to some schools and I said to the girls, "Don't be afraid to say you're good at something." Men are great at telling you how good they are. There's no embarrassment when they tell you they're the best at this, that they've achieved that, or that if it wasn't for them, this wouldn't have happened. As a girl or a woman, it's perfectly fine for you to do the same. The confidence you give to yourself by admitting you're great at something is a huge boost. That's definitely something women should do.

The other thing is to be true to yourself. If you're not good at writing, but you're great at playing, or if you're not good at playing or writing, but you're good at being a nurse, or if you're not good at playing or writing or being a nurse, but you are a great mathematician—that's the thing you should be concentrating on. Concentrate on the thing that gives you a lot of confidence and feeling. You can also do things outside that, but firstly, try to do something you love.

SF: It's such simple advice, but so many of us go out of our way to make things more difficult. Did you feel like an anomaly when you

were coming up in the music business? You were completely unique and you've taken this path of your own. Did you ever find that that was a lonely path?

JA: I'm not a lonely person. I do a lot of things on my own, but I don't feel lonely.

SF: Have you been independent your whole life?

JA: Always.

SF: I read that you had to leave school at sixteen.

JA: Yes, I had to leave school to help out with the family. But I was very happy to do everything by myself.

SF: Were you driven by commercial success, or did that matter at all?

JA: No. I was driven to get people to know my songs, to get connected. When I hear things from people like, "I used your song at my wedding," or, "My daughter was christened to your song," or, "We fell in love to this"—that's what I wanted to happen with my songs. And that has happened.

SF: You seem to have stayed so grounded, but a lot of people who have achieved commercial success don't. They get thrown off by the pressure. How do you strike a balance between being a commercially successful artist and keeping your integrity?

JA: I have no idea. I just do what I do, and I can only do what I do. There's no point of somebody telling me to do something that isn't me, because that's just not going to happen. When I made my first album, one of the first things the record company said to me was that I was going to have to change my name because nobody would remember or pronounce "Armatrading." Well, that didn't happen. One of the other things they said was that I would have to start dressing differently. That didn't happen either.

SF: That's so great. There are so many challenges in our business.

JA: Well, I'm probably an idiot. I probably don't realize what's going on (*laughs*).

SF: What is the greatest challenge for you as an artist right now?

JA: It's always writing the next great song. I'm always trying to write something that's better than the last thing. I keep trying to write another song that people would want to hear for the next thirty years.

SF: Did you ever have any mentors?

JA: The closest I would say to anybody mentoring me would be my first producer, Gus Dudgeon. Gus went through some hard times, but he would never show anything negative. He just always stayed upbeat, generous, and kind—everything you want in a human being. When he died, in his little village, everybody came out. They did not come out because he was a celebrity. They came out because he was such a genuine person and such a great human being.

SF: And do you try to stay positive as well?

JA: I'm positive to a fault.

SF: But you hit a lot of melancholy moods in your music, too.

JA: Not all of my songs are all about me. If I had gone through everything I've written about, I'd probably be in therapy (*laughs*).

SF: How do you stay inspired?

JA: I'm alive. That's it. Why are we here otherwise? What are we here for if not to explore?

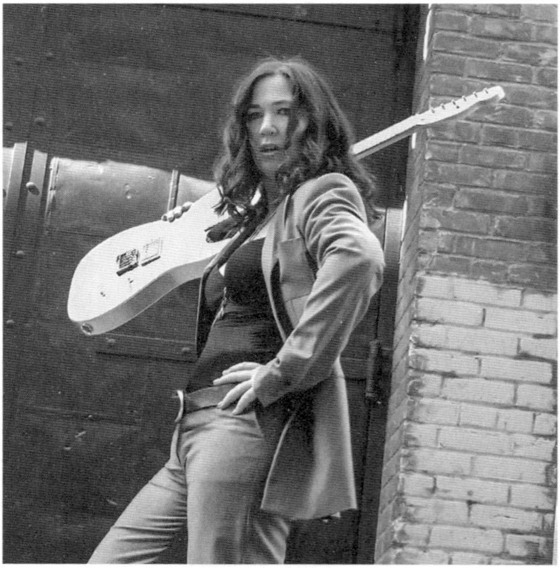

Kathy Valentine

KATHY VALENTINE

I first knew Kathy Valentine as the bassist of the Go-Go's. It wasn't until we met in person that I learned she was a dedicated lead guitarist. Kathy fronted and played lead guitar in several well-known bands in Austin, so we kind of came up in the same scene, in slightly different eras. We connected on many levels: our shared love of the blues, the challenges of motherhood, the realities of being women in music, and the trials of maintaining independence as an artist. Kathy struck me as thoughtful, articulate, and driven. She had a deep curiosity and a relentless passion for her craft, qualities that have kept her firmly rooted in music long after the Go-Go's heyday. Undoubtedly, she was the most serious musician in the group.

I remember seeing the Go-Go's on TV and being awed by these five young women who seemed to snub their noses at the world while having an unabashedly fabulous time. Their energy and enthusiasm radiated a defiance that was intoxicating. The Go-Go's, who evolved from punk rock, carried the same rebellious spirit, but their rebellion was joyful, rooted in claiming their space and unapologetically celebrating their femininity. They were the first all-female band to break through and command widespread attention. Watching them, I felt equal parts longing and envy. I admired their camaraderie and confidence, which felt worlds away from my tomboyish, loner tendencies. What they were doing seemed almost impossible for someone like me.

Kathy Valentine's story began in 1959, as the only child of an often-absent single mother in Austin. Her unconventional path emerged early when she dropped out of school in ninth grade to attend an alternative program, where she discovered the guitar. A pivotal moment came when she saw Suzi Quatro perform.

Her first band came together when she was just sixteen. By her early twenties, she had relocated to Los Angeles to pursue music seriously. A chance encounter with Go-Go's guitarist Charlotte Caffey in a nightclub bathroom changed her life. Kathy was invited to join the group as their bassist, though she also contributed significantly as a songwriter, penning hits like "Vacation" and co-writing "Head Over Heels." In 1981, the Go-Go's made history as the first all-female band to have a No. 1 album in the United States with *Beauty and the Beat.*

Despite their groundbreaking success, internal conflicts led to the band's breakup just four years after Kathy joined. She struggled to find her footing post–Go-Go's, forming several bands with mixed results. Beginning in 1994, the Go-Go's reunited for tours and a new album in 2001. In recent years, they have continued to perform intermittently, cementing their legacy with their 2021 induction into the *Rock & Roll Hall of Fame.*

In 1992, Valentine formed the Bluebonnets, which later morphed into the Delphines. She released two albums with the latter, in 1996 and 2001. When we spoke, she had just released her first solo album, *Light Years.* After moving back to Austin in 2006, Kathy expanded her creative pursuits, working as a producer and public speaker while continuing to play music.

Kathy's resilience extends beyond music. In 2020, she released her memoir, *All I Ever Wanted,* earning praise for its candid depiction of her struggles with addiction and recovery. Her acting debut in *The Transcendents* and contributions to the Broadway musical *Head Over Heels,* a jukebox musical based on Go-Go's songs, highlighted her versatility. Kathy was inducted into the Austin Music Hall of Fame in 2014 and continues to perform with the Bluebonnets.

Today, she remains a testament to endurance and reinvention. With more than four decades in the music industry, more than three decades of sobriety, and a legacy that continues to inspire, Kathy has proven herself not only as a trailblazer but also as an artist who refuses to rest on her laurels.

KATHY VALENTINE

— *The Interview* —

[2005]

KV: So, you're a single mom?

SF: I am.

KV: Hats off to you. It's really challenging, isn't it?

SF: Yeah. You have a three-year-old?

KV: Yeah, can you believe it? My whole life is turned upside down.

SF: Were you planning it?

KV: No. Well—kind of. I met this guy and we emailed each other because I was on tour, and we dated for a couple of months when I got back from my tour. I was forty-two and he was thirty-six. He really wanted to have a family and we were kind of worried about my age, so we got engaged pretty quickly, and as soon as we got engaged we started trying and I got this little thing that predicts your ovulation. I thought it would take at least a year, but it happened right away. So we got married. It was planned, in that we had to start soon, but I didn't think it would come so quick. Our whole first year of being married was either me being pregnant or me having a newborn, so we're just now starting to get together again and have a life and be a couple.

SF: It pretty much throws everything on its ear, right? Are you enjoying it—the mommy thing?

KV: Yeah, but I have a lot of advantages. The guy I married is an attorney and also a musician, so it's kind of the best of both worlds because he's really creative and really musical, but he has a good job and earns good money. I have a lot of advantages because the Go-Go's don't work that much and the money that I make from that, which used to be barely enough to squeeze by, now it kind of helps out. I can still do music and can afford to make a record.

SF: Congratulations, by the way. That must feel good to finally get your own album out.

KV: It's weird, because I didn't really ever want to do that. I just wanted to be in a band. But when I was pregnant, I did a few songs and I liked it. I started really liking being the boss and producing it—just getting to do whatever I wanted without it being under review by your band members to see if they like it, too.

SF: So you've always been a team player, and this is like a totally different animal.

KV: I did a few songs; then I had a baby. Then it was a few months before I started recording again. I was breastfeeding and doing my guitar overdubs in this little Pro-Tools studio. Every three hours, it was like, "Oops, gotta go. Baby's hungry!" It was funny—learning how to balance and juggle things. It took about a year and a half to finish the record. I'm not good at making them at all. I kept having to go back and I would give a person three shots at doing it, and I would still not be happy. Then I'd have to find someone else. It took eight months to get it mixed.

SF: At least you had the time to devote to it. There wasn't a lot of pressure on you.

KV: Do you play much where you are?

SF: Not too much. I kind of chill out when I'm home raising my son. I live in a little town; there's no scene. But honestly, when I got pregnant, I had been out so much on the road that I didn't care anymore. I didn't care to be out trying to make the scene. I travel still. It's kind of the challenge right now, but I still like to get away and go play. I have to deal with the separations, which someday, I'm sure you'll have to deal with.

KV: Do you have family to help you?

SF: Yeah, my mom helps me. That's another reason why I'm up here, because I am close to my family.

KV: The leaving part is hard. I've had to do a couple of tours, and each time I've taken Audrey for part of it. But it's a real hassle, because I have to pay somebody to come with me and be a babysitter. Then there's the extra plane ticket. The other two girls [in the band] that have kids, theirs are much older. I think they're probably glad to get away. I've never even spent a night away from my daughter.

SF: Are you home most of the time?

KV: It's not so bad. Luckily, Belinda lives in France and has a pretty successful career, so she doesn't want to do it that much. If she did and everyone else wanted to, I would just have to quit. But right now, it's maybe three weeks here, maybe two weeks there.

SF: Is it the original line-up?

KV: Yeah, we started again in 1999, and we've pretty much worked every year. It's mainly corporate shows, or casinos, or wineries. It's not really on the radar. Every now and then, we'll play a big venue in a major city and book other dates around there.

SF: Are you playing bass?

KV: Yeah.

SF: I don't know if I've ever even talked to you about the Go-Go's because I always saw you with the Delphines, hanging out in blues clubs and stuff like that. How do you find it now, the change in the band over this many years? How does it feel to be touring now as opposed to then? Is the music the same? Have you grown as musicians?

KV: It's been up and down with me over the years since I first started doing Go-Go's stuff again in 1999. I'd been focusing on guitar, playing in a trio, which really pushes you as a player. At first, it felt like going back to bass and the Go-Go's was sort of going backward. The band stays the same; everything is fixed, there's no improvising, and even changing a song arrangement is a major undertaking. But then I started looking at it differently: how could I just be the best musician I could be in that band. How present I could be, to pay attention to each moment and see what I could bring to it, whether it was supporting the rhythm guitar, locking in tight with drums, or putting in a bass melody or run where there was space needing a hook. Playing bass is fun in the Go-Go's because it's something I do really well, and probably the only band I should ever really play bass in. My guitar playing wouldn't fit with this band, we wouldn't sound the same, but my bass playing has a lot to do with how we sound.

The Go-Go's mean a lot to a lot of people, and it's not just about being a musician when I play with them. It's performing, being an entertainer. It's about the songs, the nostalgia people have around them, and what we represented to a lot of people in terms of what was possible, where you could end up despite a lot of odds against you. And, of course, any musician loves to operate at that level. It's a luxury to travel well, have a lot of crew and support, stay in nice places, and have sold-out shows with audiences who love you. I will go for all that every chance I get. But I'm also happy to lug my own amp out of the practice room, into the car, drive to the bar gig, and play to a roomful of people in Austin. I just like to play, and I like to play in a band, not by myself, so that's what I've done, nonstop, for a long time. But bands aren't always easy, and the longer you do it, the more history and baggage you collect. It's like being married to four people, in my case to four women.

Tell me about your book.

SF: I'm writing a book about women guitar players. I was researching it and I realized that there was no book of its kind. Not only was there no book, there really was no documentation in any one place about the contributions of women guitar players.

KV: Who's that woman that plays with Bo Diddley?

SF: Lady Bo?

KV: When I saw Lady Bo, I just flipped. I thought, *How come nobody knows about her?* I guess maybe she just had a minimal role in Bo's band. I always read and hear about how girls can't play, still to this day. I've seen articles that say women don't really play guitars, and even from other women! I remember reading something that Chrissie Hynde said [something] like, "I would never get a woman in my band because they don't really have the right feel." I'm just appalled. I wanted to produce a record that was just all women on guitar.

SF: Were you a guitar player originally?

KV: Yeah, I was playing guitar. I had just moved to L.A. and I was trying to make it—be successful. When they asked me, they had kind of gotten popular. I learned all the songs, and my first show with them was at the Whisky and it was three shows. Sold out. I was thinking, *Okay, this is what I came here for*. At that point, I didn't care: guitar, bass, tambourine—I just wanted to be in a fun band. I was twenty-two and I really liked their songs. That was what really sold me. It never occurred to me to look back. When we broke up I kind of floundered. My identity as a musician was kind of lost.

SF: Were you playing regular guitar then, too?

KV: No, I was completely a Go-Go. I would play guitar on the records here and there, because even back then, I had some abilities that were different. But I was pretty much the bass player, and when we broke up for a couple of years, I didn't know what I was. I had tried to put together a succession of bands. Sometimes I would play bass, sometimes rhythm guitar. It wasn't until 1992, seven years after the Go-Go's broke up, that I just got sick of being lost. I actually started dating a guy from Austin and he reminded me of what I had grown up with, of what I wanted and why I first started playing. I wanted to play lead. I wanted to be good. It's not too late to start now—and I did.

SF: After the breakup, did you go back and take lessons or anything?

KV: No, I just played with records.

SF: What kind of stuff? Has it always been rock and roll?

KV: The first thing I decided to start was a blues band, because I just knew that wherever I went, that had to be the foundation. I found a couple of other girls: a bass player who was pretty new at playing bass, a backup singer who'd always wanted to be a lead singer, and a pretty good drummer from Kentucky who could play shuffles and stuff. That's how we started the Bluebonnets. The whole purpose was to have fun and get better on our instruments. It was probably the eighth or ninth band that I'd put together since the Go-Go's split. It was the only band where I wasn't trying to get anywhere and, ironically, it was the band that started getting pursued by record companies. People would come up and say, "You guys are great. Do you have a demo?" We'd be like, "What do we want a demo for?" We did all covers and then, later on, started doing some original songs, but we really just wanted to get better at playing. I thought, eventually it will turn into something else. I didn't want to just be a blues cover band. I figured it would morph.

SF: How long were you guys together for?

KV: With a couple of shifting line-ups we went from 1992 to 1995. Just three years. Then we became the Delphines. We were just a trio.

SF: Are the Delphines over now?

KV: Pretty much. We just never went anywhere. It became too hard. We never really caught on. We made two CDs and right when I got pregnant,

I decided I didn't want to be driving around, hauling my amp in and out of seedy clubs. The last show I did was in Texas and I was four or five months pregnant. The club was full of smoke and I was freaking out because I was breathing this second-hand smoke and I just said, "That's it!"

SF: I wonder what it's like to go through all these stages of performing. From performing huge shows and being in a big band and then just back in clubs.

KV: When the Go-Go's got back together, I had just put the Delphines together and I was really excited. I really thought that this was going to go somewhere, and I had a really bad attitude. I didn't want to do a Go-Go's tour, but I wanted the money. I remember them being amazed that I had a club gig booked for the day the tour ended.

SF: When you traveled with the Delphines, was it just in a van, humping your own gear?

KV: Yes, a rented van or a truck. I never minded the back-and-forth. I just love to play, and I really loved playing guitar and it was really different. The Go-Go's was a different thing, and bass is a different instrument. I think bass is really sexy, and I was able to finally get my bass lines into something I would really like to play because I was a much better musician than when we did the Go-Go's records. Over the years I appreciate the simplicity of what I do in that band. And it was really about making everyone sound good. I started adapting that into my role as a Go-Go and it made me a lot happier. I love the immediacy of the guitar, how you can express your mood and emotions. Sometimes, you have to just play right on the spot, stop thinking. I remind myself that I don't have to show off, just play a note and relax. That's what I really like. The immediacy. Being right in the moment and not thinking about anything else.

SF: Who are your favorite guitar players?

KV: Hendrix, Stevie and Jimmie [Vaughan], B. B., Freddie King in the blues world. In rock or other kinds, Steve Cropper, Mike Campbell,

James Honeyman-Scott from the Pretenders. When I hear some of that stuff, I think he's coming from a similar place as I am.

SF: Do you think Chrissie Hynde was a good guitar player?

KV: Rhythm, yeah. I like girls that don't play girly, and any girl that plays guitar good doesn't play girly.

SF: I always liked the way she stood and held her guitar. Women like that were influential to me. Were there any women guitar players who influenced you?

KV: You.

SF: Ah, thanks.

KV: The woman who inspired me to pick it up again was a woman named Delphine, which is where I got the band name. I was just watching her in a club one night. She was French and Japanese. She was really into Poison Ivy from the Cramps. I remember just watching and seeing how cool she was, and how she played very simple stuff and it was just cool and it worked. I always have this thing in my mind that you have to be good: really, really good. That attitude stopped me from going back to guitar, because I didn't want to be not good. I especially didn't want to be thirty-five years old and not good, and [seeing Delphine] was like this light bulb. I realized you don't have to know a lot to be good. When I met Denny [Freeman] he became my guitar guru.

SF: I was gonna ask you about that because he's so great.

KV: I was kind of horrified because the second Bluebonnets gig, Denny came down. When I realized he was there I was kind of embarrassed. He just said, "You're a guitar player." I just thought, *okay, he didn't have to say that.* We became really close and he would tell me things like, "You don't need to know a lot to play cool stuff."

SF: How is it now with your baby? Are you getting out playing?

KV: I just did my first few club gigs where I was fronting the band and singing. It was really great, really fun. I put together a band and got together three women who played on my record. Then I got Vicki Peterson from the Bangles; she plays guitar and sings. A lot of my record has harmony guitar lines, so I needed someone who could play a little bit of lead and could sing, too. Then I had a girl named Abby Travis that played bass and keyboards. Everyone is in their own thing and I can't use this band all the time, but I want to have a really strong thing for my first couple of shows. Now I'm just trying to put together a band of people who aren't really busy. I need people who are local. I don't plan on going on tour, because I can't afford to pay a band.

SF: Does your daughter go to preschool?

KV: She goes to preschool three days a week and I have a babysitter who comes part-time. She drives and takes her to ballet. She has a band called the Rock-On's. She's got a little drum kit and a little guitar and keyboards and microphones.

SF: When she gets a little older it'll be a lot easier for you to get around. I always figure, if you're home as much as you are and I was, it doesn't damage them if you're gone for a week. I think it's harder if they have a parent or two parents that are working twelve hours a day.

KV: Steven gets up and leaves really early. Today he got up at four-thirty in the morning and he won't come home until seven at night. He's in corporate litigation, and it's really high-powered stress. The whole payoff is that we have a comfortable lifestyle, and hopefully he can retire in five years. But it's pretty bad now. When we take a vacation it's great, but then it's more of the same. Sometimes, I feel like a single mom and it hurts his feelings because Audrey always calls for me, not him.

SF: What's down the road for you? Are you just enjoying life day-by-day now?

KV: I have some goals. I have a TV show in development—a reality show I'd like to get made. It's basically a reality/music thing that would entail putting together a female band and trying to have them compete. The winning band would get the record deal. I also want to make another record and address topics that are hard to write about. I also want to learn to play drums and write a movie. We also want to have another kid, but I can't do it.

SF: Was it hard physically?

KV: It was kind of hard on my body, the breastfeeding. My left shoulder is messed up. Maybe from playing guitar all these years and carrying my baby. She just wouldn't fall asleep unless you were holding her or carrying her. I didn't realize it at the time, but looking back it was really hard.

SF: My shoulder is really messed up. I don't know if it has anything to do with having a kid hanging on me all those years. I just assumed it was from guitar.

KV: Is it your left shoulder?

SF: No, it's my right.

KV: My left shoulder is so out of whack. I've tried physical therapy and all kinds of stuff.

SF: How do you stay so healthy? You look great in your pictures.

KV: I eat pretty well. I exercise and I think I have good genes. I stopped drinking and smoking a long time ago.

SF: How old were you when you quit?

KV: I haven't had a drink in seventeen years, and I haven't smoked in ten or thirteen years, maybe less. I think I had a few relapses. It took me almost two years to lose the weight from the baby. I was up to 154 pounds. I went and did a tour and couldn't stand the way it felt to be onstage and being self-conscious. The last thing you want to worry about when you're playing is what you look like. You have to either not give a shit, or you have to look good.

SF: Why is it that you find yourself in a lot of female bands? Is it because of the Go-Go's? Or a sisterhood thing?

KV: Good female musicians have more mystique to me. Maybe because it's just not the norm—even though it's not such a rare thing. I think partly because there hasn't been the "ultimate female band." There hasn't been the [female] Stones or Beatles. There hasn't been that band, and part of me just wants it to exist. I want them to be up in the pantheon of rock.

I thought in the 1980s the Go-Go's would blow the doors down and people would think, *oh yeah, women can be successful whatever style,* but really, as far as huge mainstream success [in 2009], there have only been two all-female bands and that's the Go-Go's and the Bangles. I think maybe there just aren't that many female bands. The odds are against us. Every year, you have Coldplay, Green Day, Blink-182. All these bands have big careers and they're all guys. Then a band like the Donnas will come along and they'll do okay, but they won't really have that special magic that makes them really big.

SF: Do you find the way guys perceive you from the audience is different from how girls perceive guys from the audience?

KV: I see guys react the same way as women do, but that's changed. It didn't used to be that way.

SF: What did it used to be like?

KV: When the Go-Go's were in our peak, I heard from a lot of guys that they liked us but they didn't want to let on. We had a lot of girls and kids and a lot of gay men, gay women. Now there are a lot of heteros out there, too. There are just different personalities. I'm an only child, so I like that sister bonding, too. I also love playing with guys. As long as it's the right guys.

SF: The Go-Go's made a big impact on me. I'm a bit younger than you, but I remember watching you guys on TV and going, *man, I wanna do that.*

KV: When I started playing, there were no women, and when I started playing guitar I thought, *I'm gonna be the first one.* What changed it for me was when I was in England in 1975 and I saw Suzi Quatro on TV. It had never occurred to me that a woman could be a rock star before I saw her. I knew that women sang, I knew they'd strummed guitars, but I never saw any woman being a rock star. I went from wanting to play acoustic guitar to wanting to be a rock star. And it was all because of her.

SF: Hopefully it won't be long before we see some chick break through. Hopefully she won't be cheesy.

KV: A lot of the girls that are out there playing can be kind of corny. You'd think that if they were playing guitar they'd be immediately cool, but I know of several out there playing that are really good but they're very corny.

SF: Well, you know a lot of guitar players are dorks, complete goofs. Think about it. These people are kind of antisocial. They sit around their rooms by themselves all the time. You think they're really cool, but then you get to know them.

KV: I've known a lot of girls that are just corny. They dress corny, their hair is corny, their music is corny, and yet they have the ability to really play. I mean you gotta be cool, too. When I saw Jimmie Vaughan when I was fifteen years old, I flipped.

SF: I had the same experience when I saw him when I was fifteen. I couldn't take my eyes off him.

KV: Yeah, I freaked out. Not only was he great, but he was the coolest person to ever walk on two legs. Maybe that's the problem. Maybe a lot of girls just didn't have the advantage of seeing Jimmie Vaughan.

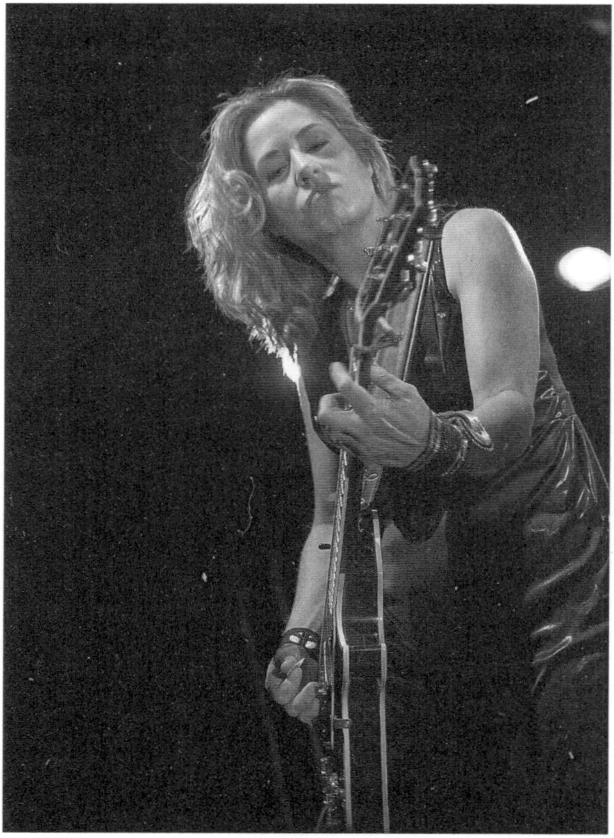

Vicki Peterson

VICKI PETERSON

The Bangles and the Go-Go's were two of the most groundbreaking all-female bands ever to hit the mainstream. Like the Go-Go's, they had a distinct femininity in both their sound and their look. It was the 1980s, an era of heavy makeup, big hair, and bold styling. But, beneath all that polish, there was an unmistakable edge to their image. Guitarist Vicki Peterson led that charge. I was naturally curious to speak with her and hear about the band's musical journey and evolution. Kathy Valentine kindly made the introduction.

Vicki's love for music started early. She and her sister Debbi, who played drums, formed a band while still in high school in California. Their parents were supportive, encouraging their daughters to pursue music and fostering an environment where creativity could thrive.

In the early 1980s, they formed the Bangs, a band that blended power pop with a strong 1960s vibe. When Susanna Hoffs and Annette Zilinskas joined, the lineup was complete. After discovering there was another band called the Bangs, they rebranded as the Bangles. As part of the Los Angeles club scene, they built a loyal following before breaking into the mainstream with hits like "Manic Monday," "Walk Like an Egyptian," "Hazy Shade of Winter," and "Eternal Flame." Their blend of harmonies, musicianship, and pop sensibility made them one of the defining acts of the decade.

Despite their success, the Bangles faced challenges familiar to many women in the music industry. Vicki spoke candidly about the constant pressure to maintain a polished image, comparing it to being treated like fashion models rather than rock musicians. The demand to look a certain way, on top of the already grueling nature of being in a band, was a reality she and her bandmates had to navigate throughout their careers.

After the Bangles originally disbanded in 1989, Vicki continued her musical journey with various projects. She co-founded the Continental Drifters, a roots-rock supergroup based in New Orleans that included Susan Cowsill of the Cowsills, an influential 1960s family band made up of six siblings and their mother, Barbara, best known for their tight harmonies and pop hits like "The Rain, The Park & Other Things." Through this band, Vicki became deeply immersed in the New Orleans music scene. Her time there also led to a personal connection that would shape the next chapter of her life. She married John Cowsill, drummer and vocalist of the Cowsills, who played drums and keyboards for the Beach Boys' touring band.

I was curious about relationships in the music industry, and our conversation turned toward the close-knit and sometimes complicated nature of relationships within bands. By "complicated," I mean the personal connections that form within groups, romantic, creative, and otherwise, that can lead to challenges, both professional and personal. I found it inspiring that Vicki has been able to make this musical partnership with her husband work so well.

Though the Bangles reunited in the late 1990s and continue to perform as a legacy act at festivals and 1980s tribute shows, Vicki remains musically active outside of the band. Recently, she and John Cowsill began collaborating musically for the first time, releasing their debut album, *Long After the Fire*, in April 2025.

As with my conversation with the Go-Go's Kathy Valentine, Vicki brought up the fact that, as of the late 2010s, there hasn't been another all-female rock band to achieve similar commercial success. While the Go-Go's and the Bangles helped break barriers for women in rock, no major all-female bands have reached their level of chart dominance in the years since. It's an interesting and somewhat disappointing reality, considering the trailblazing these bands did in the 1980s. In more recent years, bands like Haim and the Beaches have carried that flame forward, earning acclaim, awards, and devoted audiences of their own, yet the kind of mainstream chart dominance once achieved by the Go-Go's and the Bangles remain elusive.

What struck me most was that even after achieving such remarkable success and reinventing herself time and again, Vicki's devotion to the guitar has never wavered. From her teenage years in California to global stardom, from her deep connection to the New Orleans music scene to her marriage into one of pop music's most enduring families, she has stayed true to who she is—a guitarist who simply loves to play.

VICKI PETERSON

— *The Interview* —

[2007]

SF: You have a passion for cooking.

VP: I like to cook. I mean, I'm not a great cook, but maybe it's because I've been a vegetarian since 1982, that it's almost easier sometimes to just cook at home, and I have a very patient husband who pretty much eats anything I put in front of him, which is great.

SF: Kathy Valentine said some really interesting things about you, saying that you're maybe the real player in the Bangles.

VP: That's amazing for her to say that, and I do appreciate that, because I consider myself a complete and utter hack—and you can quote me on that. I think Debbi's the real natural musician in the band, my sister the drummer.

SF: Maybe Kathy said that because you play in so many different outfits. You just like to play—when the Bangles aren't playing, you're out doing something else.

VP: I tend to find these real comfortable, almost social situations to snuggle back into, musically. As soon as the Bangles went on hiatus in 1989, I immediately hooked up with the Continental Drifters, and that was a group of friends and people I've known more tangentially throughout my life as a musician, and it became my second family. It was the most incredible musical experience I'd had, even including the Bangles. The Bangles was obviously a life-altering experience in a lot of ways, but there were so many things in that soup that were nonmusical. Not "unmusical," but just things other than actually making music.

SF: Right, lots of publicity.

VP: Lots of that, lots of "you're just a band, but you're supposed to look like a fashion model." A lot of that sort of thing. I was very happy to turn my back on that when I hooked up with the Drifters.

SF: Are the Drifters still out touring?

VP: Not really, no. The Drifters right now is more of a concept. I can't imagine a time where there will be no Drifters. But at the moment, none of us are playing as the Drifters. I've always said that we'll be eighty years old and on somebody's front porch playing, because that could happen. It's that kind of a musical outfit, where we are all huge fans of each other. We, like many bands, have a very intricate complicated and interesting social dynamic as well. And a musical dynamic.

SF: That's a mixed-gender band too?

VP: Yes, it is. And you know what happens with mixed-gender bands.

SF: The Fleetwood Mac thing.

VP: Completely Fleetwood Mac. Yeah, it started out with two couples in the band, and then one couple broke up, one of the members left, the other couple eventually broke up and two of the other members hooked up, and then it got to where we decided to not play together for a while. That's a book right there. I got that stowed away in my head.

SF: Susan Cowsill is from the Cowsills?

VP: That's right.

SF: And you married her brother?

VP: I did. Something she always feared that I would do. She literally told me one day, "If you date my brother, I'll kill you." I've known them for twenty-eight years. I mean, it's even crazier because I mean, when I was nine years old I knew I was gonna marry John Cowsill.

SF: Oh my God, how did you know that? You had Cowsill records?

VP: Yeah, I was a fan, but I wasn't a "posters on the wall" fan. It's one of the reasons I have a more complex empathy for the fan/artist dynamic, because I've been on the fan side so intensely. Most artists can tell you they were a fan of somebody, somebody sparked them, somebody made them want to make music. For me, it was the Beatles, when I was a toddler. I was a really little kid singing Beatles songs. Then I had this weird fascination with the Cowsills, and it was even at the end. Their career was basically over by the time I really started paying attention to them. I don't know why, but I just knew I was gonna know them.

SF: And boy, do you ever.

VP: Yeah, there you go. But it's great; they're very special people and I'm very lucky to be a part of this family. They're hilarious when they get in a room. I don't even say a word, I just sit in the corner and watch the games, because it's amazing.

SF: Have you dated musicians a lot? I'm always interested how other women feel being on the road and doing the relationship, coming and going, "it's-on-it's-off" thing.

VP: It is hard. Through the big trying days of the Bangles, when we were pretty much on the road for four or five years almost nonstop, we'd come home long enough to make the next record, and then immediately we'd be off on a promotional tour of some kind, and then an actual tour. I dated a musician for most of those years, Jeff McDonald from Redd Kross. I just love these little things that happen: in 1995, I subbed for Charlotte Caffey on several months of touring with the Go-Go's, because she was pregnant with my ex-boyfriend's baby. She and Jeff got together right after Jeff and I split up. It's just these beautiful little threads in this very small community of ours, I guess. I was single for a good six years, and I even wrote a song called "Single by Choice." Pretty much as soon as I wrote that song, I became engaged to John [Cowsill].

SF: Do you think it's easier to have somebody who's in your own business? At least they can relate and understand what you do.

VP: I do, although I don't think it's necessary. It helps to have somebody who has an artistic appreciation, and yet I don't know that it's necessarily easier for two artists to be together. I actually was looking for a "Kathy's husband."

SF: A lawyer. I always thought that, too. She nailed it.

VP: She totally got it. You know, that was my dream: I do not want to marry a musician. I really, really did not want to marry a musician. Because to me, and maybe this is just how I react to things, I think it's difficult for two people who are artists in the same field to find a way to make music and still keep their individuality. Maybe that's a female thing. In my past I would do that, where if there was a guitar in the room, he's gonna pick it up first. And I'll go and do the dishes.

SF: Right.

VP: And it's not right, and it's probably not that way for everyone, but that tends to be what happens to me. I have kind of the perfect situation, because I did marry a musician, and I married someone who has been playing professionally since he was seven. But he's not a songwriter, and he's an incredible singer, sings pretty much nonstop around the house, he is very funny, but he doesn't see himself as an "artist." So he's not off needing a lot of personal space to create. He's just a player, and he pretty much can play anything. He's a drummer but he's playing keyboards in the Beach Boys right now, and he considers himself an entertainer. I think it would be the things that describe him as well.

For me, there is none of that funny pressure of "who's going for the guitar first in the room," and if I say to him, "I need a day, I haven't written in a long time, I just need to leave the house for a day," he is so supportive of that. Because he thinks it's amazing that I can write a song. I love that.

SF: You're still writing a lot?

VP: No, not a lot, not enough. I'm getting back into it from—I'm not gonna say it was a dry spell, I consider it not paying attention. Because the channel's always there, it's always open, but you really have to turn the TV set on. My TV's been off for a long time, I've been very distracted by other things in life, and at this point, I have to make a concerted effort to say, "Okay, I'm going to now be open, and I'm gonna write."

SF: Does it take a while to turn it back on?

VP: It does, and for me, maybe because I am a very domestic creature, when I'm home, I do want to be cooking, and I can't stand a dirty house, and I do all these things myself. I don't have a housekeeper or anything; I don't like that invasion of privacy, so I just do everything myself. I have to leave my home in order to work.

SF: I'm like that, too. I wonder if it's the balance of when you're gone, and then when you're home you just wanna take care of the home.

VP: I don't think that's a bad thing.

SF: No, and like you say, cooking probably feeds your creativity in some way.

VP: It's definitely a creative influence. I don't know if you find this, but sometimes when you're doing stupid menial tasks, your brain is freed up to wander, and to fantasize, and that's when I get story ideas and song ideas a lot of the time. Literally, while scrubbing a toilet, so there you go.

SF: Have you ever thought of doing a Vicki Peterson album?

VP: I've thought about it, but obviously not have given too much thought because I've never done it. I've always been more comfortable in the conglomerate. I'm more of a team player.

SF: Kathy took a neat approach, when she had so many friends and guests on her CD. I think she's like you; she's a team player. That's the impression I got. Are you guys playing together on anything these days?

VP: I did play with her when she first started doing music from the new CD here in L.A. I was playing with her and her band, and that was a blast. It was so fun. I don't consider myself a lead guitar player. I just sort of barely get by really, because it's never been the focus of my energy. She wanted someone to do lead [guitar] and vocals with her, but also good solid rhythm guitar playing too, which I was more happy to do. I said, "Kathy, you're a better lead player than I am, so will you please take this one? You know I'm just gonna do my hack Neil Young one-note solo here." She's a more blues-oriented solo player.

SF: The Bangles, were there two guitars or just you?

VP: No, there's two. Susanna's a rhythm player. By default I became the lead guitar player. But it's definitely by default.

SF: How did you approach your leads with that situation? More like on the melody line?

VP: I rip off the melody, or I tend to do this thing that my friend Kevin Salem, an incredible guitar player, pointed out to me. He noticed that I tend to come up with melody lines within the chords, like right there, my fingers are on the chord, and I find a way to make a little riff. I guess it's a Beatle-esque trick, something George Harrison used to do. Apparently, I do that, and I was made to feel better about my abilities by Davitt Sigerson, who produced the third Bangles CD, the one that "Eternal Flame" was on. He said, "Look you're a guitar composer, don't worry about being the great player. You have time; we can do it again."

SF: You can't be everything at all times, right? But then you must be able to serve that purpose in that song.

VP: Exactly, I can play what I write.

SF: If your sister plays the drums, are you from a musical family, or did you guys just pick it up on your own?

VP: We did pick it up on our own, but we were very, very much encouraged by our parents. They shared with us a love of pop music, and so, when were outside working in the yard with our dad, most of the time he had top-forty radio going.

SF: Your parents were pretty youthful?

VP: They were, and they were musically centered. They listened to a lot. My dad also listened to classical music, and my mom loved some jazz, and other vocal music of their generation, but they were also kind of hip. They really liked AM radio at the time, and then even FM radio a little later. They were big Beatles fans. I mean, we've told this story before, but the night the Beatles were on *Ed Sullivan*, my parents got my older sister and me out of bed to watch it. Which I, of course, just thought was the coolest thing ever—that I got to stay up that late. But I was also very tuned into [the idea that] this is something important, this is something special. Plus I had already kind of caught Beatle fever from my older sister, who was completely tuned in and got it.

SF: I've done over fifty interviews for this book now, and that moment in time has come up many times, when people have said, "Oh, it's when I saw the Beatles on *Ed Sullivan*, then I decided to play guitar."

VP: I'm sure that program was heavily hyped ahead of time; it had to have been—because why else would somebody like my parents know about it, to know to make it a special event? It was probably in an era where I don't know how many things were heavily promoted like that. Today we're bombarded with that stuff constantly, but in 1964, I think that was a pretty unusual approach to a television program. That's partially why people of my age, who were cognizant enough as young children—I mean, you think you know a four-year-old or a five-year-old isn't really gonna get it or watch, but they do.

SF: The guitar was the thing that struck you?

VP: I don't know exactly why that was, but I did immediately start asking for guitars, and I got a plastic guitar for the first Christmas [after that], and then the second Christmas I got an actual wood guitar from Sears.

Sometime in the next year I convinced my parents—with the help of a local music store, who were just trying to sell gear—to buy me a Rickenbacker copy. My first electric guitar was this very cool electric guitar, a Rick copy, and it was just like the one the Beatles had.

SF: So you were way into the Beatles?

VP: Oh yeah. And that was in the fourth grade.

SF: You were already playing your guitar then, and was songwriting what struck you first?

VP: I took lessons for about six months, just enough to be able to score the electric guitar; it was sort of the whole point. The music store was just trying to sell the gear and sell lessons, so if you were gonna take the lessons you had to buy the guitar. I took lessons for just a few months, and then gave up because I really wasn't that into playing, except that I like making up songs, and I started doing that at age nine. It was really more about writing songs, to accompany myself.

SF: Who were your influences writing, just the Beatles or were there other people?

VP: No, it was the Beatles, then by the time I was twelve, thirteen, it was the whole singer/songwriter era, so at that point I was doing Joni Mitchell, Paul Simon—big Paul Simon fan—and James Taylor. I was the girl at the park with the guitar sitting under the tree. That was me, writing these tortured, really bad, laments of long-lost unrequited love.

SF: Were you a feminine girl or were you tomboyish?

VP: I was both. As a little kid I was up the trees and over the fences, but I just wanted to be a teenage girl, because that's what it's all about. I mean, it's so true right?

SF: Right. It still is.

VP: It still is. We're still marketing to teenage girls.

SF: You and your sister, Debbi, started a band together in high school, and that is the Bangles?

VP: That grew into the Bangles. We had another female guitar player too, whom we had to fire eventually. She weighed about ninety-seven pounds, would drink one-and-a-half beers and then forget everything. I felt like her mom, telling her she can't have a beer until after the show. It became stupid, so we had to let her go, and then [original bassist] Amanda [Hills] decided to continue with her education, and she went and got married, and suddenly being in a rock band and being in academia didn't jive.

So it was Debbi and I. We were playing Hollies covers and real fast power-pop kind of stuff, until we hooked up with Susanna, and then we kind of just let our '60s hair down, as it were, and completely went in that direction.

SF: How old were you when you met Susanna?

VP: Twenty-two, or maybe twenty-three.

SF: Were the Go-Go's already going?

VP: Yeah.

SF: Were they an influence?

VP: They were, on a certain level. I mean, obviously, we were already doing it. They went to England and then came back and made their first record. Part of me was really pissed off that they got there first. And the other part of me was thrilled, because: a) it was a really good record; and b) it was just so inspiring. I won't say they influenced us as much as they inspired us to just keep going. I already believed that there was no reason why it wouldn't work.

SF: It's actually a miracle that the radio programmers allowed two all-female bands to be on the charts at the same time.

VP: Well, if you really look at the charts, the Go-Go's had broken up before the Bangles had their first hit.

SF: Okay. That makes sense.

VP: That used to piss me off, because there was also a moment in time where Belinda was doing her solo career, and she would have a single out and we would put our single out the same week or whatever. We'd be calling radio, and doing our promotion thing that we were always doing, and there would be certain instances where [we heard], "Oh, we can't add you this week, because we just added Belinda. But we'll add you next week." *And why is that? Because is there only one all-boy band on your list this week? Plus, she a singer, not a band, and why are we even having this conversation?* That can just be completely befuddling. But it was real.

SF: When you were looking for role models when you were a young guitar player, did you find any women that you could look up to?

VP: I always thought Joni Mitchell was underrated as a guitar player. She was an incredible guitar player. People say because she uses a lot of tunings that somehow that doesn't count—I don't understand why. But she's one, and then Bonnie Raitt. She's up there with any guitar player you put her against. There were great rock guitar players—Lita Ford.

SF: Do you know her?

VP: I have a connection with her, but haven't seen Lita since the '90s. I think she got tired of not being able to be heard. I think she felt underappreciated, too, and she's a good guitar player—I mean, in that metal, note-per-second way.

SF: Right, the shredder.

VP: We just did a show in February with Joan Jett. She was great, and we talked a little bit after the show. She's incredible.

SF: How did you guys do your first gigs? How did you take it from the living room to the stage?

VP: We'd been booking our own shows since high school, really. When I first graduated from high school, Amanda, Debbi, and I were playing in little sleepy bars in the South Bay area.

SF: You were just booking yourself into these bars?

VP: Exactly, we just figured we'd learn as you go. But at that time and in that level, you get yourself booked, you make your little homemade flyers, and under the cover of darkness you would go and flyer the city as much as you can. And hope that people show up.

SF: Did you have to get streetwise pretty quick, as far as hanging out in these bars, as a bunch of little teenage girls?

VP: Yes. Some places didn't care, but there were several where we had to be locked in the dressing room between sets, because we were underage. That was fine, whatever, it didn't matter. But there were definitely those nights when it was just you and the bartender and two other people.

SF: It started out as the Bangs?

VP: We started out as the Bangs, with Debbi, Susanna, and I, and a bass player named Annette Zilinskas. It was just a time and place thing, but we started playing. One of our first shows was for a punk rock magazine, a launch party, and we immediately got a write-up in the *L.A. Weekly*, just in a little gossip column, like, "Watch out, this is an interesting little outfit."

SF: Did they always call you the next Go-Go's or anything?

VP: Oh, always, yeah.

SF: It must have been nerve-racking.

VP: Musically we were very different. But it didn't matter, because we were all girls and we were from L.A., so we were just following in their footsteps. It was an interesting review if the Go-Go's *weren't* mentioned in the first paragraph. Because it followed us pretty much all the way through. Not until the very end did we actually have articles that didn't mention the Go-Go's in every paragraph.

SF: What do you think the secret is to keeping a band together that long?

VP: We were together for about nine years. It wasn't quite an entire decade, but almost. We split in the fall of '89, and then started talking again in '98. Not that we weren't talking in the interim years; I kept in touch with everybody in the band. We definitely just needed a break.

Obviously I talk to my sister more often, but then in '98 we started discussing conditions under which we would all be comfortable in performing as the Bangles again. There started to be a lot of offers for '80s package tours and reunion tours, and I was never comfortable with that. Finally I had a conversation with Sue, and said, "Okay look, the only way I think I could do this is if we actually are a viable band, and that would mean new material and preparing to make a new record. And if we actually still had something to say musically and are enjoying it, then it makes sense to proceed. Otherwise, I'm really not interested in doing the nostalgia thing. I'm just not." It was probably stupid, because I probably could have made a lot of money, but it seems disrespectful to what the Bangles were.

SF: You'd become a mockery of yourself. And it sounds like that's what the Go-Go's have done now—the way Kathy describes it.

VP: They did it a little differently, because they did split up, then they reunited and split up again several times. I've had conversations with both Charlotte and Kathy where they've said, "Okay that's it, the Go-Go's are now out of my life, that's done, and I'm onto this other thing."

SF: When you guys reunited you actually got new material together and a new album.

VP: We did. The Go-Go's did, too, they put out a record [in 2000].

SF: What are you gonna do next?

VP: Kathy, Charlotte, Susanna, and I are all producers of a TV show in development, to solve hopefully that riddle of the all-women band. Maybe we can find somebody and help make it happen for them—through the magic of horrible reality TV.

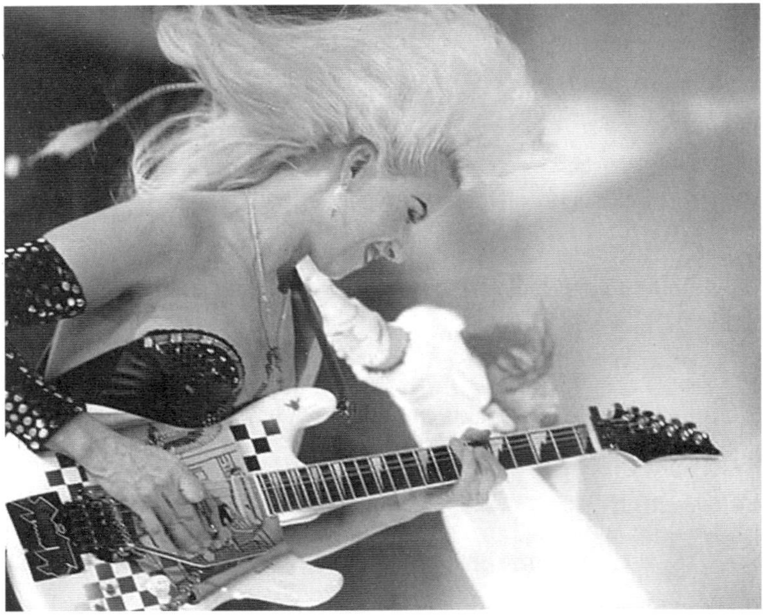

Jennifer Batten

JENNIFER BATTEN

Jennifer Batten emerged like a supernova in the late 1980s as the lead guitarist for Michael Jackson, at the peak of his fame. At the time, the idea of a woman shredding lead guitar in pop music was almost unheard of. Most shredders were confined to the heavy metal scene and had yet to achieve mainstream success.

Michael Jackson seemed to relish showcasing Jennifer's immense talent in his videos and live performances. Watching those clips today, it's impossible not to feel the electricity of her presence as she rips into solos with lightning speed, often borrowing Eddie Van Halen's iconic licks (he played the solo on "Beat It") and adding her own flair. Jennifer shattered the glass ceiling for female guitarists, proving that technical virtuosity knows no gender.

Jennifer picked up the guitar at eight years old and, by her teens, was honing her skills at the Guitar Institute of Technology (GIT) in Los Angeles in 1979, one of the few women in her class.

Her first solo album, *Above Below and Beyond* (1992), showcased her remarkable technical prowess, featuring a blistering rendition of the classical piece "Flight of the Bumble Bee." It cemented her place among the guitar elite—a proving ground she navigated with skill and determination. For women in her field, the expectations to go above and beyond were, and still are, higher.

I interviewed Jennifer twice and met her once in person. Each time, I was struck by her reserved nature and quiet intensity. She didn't seem to enjoy talking about herself, but once the conversation turned to music, she revealed a deep well of creativity and a wry sense of humor. Fiercely protective of her privacy, she also spoke of the challenges and harassment she faced as a woman guitarist in the music industry.

Jennifer's career took off when she won the coveted guitarist spot on Michael Jackson's *Bad* tour in 1987, beating out more than one hundred applicants. Over the next year and a half, she played for audiences totaling more than 450,000 people. She continued with Jackson on the *Dangerous* tour in 1992 and performed at the Super Bowl XXVII halftime show in 1993—then the most-watched television broadcast since the moon landing, a record only broken by the 2025 Super Bowl halftime show. Jennifer went on to accompany Jackson on his *HIStory* tour and later collaborated with guitar legend Jeff Beck on his albums *Who Else!* and *You Had It Coming*.

In 2011, she performed in a guitar residency for the Cirque du Soleil show *Zumanity* in Las Vegas and has continued to tour internationally, both as a solo artist and with various ensembles. She remains active leading masterclasses and guitar clinics. In 2016, she received the *She Rocks* "Icon" Award and was inducted into *Guitar Player* magazine's *Gallery of the Greats*.

More recently, Jennifer has embraced projects that blend technology and music. In 2019, she released *BattleZone*, a collaboration with keyboardist Marc Scherer that explored cinematic and futuristic soundscapes. She also developed a multimedia show combining music, storytelling, and visuals, reflecting her innovative spirit. Her latest performances mix humor, personal stories, and advanced guitar techniques, revealing a more relaxed and introspective side to her artistry.

Even though she has been part of highly commercial projects, the constant thread through Jennifer's life and work is creativity and self-expression. She established herself decades ago, proving she could hold her own with the best. Today, she has entered a more reflective and experimental phase, continuing to push boundaries while sharing her vulnerability and vision with her fans.

Jennifer Batten worked relentlessly to develop her skill and to claim her place in a world that wasn't built for her. The force with which she announced herself to the music world may have seemed bold—even defiant—but for a woman playing that style of guitar, it was necessary. That same force may have sometimes left her isolated, shielding her softer side. Yet her enduring legacy proves that she transcended those challenges and stands as a true pioneer in music.

JENNIFER BATTEN

— *The Interview* —

[2002]

SF: You started playing at eight years old when an older sister got a guitar. Am I right?

JB: Yeah. I was green with envy. I'm the only one that's still playing. I have two older sisters. The other one had a traumatic experience with piano lessons, and gave up. I took guitar lessons right away. I do remember the first lesson that I had—I cried. It was really traumatic. The teacher was trying to get me to read music and wanted me to use a pick, and I wasn't into either. But he whipped me into shape. That was when I was eight.

When I was nine, the family moved to San Diego and I took lessons. I had really varied teachers. I had one that was a folkie kind of guy who taught me a lot of fingerpicking and the next guy was into blues and rock. It was cool to have a rounded education like that. My dad is a jazz fiend, so I grew up listening to that, but I didn't get into jazz myself until I went to GIT [Guitar Institute of Technology]. That was a butt-kickin' year for me. I was twenty. The very first class they held at GIT was a guitar symposium where they had these clinics all weekend long. I went and checked it out and also auditioned to get in and I flunked. I didn't have the basic tools like major/minor scales and arpeggios and that kind of stuff.

SF: When you were young, would you have considered yourself a tomboy?

JB: Yes. I remember hanging out with guys in the neighborhood. They seemed to always be doing a lot of fun stuff. Actually, all the girls were tomboys. We were all climbing trees. Jumping in mud puddles. Being very active.

SF: Was there a time during your guitar studies that you consciously decided to make it your career path?

JB: I announced to my mother when I was twelve that that's what I wanted to do. She said, "You know, honey, that's a really competitive business." When you're twelve, you have no idea what that means. It didn't deter me at all. I sometimes think I should have listened to her.

SF: When you were twelve, were there any female guitarists that you saw or were influenced by?

JB: No, it was all guys.

SF: What was high school like? Were you serious about guitar then?

JB: I wasn't playing publicly or anything, but I was definitely a closet guitar player. I just really enjoyed playing. In my early teens, I got into blues and I would take my allowance and go buy all these records. Once I figured out the three chords, I was in bliss. I would jam along for hours. I am pretty sure I used to fantasize about big crowds. I saw the Beatles on TV. That was a hell of a shock to my system. Then I saw the Monkees and bands like the Dave Clark Five. The guitar was the main force for me. I gave a concert for my friends at one point. I spent months getting a bunch of Doobie Brothers, Allman Brothers, and Led Zeppelin songs together, and I just played by myself for my close friends. I listened to the tape and never sang again. That's what decided my fate.

SF: Do you mind if I ask your age?

JB: I pass on that question, on account of prejudice. I figure there's enough prejudice being female.

SF: Have people been forthright about that, or is it something that happens behind your back?

JB: It's mostly behind my back, but I have run into a lot of bastards in the business. I don't think it's gonna go away. Well, it depends on the person and if they have a personal problem with me. I think some of the male guitar players are pissed off that I have been successful and have had great gigs. It's always the illusion of scarcity, like there aren't enough gigs to go around, and I got a couple of the best ones.

SF: Yeah, the Jeff Beck shit is really heavy.

JB: It is, and that gig didn't exist until I got it. It's been amazing. I worked on two albums with Jeff Beck, *Who Else?* and *You Had It Coming*. On *You Had It Coming* I think I played only one chord on the whole album. I submitted twenty songs and got a couple of things going, but really, with Jeff Beck you don't need another guitar player. I did end up doing some guitar-synth stuff.

On my own *Tribal Rage*, I was really influenced by world beat stuff. I was bored with the average guitar-shredder record. I am always trying to keep it interesting for myself. My third album will be on Steve Vai's label. It should be good. The last album I made, I released myself and got my ass whipped. I don't have much of a business head and I hired people to take care of business. Now I know I don't need to do that again. I try to avoid the business side of things. I hate the telephone and I will put off making calls for days.

SF: Did other women players ever influence you?

JB: Actually, there was Monnette Sudler. When we were at GIT we were told to transcribe a solo and play it. I chose one of hers, but I haven't heard anything from her since. It was Latin jazz.

SF: At GIT, were you the only woman in the class?

JB: Yes, a bunch of guys and me. It was shocking in a way, because I hadn't realized how rare what I was doing was until I got there. I thought it might be 50/50, like a regular school.

SF: Do you think it ever will be?

JB: Not in my lifetime. MTV doesn't help things at all. You see how women are portrayed and young girls are watching this stuff and being influenced by it. Most of the girls on MTV are either singer-songwriters, which is fine, or bikini-clad-dancers shoving their ass in the camera. There are not a lot of respectful female instrumentalists. They're few and far between. As far as rock and roll guitar and soloing goes, there's an aggression to it, and I imagine a lot of girls growing up are taught that showing your aggressive side is not cool. If I'm ever in a conversation and someone sees my guitar case, they automatically assume I am a classical musician or a singer-songwriter.

I think it's going to take a very young, Eddie Van Halen-type female that gets in a pop band with great songs and great chops, and that will just turn things around instantly. Because Eddie was responsible for thousands and thousands of guitar sales and bands starting up. Doing what I do at this level isn't going to do it. The guitar-instrumental-thing is a pretty small market.

SF: When you first started out, did you feel like you had to prove yourself?

JB: The first record I came out with, I was definitely aware of having to prove myself. That's why I started out with "Flight of the Bumble Bee." This time, I'm going for sounds and moods and I'm not really trying to cater to anyone in particular. If anything, I'm going the other way—specifically, not catering to guitar players. I was so influenced by the Jeff Beck records. When we recorded, we basically walked into the studio with three songs, and six weeks later came out with an album. A lot of it was the drum programmer, who would be working away in one room, passing the tracks to another room, and the producer and Jeff would just sit and react to it. It was a real different way of working.

SF: When you play live, how do you prepare?

JB: It's pretty off the cuff as far as the solos. I try to treat the melody a little differently every time just to keep myself away from boredom.

SF: Do you enjoy playing live?

JB: It depends. I've had so many situations, and I'd say probably ten percent of the places I've found it good. It's usually such a battle. Of the whole process of writing, recording, and playing live, I'd say my favorite is writing. When the ideas start to come it's a real high, and very exciting.

SF: I read that you worked with the Julia Cameron's book, *The Artist's Way*. Do you still?

JB: I think that's the heaviest book. I've bought about twenty copies for my friends. I read through the whole thing, and then I read it again and did some of the exercises. That book is like the Bible. Her insights are so right on.

SF: Some of her insights about our business are just like what you were saying about the perception of the scarcity of jobs or gigs. Like there's not enough to go around.

JB: Staying away from poisonous people, too, that's a heavy thing. Especially when they're onstage with you. And the whole image thing. Some people think in order to be a valid or great artist, you have to be wounded and dark or tormented in some way. Funny how that kind of thinking seeps into your brain. What the hell is that all about?

SF: Do you ever teach?

JB: Yes, I am back at it.

SF: Do you think that there's anything that cannot be taught?

JB: You can't teach someone to have his or her own personality. There's a lot of work that individuals learn on their own. They have to open their receptors. You can't just pound something into them.

SF: Who are you listening to now?

JB: My favorite band is the Afro Celt Sound System. I also got turned on to a lot of British techno music through Jeff Beck, stuff I would never have found on my own. He never wants to repeat himself. He doesn't want to do a record that's already been done. He's a lot better at listening to what's out there now than I am. He'll be listening to East Indian radio when he's at home and to all these different things to try and find inspiration. I haven't had that kind of success, so there's not really any pressure on me to repeat what I've already done. I can just go naturally where I want to go. I'm just trying to entertain myself.

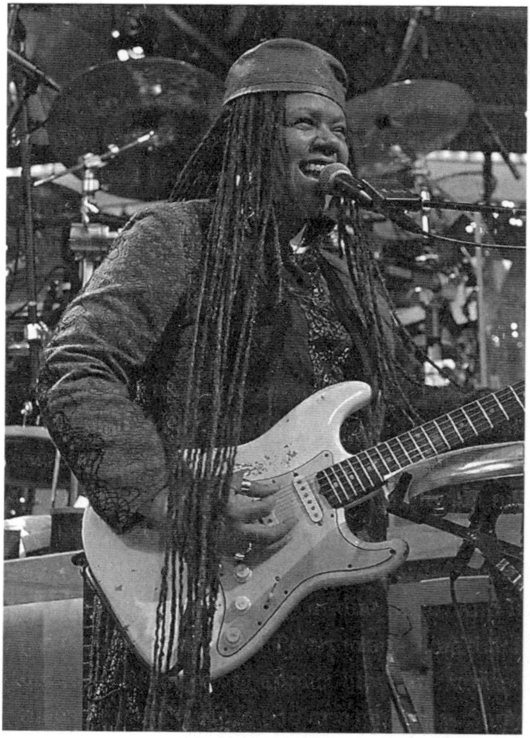

Felicia Collins

FELICIA COLLINS

Felicia Collins burst into the public consciousness as the guitarist in Paul Shaffer's *Late Show with David Letterman* band. From 1993 to 2015, she held one of the most high-profile gigs imaginable, performing five nights a week on national network television. I was fascinated by this cool woman guitarist who had landed such a major role. Where did she come from? What was her story? And how did she get there?

Watching Felicia on *Late Show,* I was always struck by how at ease she seemed. She smiled often and exuded an air of confidence that said she belonged in the band. And this wasn't just any band; it was made up of some of the best musicians in New York City. The fact that Felicia stood up there night after night for over two decades spoke volumes—not just for women in music or women guitarists, but for anyone with big dreams. Seeing her in that position was deeply inspiring.

By the time Felicia got that gig, many women were already making waves in the guitar world. Yet there was something uniquely powerful about her presence—a woman doing this on live television with millions watching. It was a quiet but undeniable statement, and I believe it had a massive impact.

When I finally spoke with Felicia, I was struck by her calm, grounded nature. You might expect someone who'd held such a high-pressure job for so long to have an edge or a fiercely competitive streak, but not Felicia. Her energy was all about ease, flow, and letting good things come to her. She had an almost Zen-like approach to success and life, which felt both refreshing and profound.

She explained her philosophy simply: "If a person is lucky enough to be totally present in their body and they don't lose that, it helps you stay fearless and easily satisfied." There was an effortless confidence in her—a sense that no matter what happened, she'd be fine. Felicia spoke warmly about her family and described feeling valued and supported as a child, a foundation that clearly helped her stay grounded in the chaotic world of show business.

She didn't view being female as a disadvantage; if anything, she saw it as an advantage that opened doors. Rather than letting her gender make her defensive, she leaned into it, confident she could "really throw down" with the best of them.

Felicia Michele Collins was born in Jackson, Tennessee, in 1964 and raised in the Bronx. Her family was full of musical talent, and she remembered being inspired by her Aunt Barbara, a singer who performed with Bo Diddley. It wasn't until she was twelve, growing up in Albany, New York, that she bought her first guitar from a pawn shop and taught herself to play.

Though she's best known for *Late Show,* Felicia's career includes many other highlights. Before joining Letterman, she worked with Nile Rodgers on several studio projects and performed with the Thompson Twins at *Live Aid* in 1985. She toured with Al Jarreau, playing guitar and singing on his 1986 album *L Is for Lover,* and joined Cyndi Lauper's band for her *Hat Full of Stars* tour in 1993. Even during her *Late Show* years, Felicia led her own bands, 360 and B!tchslap (later renamed Felicia Collins and the Life), and produced *Anarchists of Color II,* a live showcase celebrating Black rock music.

In recent years, Felicia has expanded her creative work. She joined the Atlantic Theatre Company as a guitarist in the off-Broadway production of *Marie and Rosetta,* a play honoring the legendary Sister Rosetta Tharpe and Marie Knight. When Tharpe was inducted into the *Rock and Roll Hall of Fame* in 2018, Felicia was invited to perform in the tribute ceremony, a fitting honor for someone who has carried forward Tharpe's legacy of boundary-breaking artistry.

Felicia Collins's story is one of talent, perseverance, and authenticity. Whether playing guitar on television for millions or honoring the women who paved the way, she has proven time and again that she belongs at the top. Like her playing, her journey radiates ease, fearlessness, and grace.

FELICIA COLLINS

— *The Interview* —

[2007]

SF: You're working on a Felicia Collins album? You've never released an album of your own, have you?

FC: Not a whole one. I've done some EPs and played on other people's stuff. In a way, it's just that the age has come where the typical things that I once shied away from are just gone now, and I can just carve my own niche. I never was attracted to record labels and stuff like that. They always just had such an attitude. If somebody wasn't coming out and going, "Come on, I'm bringing you in," then I was never the type that would bang down a door. You know what I mean? I like to enjoy it. This other stuff I can do for work. I want to dare to get through it just doing my whim, which is playing music—playing the guitar.

SF: It's funny that you say that, because so many people spend so much time networking and doing that very thing. You've had all this great luck in your career. All the gigs you sort of stumbled upon—that doesn't happen to everybody, that they just "happen" onto Nile Rodgers and then they "happen" into Cyndi Lauper's band.

FC: I know. With me, it just always happens that way, which makes me think it's not just by chance.

SF: Do you ever wonder how that came about? Or is there any kind of inspiration in your life that you think has helped you with that?

FC: Honestly—and this is so simple and got nothing to do with networking or even music—I believe that if a person is lucky enough to be totally present in their body and they don't lose that, it helps you stay fearless and easily satisfied. I never put any big pressure on myself about how my little journey was going to end up. I never thought about the end of it, just what's happening now. I've always been lucky. I started off life in a good place where people must have made me feel good and comfortable, because I've always been okay with myself and making friends and trusting what I can see in people and just being satisfied with being satisfied. If I become a big huge star, that'd be fine, and if I don't but I'm just playing my music and I'm not getting up and going to work with a boss that's trying to be inappropriate and having to wear spiked heels and kill my feet. If I can afford to live in a place without three roommates and I can have a pet, then I'm fine.

I was always willing to just go where it took me, and I always tended to drift to where people wanted me. I knew I was offering something. With the music, it's like I'm over here because I'm funky. It just helped that I was young at the time.

SF: Was your family really supportive?

FC: Yes. I mean, just like they are with each other. It's just as long as you're not messing up, of course. They're supportive.

SF: Did you have brothers and sisters or anything?

FC: I got brothers. I'm the oldest. We got twins.

SF: And do they play, too?

FC: No. I think I kind of messed that up when we were little. I remember one day, I think we were watching *The Partridge Family* or something, we were always into the Jackson Five and stuff like that. I just wanted us to have a group, so I tried to force them to play the guitar one day. They were four years old and their fingers were hurting. I decided that day they were going to get it, but I was a little kid too, and I had no idea what I was doing. I think they hated it from that day on.

SF: I read about you seeing Bo Diddley or your aunt perform with Bo Diddley. Is that how you got into guitar?

FC: It might have been.

SF: Did he have Lady Bo on guitar? Did he have any women in the band?

FC: It's possible, because that seems to be some faint memory, seeing something like that. I think I saw that with my own eyes. This was some afternoon performance somewhere. It wasn't a nightclub, because I was a baby. My aunt Bibi opened up for the Coasters and then Bo Diddley.

SF: What was your aunt's name?

FC: Bibi Butler. Man, she had a voice that could hang with anybody.

SF: Did she have recordings, too?

FC: Yeah, she did. I went online looking for something about her, and I found this guy in Australia that's got her single, and he mailed me a picture of the cover of the 45 because I told him I remember it looked sort of like a racing flag with red-and-white checkers. He sent it to me and I'm like, "That's it!"

SF: Is she still alive?

FC: Yeah.

SF: She must be proud of you.

FC: Bibi's going strong. She just sings in the church now. I think the reason why she didn't go even further was because she had a whole family. She had five children. She and my uncle Robert lived in New York, and I think it really came down to the kids and stuff. Because believe me, I mean, everybody knew she was the bomb. I remember when she was working with [legendary bassist] Chuck Rainey on a lot and stuff—they would make arrangements for her, because she was doing it right up until I was about maybe seventeen or eighteen.

SF: Was she a real inspiration, do you think?

FC: Definitely. How could she not be?

SF: Anybody else in your family do it?

FC: Not that I know of. The only one I remember is her, up there on the stage with the gown. And I remember them carrying her up the stairs or down the stairs. I was really little, and I got so alarmed because I thought something was wrong with her. Then my mom explained to me that her gown was so tight she couldn't go up the stairs. The men would carry her up the stairs in her gown. All she could do was just stand there with one knee in front of the other and belt it out, baby. Yeah. She was the bomb.

SF: So, how come you picked up the guitar and didn't become a vocalist like her?

FC: I don't know. It goes back so far. I remember when I started playing, because I had a guitar for years before I ever could actually play the thing. I think I was about maybe eight.

SF: Did you ask for one and your parents bought you one?

FC: Probably, yeah. They knew that I liked the thing. It's easy to figure out what your baby likes. I must have indicated that I liked the guitar, so I had little toy ones, little plastic ones. Then, as I got older, they got more useful. More real.

SF: Who were your first guitar inspirations? Who were the first people you saw playing that really turned you on?

FC: I'm thinking that the Bo Diddley thing did something. My great-grandmother had this picture—and of course nobody knows where it is now—but I remember for years seeing this picture. It was after that same gig with the Coasters. Me sitting on Bo Diddley's lap, almost three years old, and he's pointing to the camera, probably telling me to say "cheese" or something. And I'm touching the guitar.

SF: That would be so cool to find.

FC: I can't believe they'd let that go. Therapy over that, man . . .

SF: Have you seen him since? Like, on the show or something?

FC: Yeah, I've got another picture of me sitting with him. Not on his lap this time, but just sitting there talking. It would be great to put it side by side with this other photo.

SF: You grew up in Philly?

FC: Actually, I grew up between New York and Albany—that's where my mother stayed after she finished school. I heard that my father's sister was a singer. It's like both of my parents had sisters the same age who were singers and they sang in the jazz clubs. I never met her.

SF: So, how did you get started playing gigs? In high school?

FC: There actually wasn't anything really happening in high school. I did a gig when I was a teenager; we were just jamming. People didn't care. I remember having a wah-wah pedal that was wired backward for some reason. Like, the wah would go when I depressed my heel, not my toe. And it had a siren in it. You step on the pedal and you have a siren go off. I was like hot shit with my little pawn-shop guitar.

SF: You played all through high school?

FC: Yeah, but just by myself. Not in bands or anything. I just played my guitar. I didn't know that it was practicing, because I never had any lessons. I just didn't have a clue.

SF: Really?

FC: Not a clue. The only thing I wanted to do when I came home from school was jam on my guitar.

SF: And how would you go about learning stuff? Just by ear? The radio or whatever?

FC: Yes, exactly. Just by ear. A lot of times it was like hood chords—not the real chords.

SF: In college, did you ever study music officially?

FC: Nope. I went to school for advertising design. The name got changed to graphic communications. I had a twelve-string acoustic guitar by the time I went to college, so of course, I took it with me and there was a guy down the hall, Matt, who was a jewelry design major and he had an Ibanez twelve-string. We used to sit out on the stairwell and just jam. I always played the guitar, but that was the first time I wanted to be a guitar player. I was eighteen by then, and I could play anything Matt could play. I learned a lot from him, though, because we'd just take turns. Like, one holds down the rhythm while the other one solos. I made him practice his rhythm. I used to tell him, "Look, don't fall apart when it's my turn to try, man." He enjoyed it too, because he got more into the rhythm thing, which I think he never really would have thought of. I used to play funk records on my twelve-string because I didn't have a decent electric guitar at that time.

SF: And rhythm is so important. It must be a huge part of what you do now.

FC: Of course it is. Soloing was the last thing to come about. I wasn't really interested. It would be nice if I could just blink and be ripping one off, but I thought I would have to become somebody else, or I didn't know what it entailed to learn how to do that. I met a couple of guitar players who were more advanced, and they showed me stuff. I didn't know that until then.

SF: Were you shy about performing or standing out front? Or did you prefer to stay kind of in the background sort of thing?

FC: It didn't matter. I would have done either one. It was just that being part of the support team is where I had more opportunities. I'd notice that even if I played with the hugest people on Earth, I would get all the props in the world necessary for them to shine, but if I started making noises that I wanted to do something solo, those same people would put me in my place. That's just how the world is. You can't really pay any attention to that.

SF: It's funny, because you've had a pretty long career as a guitar player.

FC: I know. It's ridiculous.

SF: It's amazing though, because you're self-taught and the stuff you guys do on this show alone, there is quite an amount of theory that you have to know.

FC: My theory is that you learn it and then you memorize it. That wasn't even so much a theory. That was just a formula.

SF: So for everything you do on the show, you do it by ear?

FC: Actually, working on *Letterman* is where more formal education has come in, because from one day to the next is how I have to be prepared. There's no time for me to take stuff home and learn it for a week and then come back and I got it under my fingers. It forced me to get other ways for it to get into my brain. The retention thing is still a big strong part of it, but I have to learn what to retain, and being on this show is helping me read better and to follow charts better. I was completely clueless. I mean, you could put a chart in front of me, turn it upside down, sideways, ninety degrees to the left, and it would all have been the same to me.

SF: Did they know that when they hired you?

FC: Yes. I asked first, like, *what are you going to need me to do?* Paul [Shaffer] said, "Well, it's just like how you do already. You hear it by ear, and then we play it. It's just pop music." I was like, all right, I can hang with that. Then I wanted to be a little quicker with stuff and they were all very, very supportive. Sid [McGinnis], the other guitar player, is the one that taught me the country chart. I said, "There's a country chart?" And he said, "Yeah, after they hit the key, their whole chart just says one, four, five, six." I had to learn how to communicate with the numbers like that with them, and then charts would go in front of me and I could follow the chord chart. It just got better and better and before I knew it, I was reading music and I was like, *wow I never did this before. I love it!*

SF: Being a female guitarist, did you ever feel like you were standing out? Or when you were in a group, you know, did you ever feel like there was any kind of pressure to prove yourself?

FC: No. I guess if I tried to get into a jazz situation, but it was always rock and roll. Even Al [Jarreau] with pop music: I was trying to turn his gig down, and his manager was assuring me it wasn't what I thought, because I was telling him, "Look. I don't play jazz. I don't think he wants me." They were thinking *Oh, we just got to have this guitar player.*

So I never felt the pressure of being a girl. I always felt like that was my ace in the hole, because I knew I could rock it whoever's band I was in. I can throw down in the Thompson Twins. Give them a little extra funk. You know? I could definitely play.

SF: I don't know if you ever think about this, but I have when I've seen you on *Letterman*, it's such a high presence that you have on that show and you're there every night. You're in the band. You're visual. You're the only chick in the band, and you're one of the guitar players. I'm a guitar player, so I always notice other women players.

FC: Right, I usually do, too.

SF: Have you noticed since you started playing now that there are more women players out there?

FC: Yes.

SF: I'm not saying you're responsible, but I think there's been sort of a paradigm change somewhere.

FC: I didn't think you meant that I was responsible. I think it's just this time in the chronology that you see it. That's all. I'm just an example of it happening more. I'm not the cause of it.

SF: You're also an example in women's minds that it's a possibility. Thirty years ago, you didn't see women in the public eye bearing down

on the guitar, unless you really looked for it. But here you are every night on an international TV show, bearing down.

FC: To people that know me, it makes all the sense in the world. They're just like, "Yeah—and what's your point?" Because I've been playing all my life. You find people in [my] grade school and go, "Do you ever remember Felicia Collins playing the guitar?" And they go, "Yeah, she played."

SF: Did you know other women players when you were growing up? Or other girl players?

FC: Not when I was growing up. I remember being a kid in Albany and there was somebody older than me named Elaine who played the guitar. That's all I know. I never saw her play, but I knew about her because Albany is a small town. Most people didn't know that I played. Only other musicians that I played with knew, because I didn't do gigs or anything like that when I was growing up.

SF: Right, and it never mattered to you at all?

FC: Not that it didn't matter. It wasn't driving me nuts. I wasn't like Miles Davis or somebody, who, every day, had to become this. It was just something I did. In my mind I was still attached to all of my records, and this world of music was out there. I didn't think it would take playing in bands in Albany or taking classes. I thought I would get to it when I got out of Albany. I thought, *let me get out of Albany and I'll meet these people and they can hear I can play*. I didn't think that I was going to have to show papers that I had been in x amount of bands. So yeah, I guess you're right. It didn't matter.

SF: I totally get that impression from you as a player. You're just so into playing that it wouldn't occur to you that it had anything to do with gender.

FC: Yes.

SF: It also occurs to me that there are more women players now, and I'm just wondering if you've ever thought about the fact that you're actually having an influence out there.

FC: I mean, like, well—it just makes sense that I would.

SF: Do you ever get women that write to you and say, "I'm a player and it's so great to see you playing?"

FC: Occasionally. Yeah, sure.

SF: You're so casual about all of it.

FC: Because I don't assume that it's the biggest thing that's happening today. It's logical that it must be taking place in some cases, and I don't want to take anything away from it either. I'm not going to say it's nothing. It is what it is.

SF: Do you know a lot of great female players now?

FC: Yes, I do. Kat Dyson [who has played with Prince and many others]. I met her when I was on a Thompson Twins tour and was shopping when we got to Montreal. I was talking to a shop owner and then she told me about a girl she knew named Kat Dyson. She says, "The band won on *Star Search*" and all this and I'm like, "Really?" We invited [her] to come to the concert, but she goes, "No, I'm an old lady now, but would you mind if I gave the tickets to my daughter and to Kat?" That's how I met Kat.

SF: You guys have a lot in common.

FC: I know. She's even got twin brothers.

SF: She's funny, because I asked her the same thing: "How did you get all these good gigs?" She said, "Well, this happened and this happened, and next thing I'm playing with Prince!" It doesn't happen to everybody!

FC: Well, see, you said, "Did I find it any pressure being a woman?" I was like, "No." If anything, that was my ace in the hole.

SF: Because you were unique?

FC: Yeah, and they didn't have to settle. You know, they didn't have to go, "Well, it's cute having a girl, but she can't throw down." It's like, "You mean we can get somebody that throws down and is a unique thing?" I knew whatever gig it was, I would have it.

SF: You play a lot of different styles, too. But funk is your mainstay?

FC: That might be the most impressive part to some people, but that's not my mainstay, because I grew up in Albany. Albany is the funkiest town in New York, but it's also rock and roll every day and pop music every day. I like Henry Mancini. If I hear a sonic piece that I like, I don't tune it out or tune it in automatically.

SF: That's another thing you and Kat have in common, that you both play a lot of different things musically. She says she just listened to the radio and whatever came on.

FC: Same here. I didn't even have a record player really until we moved into a nice place and my parents got a hi-fi. After the first year, it ended up in my bedroom somehow. Nobody missed it. They didn't care. They didn't miss it in the living room, because I was the one getting the records at that point and just sitting in my room. I remember when my mother gave me *Songs in the Key of Life*. It was a double album and it had a little forty-five that came with it, with three more songs on it and a song book. I listened to that over and over again for a month. Then she gave me a Wes Montgomery record and one by Ahmad Jamal. She knew I didn't care who it was.

SF: What's next for you when your solo CD comes out?

FC: I have no idea, because it's just so bizarre.

SF: Have you got a deal for it? Are you looking for a deal? Do you care?

FC: Actually, no. I'm really not. No, and thank God I never needed one in order for me to enjoy getting up and playing music for work—instead of going down to Barney's and standing in high heels for six hours.

SF: No more high heels.

FC: That was my first job when I was still in school. *You know how much I do not want to be doing this?* And you can't sit down. Oh, and I worked in the men's outerwear [section], so it was all men shopping all day. I had to have my little skirt on and my high heels. I went to lunch one day and didn't come back. I wasn't afraid. I was like, *I know this is really, really irresponsible.* But the minute I decided not to go back after lunch, [I felt] enormous relief. That's what I meant about just staying tapped into not being afraid. Just keep yourself happy. Just know what it's gonna take to make you happy, have some discipline—which you need for that—and then take what life gives you. That's the way I look at it.

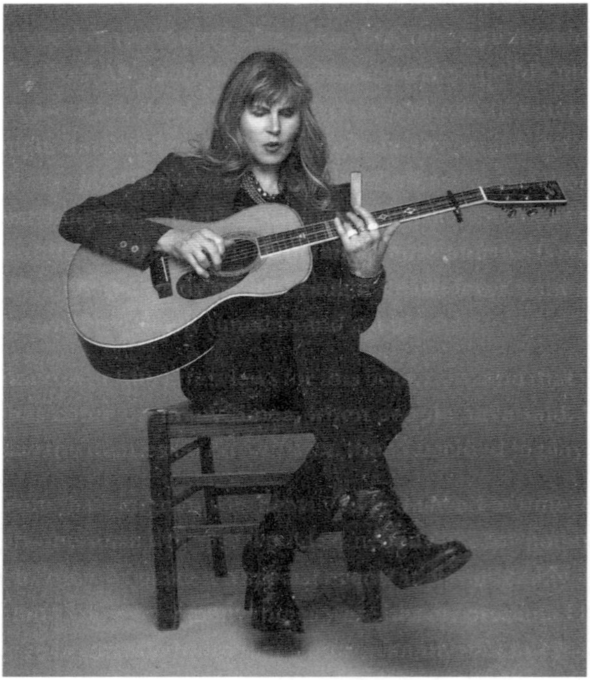

Rory Block

RORY BLOCK

I first saw Rory Block perform when I was about eighteen and had just moved to Vancouver. I was feeling a little out of place, three thousand miles from home, when I took a chance and bought a ticket to an acoustic blues show. I had never heard of Rory Block before, but I was already an avid fan of country blues and on my way into a career as a guitar player. I sat by myself in the crowd, awestruck by her performance. She played solo, deep and stark, even singing a cappella at one point. Her passion was palpable. Some songs were heartbreakingly raw, while others, full of humor, showed her wit and versatility.

From that moment, Rory became one of the women I turned to for inspiration. Too shy to approach her after the show, I walked away knowing I had found someone I could look up to. Every time I've seen her since, her music has brought me to tears with its honesty and emotional depth.

Rory has a unique ability to connect with her audience, laying herself bare with rare transparency. She openly shares the details of her life, her struggles, losses, and triumphs, and channels it all into her music.

She's also an extraordinary guitarist, one of the foremost interpreters of Robert Johnson's intricate and demanding repertoire. Her performances are dynamic; she slams her guitar like a drum, strums with ferocity, and demonstrates astonishing dexterity in her slide and single-note leads. Her voice is as rich and expressive as her guitar work, carrying the weight of every story she tells.

Born Aurora Block in 1949, she spent her early years in a tiny wooden shack deep in the hills of New Jersey before her family moved to Greenwich Village. Her father, a sandal-shop owner and fiddle player, regularly jammed with local musicians, and Rory grew up surrounded by music and creativity.

As a young girl, she wandered the streets of Greenwich Village, soaking in the legendary folk scene. When she heard the album *Really! The Country Blues* in 1964, her life changed course. She dedicated herself entirely to the blues, studying with guitarist Stefan Grossman, who introduced her to Reverend Gary Davis, Mississippi John Hurt, and Bukka White. At fifteen, she ran away to California with Grossman, performing in coffeehouses and small clubs, crossing paths with some of the greats she had idolized.

Since then, Rory has released thirty-six albums, won seven Blues Music Awards, and toured the world extensively. *Rolling Stone* credited her with recording "some of the most singular and affecting country blues anyone, man or woman, black or white, old or young, has cut in recent years." Today, she is not only a musician but also a producer, author, ordained minister, festival promoter, and mother.

When I interviewed Rory, our conversation ranged from her early mentors to staying healthy on the road and her love of raising dogs. Her warmth and wisdom were unforgettable.

It is her soul, her courage, and her devotion to her craft that make Rory Block so remarkable. She embraces her age as a badge of honor and sees this stage of life as a time to give back. Her music has long been a source of healing, both for herself and for her listeners. After losing her nineteen-year-old son in a car accident, she recorded *House of Hearts* as a memorial album. Letters from fans poured in, sharing stories of their own losses. One man even credited her song "Lovin' Whiskey" with saving his life.

Rory's *Power Women of the Blues* series began with her 2018 release *A Woman's Soul: A Tribute to Bessie Smith*, followed by tributes to Robert Johnson and other blues legends. Most recently, she released an album honoring Bob Dylan, a nod to her formative years in Greenwich Village. She has also collaborated with artists such as Stevie Wonder, Mark Knopfler, and Bonnie Raitt.

Rory Block's life and career are a testament to resilience, artistry, and the enduring power of music. Her ability to turn pain into beauty and truth into song continues to inspire generations of musicians. She remains one of the most vital figures in the contemporary blues scene, deeply connected to the source yet always pushing the music forward.

RORY BLOCK

— *The Interview* —

[2001]

SF: Where are you living?

RB: I live in upstate New York. It's quite beautiful. I love it.

SF: I was really surprised to see you grew up in New York City. For some reason, I imagined you in the country.

RB: I am, by nature, very earthy so I never knew what I was doing in the city. I liked it when I was growing up there, and if I hadn't lived there I would never have met all the blues people that I knew.

SF: You've brought me to tears each time I've seen you perform. It seems like you've got this urgency, something you're trying to communicate. Like you are trying to get some message into every person in the crowd. Could you describe what that is?

RB: I don't really have a conscious choice about what I am doing when I am onstage. Your word, urgency, I think of as maybe an intensity. A passion. It gets described that way sometimes. That's always been a part of the way I perceive the music and the feeling that I have for this music—or really any music that I love.

There's this feeling of passion I can't seem to get away from. It's just there and is a part of me. Sometimes when I am performing and I am playing blues, I feel so connected to the music I don't even know what I am projecting. It's like making love to someone you love. It's purely passionate. Powerful. Intense. I fell in love with blues. I fell in love with soul music. There's this out-of-control, passionate, loving feeling about the music and if that comes through, great.

SF: When you were fifteen you ran away from home. I had a similar experience. Were your parents worried about you running away to California?

RB: They just didn't care at all. I probably shouldn't say too much about that, because my dad's still alive. I sometimes say to my audiences that my website has my life story for anyone who has the interest and the energy to get through it, but there's unbelievably heavy, dense stuff that isn't even there. So, with my parents at that time, it was like nobody really noticed. Everybody had their own agendas.

SF: Everyone was going in his or her own direction.

RB: It didn't seem to really get anybody's attention. In one weird way, I was free and that was good. In another weird way, nobody cared and that was bad.

SF: Stefan Grossman was a mentor to you, but he wasn't that much older than you, right?

RB: He was actually only four years older than me, but in the days when you're fourteen and someone's eighteen, they seem like they're thirty-five and you're twelve. When I met him, he was this big guy who was playing this amazing music, sort of ragtime-style. I started listening to his music and I thought, *God, this is fantastic. What is this?* It was like bells going off in my ears. Then we started talking and he gave me some records. I thought it was the greatest, most beautiful thing on earth.

SF: It must have resonated because of everything that was going on at home, too.

RB: Stefan said, "Let's go to Reverend Gary Davis's house," and from that point on we became this partnership—always being where there was music. If Mississippi John Hurt was coming through town to do concerts, we were there backstage. If Bukka White was playing at the Bitter End or the Village Gate, we were there backstage. Whenever there was somebody at someone's house, we were there. Stefan knew all these people, so it was like stepping into that crowd by knowing him.

SF: Did you feel unusual at the time, being fourteen and being a guitarist? I know people probably said the odd thing to you.

RB: Not really. I just saw myself as a player. I did get a lot of comments like, *she plays like a man*, or, *where did she learn this music?* There may have been an initial surprise when people saw me, but I chose not to register it. I was just proud that I was playing. I wanted to play my music for people. I just wanted to get in there, in the middle of things.

SF: Did you have any interactions with other female blues guitarists? Were there any others around?

RB: There was Jo Ann Kelly. She was basically the only other blues player around in 1968 or '69. Tragically, she died of brain cancer about eight or nine years ago. She was great. The two of us would sometimes sit around, and we definitely had this bond. We felt like the only two twenty-year-old women on earth playing acoustic country blues. Nobody cared about what we were doing. There was no chance in getting signed as a country blues artist. You'd have to become a songwriter and you'd have to fit their mold. You know what? It's not that much better now.

In the pop market that's really big. Every time somebody makes it, that's when the mold thing comes in big time. That's when the record companies are all looking for a duplicate of that one thing. Then you get an overload of that for a while because they thought, *well it sold over here, so this will sell again.*

There is a lot of interest in acoustic blues, but still, there are not that many female players. They're out there, but I just don't know all their names. I meet a lot of women players at festivals and I always say, "Don't stop playing until everyone knows who you are." That's my blanket advice.

SF: Were you influenced by any of the recorded female blues artists, like Memphis Minnie, Mattie Delaney, or Geeshie Wiley?

RB: Lottie Kimbrough was an influence, but mostly I gravitated toward Robert Johnson. I don't really think it's a gal or a guy thing. I just think it was that the style he was playing was just so intense. I also loved Tommy Johnson, Skip James, and Charley Patton for whatever reason. Robert Johnson was the most brilliant guitar player, in my mind, and I wanted to be a guitar player. That's where my interests lay.

SF: You wanted to really state yourself with your guitar. You didn't just want to be a strummer.

RB: It wasn't even a conscious thing. It's just what I was fascinated by and what I was driven to do.

SF: What age were you playing from?

RB: Ten is when I started.

SF: I want to talk about interpretation. There's something in blues that when you pick up someone else's songs, you're jumping into their whole style. Was there a point when you found it easier to find yourself in the midst of that?

RB: Yes, but I don't know when that happened. But that's true. In the very beginning, you're emulating all you can. It may be impossible to say when your style becomes your own. I've heard other players that are superb at the imitation part of it, but I don't feel that they fly on an individual basis. I don't really feel like they're giving as much.

SF: That's one of my beefs with modern blues. There's a lot of interpretation. I mean, a lot of guys come up and they do their best Muddy Waters and it sounds pretty good, but there's not a lot behind it. All the masters defined their own blues. I mean, Lightnin' Hopkins sounded like himself. He didn't play Muddy Waters.

RB: Right! That's one of the things that distinguished early Motown, too. I mean, Stevie Wonder didn't sound like Smokey Robinson. All of them were so outstandingly unique. That's what I look for in music. I look for uniqueness. Robert Johnson only sounds like Robert Johnson. Charley Patton only sounds like Charley Patton. I am looking for that in the present day as well.

We have to make it real—from our own lives. One of the greatest compliments was when some guy came up to me after a show and said, "You're the only person I've seen do blues in the present day, and I feel like you're making it new. I've never liked blues before because of this, but seeing you now, it feels totally different and meaningful." I am sure he's found others since then, but it was the greatest compliment.

SF: You're not aware of any time when it went from being interpretive to just feeling like yourself?

RB: Maybe when people started saying that to me, but I didn't really know that anything was different. I can't see myself terribly well at all.

I have a record called *The Early Tapes*, the earliest stuff on tape thus far. I listen to it and, honestly, I think it sounds pretty much like I do now. I sound younger. The voice is higher and sweeter. It's not quite as textured. But I am singing the same way.

SF: I think there's a lot of depth to your sound. I think that comes with all the experiences you've had—the experiences you openly share with your audiences. I think at eighteen, you didn't have all those experiences. I could be wrong, but all the artists I like are well over fifty because I love that sound and that richness of tone. All that comes with age.

RB: I embrace my age fully. I am always telling the audience, "Now that I'm fifty-one I can do whatever I want." They cheer and everything. I do think it increases the intensity of my mission. The first fifty years were great, and I had all those experiences, and now in the second fifty years, I've got to give back a lot more. I really feel like I have to give back.

SF: How much do you tour now?

RB: It varies so much. Sometimes there's so much going on, and then I might get these quiet periods where I get to be my little homemaker-self. I can be into my flower garden and into my cooking or my organic-domestic thing that I have going on here at what I call "the dog ranch."

SF: How many dogs do you have?

RB: I have three. We're really into the dog thing and I know I'd have a whole lot more if I could. It just doesn't make much sense because I wouldn't go on the road anymore. Then I might just have a kennel and save and rescue dogs. I would love to do that. Dogs are basically wild animals. They could kill us, but they're conditioned to love us. God knows why they put up with us, because we're so cruel to them so much of the time.

SF: Do you live on a farm?

RB: It's not really a farm. It's a farming area that's been rediscovered after almost being abandoned. It's two hours north of New York City. I live in a 230-year-old house. It's a very beautiful area. I'm doing a benefit for the land conservancy in Columbia County here locally because that's one of the things I really care about—preserving some wilderness and some open land and so on.

SF: When you first had your kids, did you stop performing?

RB: I did, considering that I was seventeen when my first son was born—seventeen by four days. I was really, really young and I didn't have a career at the time. I had done that early recording with Stefan Grossman and had traveled around with the blues men and then I had this kid. I was married and I stopped doing everything. For about eight years, I didn't do any music at all.

SF: You got married at sixteen?

RB: I sure did. It was just like out of the storybooks. I ran away from home and got married and lived on my own from that point on.

SF: From seventeen until twenty-five, you just mothered your son?

RB: It was seven or nine years or something like that until I kind of decided to play music again.

SF: What did you do when you got back into it? Did your son come with you to shows?

RB: He was with me everywhere, and then when my second child was born, he was also with me everywhere because I would nurse them and carry them around. I was a free spirit. I didn't worry about what people would think. I just figured, *well I have kids, so I should take them everywhere with me*. I wasn't doing serious, long touring things then. That came after they were older. If I had little kids right now, though, I would take them on the road with me. Right now, I have my wonderful tour bus that I love like crazy. I have someone to drive it and do the sound at the shows.

SF: You own your own bus?

RB: I do. I keep it in the back of my barn here at the house. But if I had to do that now, I would take along a babysitter.

SF: I am very interested in how women balance having kids and playing music.

RB: There's no great answer. What I feel like I'd like to write about someday are the methods that I use to stay sane and healthy while I'm on the road. I've worked it into a kind of science. From the start, I toured in a station wagon, and one of the things I noticed was how unhealthy you can get. Eating road food, having no exercise, loading in and out of hotels—the basic road stuff.

I started developing this routine. I went out and bought a fair-sized cooler and carried it around in the back of the car. I also had a bed in the back. My husband at the time drove, and I went shopping at all the health food stores and got all my good food and then I had a box of kitchen stuff like a hot plate, and unbreakable dishes. Basically, it was all you needed to take a box into your hotel room, plug in your hot plate, pull out a pot and boil brown rice and vegetables and make a real meal. For years, I had a water boiler that plugged into the cigarette lighter in the car, and I could make miso soup and teas. I would be in the back of the car and chop away on my cutting board and make salads while we were rolling down the road. I had the whole thing down.

Then I got the crazy idea that I would make the people who worked with me play softball at the rest stops. That was cool for a while. It was really great to work up a sweat at the rest area, then get back into the car or van and keep going. At one point, I started coming home from a tour healthier than when I left.

SF: Do you do anything or try to get into a particular headspace when you prepare for a show?

RB: Actually, I am glad you asked that because that's been the oddest thing from day one. I don't do anything. I don't practice.

SF: You really never practice?

RB: I will only practice if I am getting material together for an album. It's so intense when I play that as soon as I get off the road, I don't even want to look at my guitar. I did play at the beginning of my musical life without stopping: morning, noon, and night. That's when my guitar was glued to me. Now I just set it aside right until I go on the stage. When I get up there, I feel like I receive energy from the audience, and they are like my sustenance. I am always overwhelmed by their enthusiasm and the power of their affection. My fans are saints. They actually put out their hard-earned money. Some people will come and say, "I drove four hours."

SF: You receive from them before you start to give?

RB: Absolutely. From the moment I walk out there, I just feel goose pimples from the energy of the audience. I think, *if I can go out there and do one good thing for one person, then everything is worth it.* I know it's not about me. It's not about the outfit that I'm wearing. It's not about vanity, form, or fashion. I have this real strong desire to not waste my time here being a self-oriented person that lives their life thinking, *what can I get for me?*

Like this one guy said, "I never heard you before, but when you started in with that slide and that percussion on 'Gone Woman Blues,'

I about had a heart attack. It changed my life." You don't know what you might do for somebody. Then there are all the people who say, "You know, I used to play guitar and I put it down, but I think I'm going to go home and practice." Men and women say that, but I especially feel attached to it when it's a woman, because I feel perhaps that society still makes it harder for women to follow their dreams. It's much easier than it used to be, but there's still that sort of vibe in the air, and I really like it if a woman has a special dream to see her follow it.

And even more profound, perhaps, is when people come and say something saved their life or they tell me that a certain song changed their life. It's a tremendous privilege to be able to sit up on stage and do what I love, and to have all these incredible, wonderful people come and see me. They're making it happen.

SF: I sense a deep spirituality within you. Is that instinctive or have you studied any formal paths?

RB: I think it's instinctive. I always felt like I was an outsider, because I was raised in a sort of unspiritual environment. I was raised in the modern age of skepticism. The "God is dead" generation. Many times as a child, especially out in nature, I would celebrate the beauty of being out there. That was my number-one source of comfort, because my family life was not a source of comfort—it was a source of rejection. I would be loving it in nature and feeling somehow loved. It startled me when I told this story to someone, and they said, "That's God"—meaning the feeling I had out there in nature. I felt surrounded by this beautiful intensity of a presence. That was a good moment. Then I thought, *I guess I am a spiritual person.*

SF: Do you ever wonder why there are not more women guitarists? Do you think there's a stigma or a symbolism attached to the guitar?

RB: I do think women are breaking through that mold in a very nice way, but we have more mold-breaking to do. When I first started playing the guitar, the attitude at the time was that women who played guitar were expected to play with the lightest possible touch.

I went to Australia once, years ago, and people were very startled by my guitar playing. Almost offended. I was on tour with John Hammond, who also plays very strident guitar, and I noticed criticism in the reviews—not criticism of my playing, but it was like people were taken aback by it. They applauded his strident approach, but mine shocked them. I've also had people at concerts in Europe come up to me after a show and say things like, "But should you do that? I don't know if you should play guitar like that." Now people recognize my name and know what I do and how I play. People come to my workshops wanting to learn how to play like that.

SF: I think with a woman, playing guitar like that comes from a place of real power. The guitar is such a sexual instrument.

RB: Which brings me back to your original question of why there aren't more women playing like that. I still think there is this expectation that a woman will have more of a laid-back, folksy approach—more mellow and gentle. *Why can't she play it like a battle axe? Why can't she slam it and make it like a drum? Why can't she do the whole thing?* It is very sexual, and maybe that's the reason. I think it's changing, but perhaps it will take more time for women to feel encouraged.

SF: It will take more time for other people to feel comfortable seeing a woman play like that. I've noticed resistance from people for years.

RB: People were just sometimes not ready for that. It was like, guys can do that, but women can't. Well, why not?

SF: One of my main focuses with writing this book is to dig into that question. It's just a musical instrument, after all. It's no different from a cello or a piano. In Spain, it's very difficult to find a woman who plays flamenco guitar. In Romani culture, it was strongly discouraged for a woman to play the guitar. That's thought of as a man's role, while the women sing and dance. I've spoken to a few women flamenco guitarists here in North America and asked them why there are not more. They just said they hardly knew of any besides themselves, and they really didn't know why.

RB: Is the guitar like a phallic symbol or something?

SF: The guitar shape is like the body of a woman, with a phallus. Maybe there's something there that affects humans on a subconscious level. I also want to see if women actually express different things with their guitars. I have the opinion that the electric guitar is one of the most highly abused instruments on the planet. There's a whole lot of posing and wanking going on out there. I was just wondering if women are less prone to approach music in that way. Less testosterone perhaps?

RB: Maybe it's like the little-red-sportscar mentality. I was once on a tour somewhere in Europe, and the driver and the booking agent came along with us. I used to ask them to drive slower than they were used to driving. I always gave them a speed limit. In certain places in the world, they just consider that almost impossible to co-operate with. Somebody came up around us in a little sports car and looked at us almost contemptuously as if to say, "You turtles. You're hardly moving! Are you a man or not?" I asked, "What was that all about?" Our driver explained, in this sort of broken English, that he was being told he wasn't masculine because he was driving too slow.

Could that be connected to this subject? The expectation is that something has to be done in a masculine way. But, these days, I really feel like I'm accepted and no longer looked upon as an oddity. I feel celebrated for what I do. I'm not coming from a disgruntled perspective, either. I'm trying to be objective. This is not a feminist or anti-man thing. When you close your eyes, it's just music.

SF: Did you ever take formal vocal lessons?

RB: I've gained vocal power and range over the years. I started out with no vibrato, and I did my studying by listening to the great R&B and Motown singers, practicing in my car mostly. I always tell people to roll the windows up and sing. No one on earth will hear you, and you can do whatever you want. The vocal has to move independently of the guitar part, and that's where I hear most people don't get it right. Their vocals are controlled by the rhythm guitar part. I remember sitting on a rock in the Rocky Mountains when I had run away from home at the age of fifteen, playing Willie Brown, "M & O Blues," and repeatedly trying to get the vocal independent of the guitar part. Once you get it, you can apply it to everything else you do.

SF: When you write songs, do you take it from that perspective? Do you write the vocal line first and follow it with your guitar?

RB: Actually, I almost always do it the other way around. A lot of time I do something on guitar and record it with no vocals. Then I'll travel around with a cassette in my car until I have a plan for what I want to sing with it. The way I sing is never the same two times in a row, so I never really write a melody. I used to get criticized by record company guys for that in the beginning of my career. They'd say things like, "How is anybody going to sing along? You can't do that! Where's the melody?" I thought, *what melody? You just sing.*

SF: Are you listening to anyone right now?

RB: I tend to listen to what people give me. I check all that out, but I am almost never listening to music at all, or I listen to classical music because it's a break from what I do. But people send me CDs and I always give them a cursory listen so I can be informed and so I don't dishonor their request. A good thing I got recently was John Hammond's new album. The funkiest stuff in the world for me is still probably the rhythm tracks on the old R&B songs. The best time for me to listen is on the road. When I hear music that moves me, I try to contact the person and tell them that they are special. I try to give them some inspiration and support.

SF: That seems to depict your spirituality.

RB: I don't criticize other players. I don't want to be in a position of downing anybody. I'd rather just give support, and if I have nothing good to say, I'd rather say nothing. You don't want to be the reason that somebody else is discouraged.

SF: Who have been your favorite collaborators? You have worked with a lot of people in your career. Is there anybody that really stands out? Stevie Wonder?

RB: He jumps to mind. He was beautiful. Not only because he was an extreme genius, but also because of his attitude in the studio. He said, "I want to do what you want, because you're the artist." I was so honored that he valued me as an artist, and I felt so uplifted, as soon as he started playing, I started crying. I tried not to cry, but I couldn't help it. I just started to bawl. I felt the waves of what he was playing just washing into my life. That was beautiful.

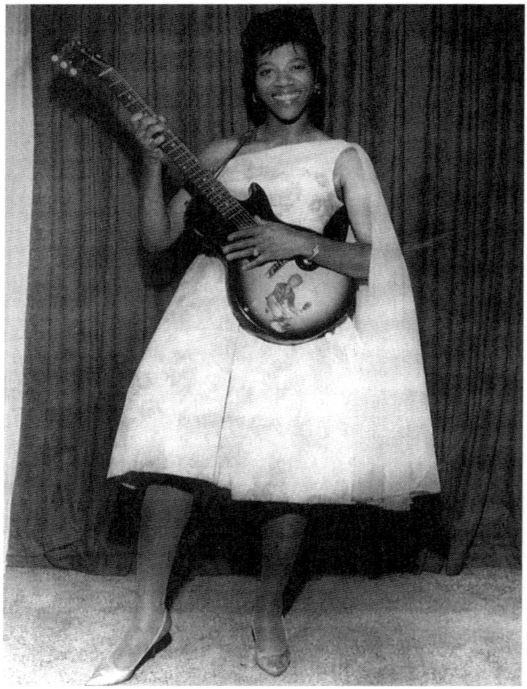

Barbara Lynn

BARBARA LYNN

I first met Barbara Lynn after moving to Austin in the early 1990s. I was twenty-one, freshly signed to a local independent blues label, Antone's Records. Not long after, Antone's released a compilation album called *Antone's Women*, featuring Barbara, myself, and several other Texas-based female blues artists. To my delight, the label organized a tour with all of us, giving me the once-in-a-lifetime opportunity to travel and perform alongside a group of strong, soulful women I deeply admired.

Every artist on that tour was extraordinary, but Barbara stood out, not just for her talent, but for her history. She had accomplished so much since the 1960s. Barbara was a Black artist who wrote her own songs, many of which became hits. She played lead guitar, left-handed, and did it with effortless style. Even after more than half a century in the business, Barbara, now in her eighties, still performs and headlines shows across the United States.

Barbara Lynn Ozen was born on January 16, 1942, in Beaumont, Texas. She began her musical journey as a child taking piano lessons, but after discovering the music of Elvis Presley and other rock and roll greats, she knew she wanted to play guitar. She taught herself on a right-handed guitar that she flipped upside down and restrung.

While in high school, Barbara formed an all-girl band called Bobbie Lynn and Her Idols, performing in clubs across Texas and quickly gaining a local following. Her big break came in 1962 when record producer Huey P. Meaux discovered her. Meaux brought her to Cosimo Matassa's legendary studio in New Orleans, where she recorded her debut single, "You'll Lose a Good Thing." The song soared to number one on the Billboard R&B chart and reached number eight on the Billboard Hot 100, making Barbara one of the first Black women to achieve such success with a self-penned hit.

Meeting Barbara for the first time made me nervous. I had been in awe of her talent and legacy, but when I finally mustered the courage to approach her, she put me at ease right away. Barbara is one of the kindest, gentlest people I've ever met in the music business. She speaks with a slight stutter, which gives her an air of vulnerability that instantly draws you in.

On tour, I stuck to her like glue, soaking up everything I could. I stood side-stage every night, watching her perform and learning how she worked the crowd, carried herself, and connected with fans. I even carried her guitar and changed her strings between shows. Barbara was always gracious and warm, thanking me with genuine sincerity.

Her humility belied her incredible career. Barbara had toured the world with legends like Stevie Wonder, Gladys Knight, B. B. King, the Supremes, Chuck Berry, Guitar Slim, and the Temptations. Her songs have been recorded by major artists including the Rolling Stones, Aretha Franklin, and Petula Clark. "You'll Lose a Good Thing" remains her signature hit, yet Barbara has never been boastful about her accomplishments.

Her performances were a revelation. She exuded a sweetness and down-to-earth charm that drew audiences in. Her sultry voice and heartfelt lyrics could captivate any crowd, but when she launched into a guitar solo, it was like she revealed another dimension of herself. Her playing wasn't flashy or showy; it was soulful, pure, and unpretentious, a natural extension of her spirit.

Barbara stepped back from the music industry in the 1970s to raise her children, returning triumphantly in the 1980s. In 1984, she toured Japan and recorded the live album *You Don't Have to Go.* After her husband passed away, she returned to Beaumont, where she still lives today, continuing to perform and record. Her contributions to music were honored with a Pioneer Award from the *Rhythm and Blues Foundation* in 1999, and she remains an icon of the genre.

It took me years to ask Barbara for an interview, and when she finally agreed, I was deeply grateful. Like many early R&B artists, Barbara endured exploitation, and some chapters of her life, particularly her association with Huey P. Meaux, were painful to revisit. Meaux, once celebrated for discovering artists like Barbara, was later convicted of serious crimes involving sexual abuse and exploitation. His harmful actions in no way diminish Barbara's immense talent or the enduring power of her music.

Barbara Lynn's playing is as authentic as it is inspiring. Her music flows from a place of joy, creativity, and God-given grace. Watching her perform and learning from her left an indelible mark on me, and I remain forever grateful to have shared that time with her.

BARBARA LYNN

— The Interview —

[2009]

SF: Is there anything I shouldn't ask you about?

BL: Well, not too much about Huey Meaux. A lot of people ask me about him, but I would rather focus on other things.

SF: It's probably better to focus on the positive.

BL: Yes. I have my family, and so far, I've got my health.

SF: Well, you look great. Are you playing a lot these days?

BL: Yes, I just finished in Pittsburgh. I've been to Fresno and Bakersfield, and now I'm getting ready to go to Dallas.

SF: Have you got your own band or are you using bands along the way?

BL: For the Dallas show, it's going to be like an orchestra backing up many acts. This is going to be at a theater, and it's concerning seven or eight acts—some old groups from way before your time like the

Moonglows. All of these guys are around my age, in their sixties and seventies.

SF: How does it make you feel when you run into all of these older R&B legends?

BL: It makes me feel great. I got to play shows with bands like the Chi-Lites, the Stylistics, the Drifters, and everybody. All of these people are around my age and we communicate so beautifully. A lot of Hispanics are really crazy over our old music. They are lining up around the buildings trying to get to see these acts from the '50s, '60s, and '70s. It was my first time working with that clientele of people, and I was really amazed because I didn't know this. When I get on stage, them little young girls and boys go crazy. I spend all night signing autographs backstage. I mean, eat your heart out, Diana Ross! I didn't know there was this whole new group of people into my music.

SF: That must make you feel really good. It's great that you can keep going. Are you playing as much as you want right now?

BL: I wouldn't say as much as I want, but then I'm not getting any younger. I try to go out and then I try to rest a little while.

SF: Is your mother still alive?

BL: Yes. Oh, Lord. And she's the main person I try to spend as much time with. As much time as God can give me to be with her. She's eighty-seven and Lord, have mercy, she still moving around and doing her thing.

SF: Do you still live with her?

BL: Yes. When my husband died, I moved back to Beaumont. This is the home that I had built from the ground when I recorded "You'll Lose a Good Thing." With my first check, I bought me a lot and a half right here on this corner, and that's where we still are today. I had this company build me a brick home, and that's where I am right now. And I designed my own house. I told them what I wanted. I wanted a second living room and that's what I have, and I have a large wall mirror against my living room wall. In fact, when my grandchildren walk in, they look at themselves and dance and pose in front of the mirror. I've even got a heart-shaped bath, and that's what I wanted. At that time too, one hundred thousand dollars to draw off one song at one time in the 1960s—that was considered a lot of money.

SF: It's still a lot of money.

BL: When I got that $100,000 check I was excited. I went and bought two Cadillacs. I was really young and excited. Nowadays, I've calmed down.

SF: You were really smart to build that house.

BL: A lot of people said that I did something right with that. I told my parents if I ever made it big that I was going to buy them a home built up from the ground, because we stayed in a little two-bedroom house.

SF: Did you have any brothers or sisters?

BL: No, not by my mother and father. My father, he divorced my mother when I was a young girl. My mother tells me I was maybe a year old. All I really knew for a father was my stepfather, who my mother married later. He raised me, and when he died, he called me his child because he was such a good husband to my mother and a good stepfather to me. When I was down or something, or if things were going rough in the business and I needed another car, my stepfather drew some money out and bought me a brand-new Chevrolet. Lord, I needed that car. That's just the kind of stepfather I had.

SF: How did you come to play the guitar?

BL: When I was young, I always pretended that I was playing piano on the windowsill. Then I saw Elvis Presley and other guitar players and I thought I would like to play guitar. I told them that I wanted to play something odd, that you don't see a woman playing too much. You see a lot of women singers, and I would see a lot of white women playing guitars, but I ain't never seen no Black woman guitarist. That's what I told my mother. And Sue, it really paid off. When I was in high school and when I started playing clubs, you should have seen the people throwing money to me. They had never seen a girl playing left-handed guitar. In fact, the money they were throwing at me was bigger than my salary. I was really excited then. I thought, *this is it*. After seeing Elvis Presley playing too, I just knew I was born to play that guitar. So, my mother went out and bought me an Arthur Godfrey ukulele. She worked at a box factory place where they made boxes, and she took her little bit of money and went and bought me a nine-dollar-and ninety-five-cent ukulele.

SF: How old were you then?

BL: I had to be about maybe nine or ten. At that time on the radio, we were listening to people like Guitar Slim and Muddy Waters, Jimmy Reed, and then also women like Brenda Lee and Connie Francis. I liked all those people.

SF: You just listened to everything? You didn't care if it was black music or white music?

BL: I just liked all of it. Barbra Streisand—I love her.

SF: Tell me about your first band, Bobbie Lynn and her Idols.

BL: That was my first band and I formed it when we were in elementary school. We would play a lot of talent shows around then, and I was getting so much encouragement from all the girls and boys that I thought I'd form a band. It was three girls and myself. The reason it was called Bobbie Lynn was because a lot of people call me Bobbie. Then we really started playing those record hops and talent shows, and we would win them all. We were tearing it up.

SF: Did the other girls play instruments?

BL: It was a singing group. I played guitar and they would sing behind me. Sometimes, I would get a piano player to follow me or a bass player from school.

SF: Was your family supportive and proud of you from the start?

BL: Yes. My stepfather and my mother, they would say things like, "It looks like Barbara is going to be a singer." I was still in the eighth grade.

SF: Did you ever take lessons?

BL: I took some piano lessons for about a year and a half. But I didn't stick to piano. I just wanted to be on the guitar.

SF: And you never took guitar lessons?

BL: No, I ain't never took guitar lessons. I know my keys, but when you say them notes I can get really mixed up.

SF: Tell me about Clarence "Bon Ton" Garlow.[1]

BL: Clarence tells everybody that he discovered me, not Huey Meaux. He was mad at Huey Meaux for a long time and he would say, "You took my artist." He would say, "Barbara, Huey stole you from me." But that wasn't true. It was just that Huey offered me more. At that time, Clarence had this little studio he would run and he would let me and some of the boys go in there and mess around. He was trying to record us but it just seemed to not work out. Then, when Joe Barry heard about me playing across the state line in Louisiana at the Palomino Club, he told Huey Meaux about me and Huey got in contact with me and came here and talked to my parents. He told them that he would like to do an album on me if it was all right with them. They gave him their consent. Then, for a long time Clarence went around telling people that they let that white man take me away from him. But that is not the case. Huey Meaux had more money to push me. With Clarence, I wasn't getting pushed the way I should have. And I was playing all kinds of clubs around here—the white clubs, the black clubs—because my name was getting around.

SF: Your first hit was "You'll Lose a Good Thing," right?

BL: That was my first hit, but just before that Huey had released a song called "Dina and Patrina." That was a song I wrote about two girls from my neighborhood who grew up down the street from me. I recorded that song and Huey put it out locally to see what kind of noise it would make,

1 Clarence "Bon Ton" Garlow (1911–86) was an American R&B, Texas blues, and cajun guitarist best known for recording the song "Bon Ton Roula."

but it didn't generate too much. Finally, he took me to Cosimo studio in New Orleans and he recorded me there. I had a whole lot of other songs ready, and one of them was "You'll Lose a Good Thing." So out of all those songs, we made an album, and out of that album "You'll Lose a Good Thing" was the single. First, it didn't make much noise around the area, but then when Jamie Records out of Philadelphia heard it, they put it out nationally. Then it soon started going internationally.

SF: And the rest is history. When did you write your first song?

BL: Girl, I started in grade school. I would come back home in the evenings and I would get my homework done, and then I would just mess around with pencil and paper and write words and poems down. I would work on rhymes. I would listen to the songs on the radio and hear how they made things rhyme. I just taught myself how to write that way. I wrote a lot of poems. When they came to put me in the studio, I must've had about twenty songs ready.

SF: That's so unusual. Most women didn't write their own songs or play their own guitar.

BL: My stepfather said, "If that record isn't a hit record, then you are going to college." I said, "Okay." Then that song came out and my stepfather was grinning from ear to ear. He was excited then.

SF: Did you tour throughout the 1960s?

BL: Yes indeed, with people like Smokey Robinson, Stevie (Wonder), Dion, the Supremes—I mean everybody. Chuck Jackson. I did a show with Chuck Berry and he forgot his guitar strap and he asked me if he could borrow mine. That song took me all over the world. Japan. Germany. I was everywhere.

SF: Did your mother come with you everywhere?

BL: Yes, my father made sure my mother came with me. He was worried about drugs and all the things that go on out there on the road. And strangers. My mother took off from her box factory job. I told her that she didn't have to worry about working anymore anyway, as I was gonna take care of her. When I played the Apollo Theater, I sent her a bus ticket on the Greyhound bus and she came and met me. Ever since then she was traveling with me. All the music people got a chance to know her. B. B. King and Stevie [Wonder], they'd call her Mother Dear, because on tour they would hear me call her Mother Dear.

SF: What would be some of your absolute highlights from those years?

BL: Dick Clark's *American Bandstand*. That was one of my worst moments, because my wig was crooked. I had to hurry and go backstage and cut my wig and I cut it crooked. Nobody noticed, thank God. I've got that picture hanging here, right up on my wall. Some of my nice memories are meeting all these people I had always heard of, but I never thought I would be able to meet, like Patti LaBelle and Gladys Knight. People like that. I had heard about them, and finally I was able to meet them.

At one point, Huey told me that my record was climbing up the charts and that they got me a show at the Apollo Theater in New York. At that time, we were hearing things like, "If they'll like you at the Apollo Theater, they will let you know." I was told they would boo me off the stage and throw things at me if I didn't do good. Well, I was so nervous when I was standing backstage, and then I heard them introduce me and people started clapping. When the announcer told them about my song, "You'll Lose a Good Thing," well, people started to go crazy. When I picked that guitar up, them people ate me up. They really accepted me and they were screaming and everything. They came close to the stage and everything. After I did that, I calmed down because rumors were they would throw banana peelings at the artist if they didn't like them, but they didn't do any of that. I just thanked God that I made it.

SF: What have you learned the most in the music business to keep going? What do you think is the most important thing for you?

BL: Well, the main thing is to give thanks and praise to God for letting me stay out there as long as I have been. I am still playing and I'm sixty-seven. And I still have my voice. I thank God for all of that, and I thank him for giving me the strength to turn down drugs and smoking. Today, I still don't drink or smoke. I never did any of that. I just stuck to my water or orange juice and soda pop. I tell everybody, including the young kids of today to just stay off drugs and do what you love best, and if you're very determined you will make it. You have to have a lot of faith and patience.

SF: How has the music business changed?

BL: Very much. The generation of today is really into rap music. When it first came out, I didn't think the rap would last but it did and today it's the number one kind of music there is. Today's generation is so different from the time I was growing up.

SF: I think you grew up in one of the best times for music.

BL: I think you're right. And I see so many young people who are wasting their lives with this. My son is a rapper. Now he's thirty-five and he has a mini studio in his house. But he knows not to go bad-mouthing any women. He has a wife and three children. I tell them, "To make it, baby, you don't need to do that. Go on and rap like LL Cool J or Will Smith and them." My daughter said, "Mom, when you do your interview, will you mention me?" So, my kid's names are Keisha Sims, Elkie Chambers, and Batchlor Wise IV. I have also got seven grandchildren.

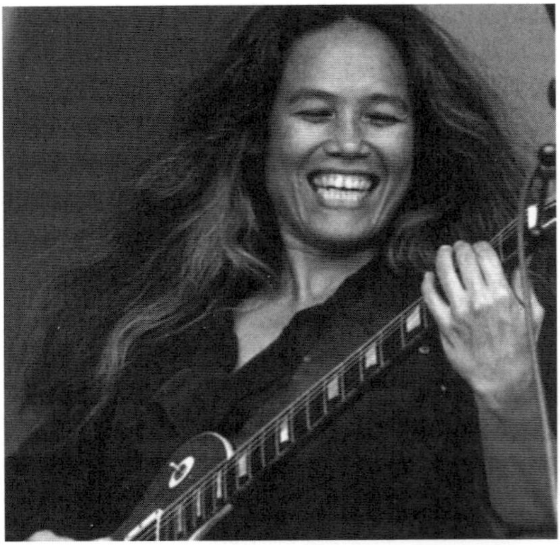

June Millington

JUNE MILLINGTON

Emerging in the late 1960s, Fanny became the first self-contained all-female rock band to sign with a major label and earn widespread critical acclaim. They weren't a gimmick or a novelty act, Fanny was as serious about their craft as any male band of the time. According to guitarist June Millington, who formed the band with her sister Jean, they often had to work harder to be taken seriously, pushing themselves to master their instruments and refine their sound to prove they belonged alongside their male counterparts. Today, June exudes a sage-like wisdom and depth, paired with the legacy of a groundbreaking musician.

June and Jean were born in the Philippines and moved to northern California with their parents when they were in grade school. As immigrants, they often felt out of place, navigating the challenges of assimilation and acceptance. Music became their bridge to American culture and their peers. In high school, they formed their first band, the Svelts, playing gigs in towns around Sacramento and Davis.

As Fanny, the Millington sisters rubbed shoulders with the Grateful Dead, Santana, Little Feat, and Jefferson Airplane. June's reflections on that era reveal the unique pressures they faced, not only the usual challenges of the music industry. Despite the odds, they carved out a place for themselves and inspired future generations of female musicians.

When we spoke, June described her early inspirations that drove her to pursue music. She recalled seeing her heroes perform when she was a teenager, a veritable "who's who" of many of the major acts the defined the 1960s. These seminal musical experiences left a lasting mark. Her passion for music was never just about personal fulfillment; it was about breaking barriers and opening doors for those who would come after her.

Fanny's accomplishments are deeply significant in rock history. They were the first all-female band to release albums on a major label (Warner Bros), and they earned the respect of critics and peers alike. David Bowie was one of their most vocal supporters, famously declaring that Fanny was one of the most important bands in rock history. Despite critical acclaim, they never scored a major hit, yet their influence extended far beyond the charts. They proved that women could rock, inspiring artists like Suzi Quatro (whose sister Patti briefly joined Fanny), the Go-Go's, and Joan Jett.

The challenges Fanny faced weren't limited to musicianship. They also endured the loneliness of being trailblazers in a world unprepared for them. June spoke candidly about those isolating years and the extraordinary effort it took to establish the band's legitimacy.

By the late 1970s, after years of grueling tours and industry pressure, June left Fanny and turned inward. She explored spirituality, embracing Buddhist practice and vegetarianism, seeking balance and healing. This new phase led her to the "women's music" movement, which emphasized collaboration and mutual support among female artists. She later co-founded the Institute for the Musical Arts (IMA) in Massachusetts, a nonprofit dedicated to mentoring young women in music. Through the IMA, June continues to share her wisdom and experience with new generations of artists.

June spoke about the changing landscape of live music, lamenting what she called the loss of "direct transmission," the electric connection that happens when an audience experiences music live and unfiltered.

For her, that authenticity is irreplaceable and it's something she strives to instill in her students.

June's story is not just about her musical achievements but also about resilience, innovation, and the power of mentorship. Her journey from the Philippines to the forefront of rock history is a testament to her determination and talent. Fanny's contributions to music were groundbreaking, yet their influence is often overlooked. While June is undoubtedly a trailblazing figure in rock history, her role as a mentor might be her greatest gift to the world.

JUNE MILLINGTON

— *The Interview* —

[2008]

SF: When you first started, you guys were always independent as far as how you got the band going?

JM: We were totally self-created. We were self-contained and we could play (*laughs*). You know, nobody was around to teach us the ropes because I was booking the band when we were in high school. We would play Air Force bases, we would play for charity parties, teams, there was so many gigs. Sometimes we'd do three gigs a night. Even when we were in high school. And in the summers we would play five sets a night.

SF: Unbelievable.

JM: We'd lie about our ages, you know. I would go buy 45s, a lot of times I'd just sit with my turntable and then learn them and then teach them to the rest of the band.

SF: Who were your main influences?

JM: Anyone you could think of who was on the radio. Top forty. Mid-'60s. When flower power hit, all these bands. I went to UC Davis for a year and UC Berkeley for a quarter so all these bands were coming to our colleges and I saw the original Buffalo Springfield. I mean, we saw the Grateful Dead so many times when [original keyboardist] "Pigpen" was in the band. We did a lot of gigs in Lake Tahoe because it was only a couple of hours from Sacramento. We did this team center gig once and we were opening for this band that I'd heard of in a club, the Lemon Tree in Reno. Some soldier came up to me and said, "Yeah, I just came from Las Vegas and there was this amazing band there. You know, they're really great. They're hot." I said, "What's the name? Sly and the Family Stone." Fuck, I'd never heard of them. They weren't on the radio yet. So we do this gig and we dropped acid. It had to have been '67. And lo and behold, we opened up for Sly and the Family Stone and there was nobody there. I think there were fifteen people. We played our set and then I went and lay down on the floor in front of the band and we just watched Sly and the Family Stone. Like a private show.

Then when Fanny was recording in L.A., this was when Sly was getting into his own world, he had not a trailer, but a bitty house, what do you call that? An RV, possibly, in front of the studio. He slept in the RV and he would record for hours and hours and hours. They had this special assistant who had to go through the tapes and find the places that worked. But he used to come into our sets and just sit on the floor and listen and say, "That sounds great!"

So, you know, interesting times. I was at the same studio and, I used to run into this girl in the halls but we never said anything to each other. She looked like she was shy. And what's her name. (*sings*) "Just like me, they long to be close to you . . ."

SF: Karen Carpenter?

JM: Yeah, it was Karen Carpenter. We ran into each other in the halls—quite a bit. Never even said hello. Too shy. Way too shy, both of us. I was so shy I had to be introduced to somebody.

SF: You were so shy, but you still booked the band and everything.

JM: I know. I have Moon and Venus in Gemini. If it's a business thing and it has to do with music and getting the job done, I would do it. Whatever it was I had to do. But in terms of having a social life, no. I'm very work-oriented. I always have been. In fact, our second good drummer, her name is Brie Brandt; she actually ended up being Carole King's percussionist for many years. And she's half-Filipino, just like me and Jean. Exactly the same. Her mom's Filipino, but her dad is American, and she lives in Folsom. She and Jean were best friends. And, what was my point? What were we talking about before?

SF: You were shy and you booked the bands.

JM: Oh, yeah. I was in L.A., right around the time that the Fanny collection was being mastered, and so I called Brie, and she came over and sometime during that visit she turned to me and said, "You know, June, you were right. I hated you because you always made us practice, but you know what? We were good *because* you made us practice. So, I'm sorry. You were right" (*laughs*).

SF: Was she the drummer after Alice?

JM: She was the drummer before Alice. I had three really good drummers. The first one, the original one, her name was Kathi Terry. She was the one who called our house out of the blue. She came from our rival high school. And she just said, "You know, you want to start a band. I play drums. I heard you guys play; you want to start a band?" And we were like, you know, about a half-second later we said, "Yeah, sure!" Oh, my God (*laughs*). And that's how it started. Before that we were playing folk songs.

SF: Yeah, did you always want to be in an all-woman band?

JM: Never thought of it. Never even thought of it. Way too shy. How could I even think of something like that? We were just trying to be American. In 1961, I just turned thirteen. We were just switching to guitars and we didn't know anybody. And everyone assumed we were Mexican, which was fine. It was really, really hard. We were way behind the times. Music was what made the difference. All the difference.

SF: So that's how you integrated.

JM: Definitely. Music was our lifeline. No question about it.

SF: I just assumed you guys had made it a principle to be an all-girl band.

JM: We were hanging out with our boyfriends, who were in a surf band. And we were singing with two other girls who also played folk. The four of us got together, like four acoustic guitars in a heat wave. We'd do these all-girl songs, and then we played songs of the Beatles, "No Reply," stuff like that. Which is also a great song, kind of underrated—nobody plays that song anymore. And "Dancing in the Street" and "Nowhere to Run." Oh my God, we loved "Nowhere to Run," Martha and the Vandellas. And these guys would let us sing in between their sets at clubs because we're just the girlfriends. They let us use their equipment, just [to] start rehearsing. We started to do little numbers in between, using their equipment. Then we'd all audition for the same gig—and we got the gig. And that was it, man. We had to buy the equipment.

SF: (*laughs*) Were the guys pissed off?

JM: Yeah, they were (*laughs*). One of them was Jean's boyfriend. We ran into him about ten years ago. Really nice—but not mad at us anymore (*laughs*).

SF: You guys had a really amazing run.

JM: We were a hard-working band, let me tell you. Hard-working before we got to L.A. That's the thing that people don't realize—we worked non-stop, 24/7, sincerely. Let's say I did a gig, whoever was good on the bill, I'd ask them if they wanted to play or jam, could they teach me something or whatever. I would go and watch a really good band and sit in the front row, and I'd watch how they did it. I remember standing in front of the Grateful Dead at UC Davis and that was the first time I thought to myself, *How does this guy do that?* I had not the slightest idea because, it was rhythm and singing, it was great. In fact, I'd rather play rhythm than play lead guitar for the most part. I'd always stand right in front of the guitar player at the Filmore West and at Winterland, which were the two places that you would go. By that time I must have been sixteen or seventeen. I could drive myself to San Francisco. Jimi Hendrix, I was standing right in front of him. Albert King, or Cream, it didn't matter who it was, I'd be standing in front of the guitar player. There was this little kid standing right next to me, and we'd definitely be always jockeying for that spot, always standing right next to each other. And then when the first Santana album came out, I saw Carlos's picture and, "Oh my God! That's that kid!" (*laughs*) He and I were doing the same thing.

There wasn't any place you could get the information, moreover, you couldn't get the information because people were making it up on the spot. You had to just go be where it was, if you were bitten by the bug like I was. I was just so passionate about it, just was everything to me. Music still is. It transports me to wherever it does, where you don't exist. And of course, that's just where we all really want to go. It just depends on what your magic carpet is. That's what I did, 24/7, and essentially, that's what the band did.

SF: Who were your favorite guitar players?

JM: There were a whole bunch of names I can't remember, who were in bands at the time when we were first starting out in Sacramento. But in terms of people who you would remember, definitely Jimi Hendrix is the top, top of the list. I have to say Albert King because the first gig I saw other than Jerry Garcia play, in terms of roots music, was in San Francisco and it was a double bill with both Jimi Hendrix and Albert King. I don't think I really knew who they were and I'm telling you, the top of my head exploded. It was unbelievable. I was standing right in front of them. That viscerally put it in my DNA. From that point on, I just was non-stop.

SF: How old were you then?

JM: I was probably seventeen. So much happened to me in that year, in terms of really getting it. By the time we went down to L.A., Lowell George [of Little Feat] became one of my best friends. We spent a lot of time playing together. So did our two bands. He used to come over to our basement and jam and then we signed with Warner [Brothers subsidiary] Reprise. I met Lowell at a jam in Van Nuys, in the Valley. I remember specifically him asking, "How do you get a record deal?" (*laughs*) I said, "Why don't you just call Warner?" Then they ended up with a deal.

Since Warner owned the movie lot, all the time there was a sound stage that wasn't being used. In fact, they usually had two. So if we weren't jamming in our basements, we both had a sound stage at the movie lot. We would be rehearsing at the same time, and we'd visit each other during breaks. I mean, we were really close.

I didn't play the blues. Even though I'd seen Albert King, I hadn't even thought of playing the blues, because I didn't hear it in the Philippines. All I heard was pop music. Lowell came over one evening. He didn't tell me he was coming; he'd just drop by anytime. He said, "June, you can't go rock and roll and have this career without learning how to play this kind of music." He pulled out a doobie and he got really high and he put on Howlin' Wolf and Muddy Waters.

The whole time I was in Fanny I was playing the blues simultaneously with what it was that we did. It was like being in college. Lowell was a great teacher, because it was tone: It wasn't just your licks, it was your tone. There was a whole bunch of us working on how you get sound from amps; we were always changing amps and fooling around, different tubes and all that stuff, developing our sounds.

Skunk Baxter was my guitar repairman. He wasn't even anybody that anybody knew. I brought my Les Paul to him, and he picks it up and says, "Yeah, this plays great!" I'm looking at him and I remember thinking, *Why don't I know this guy? He's so much better than me. This guy is amazing.* The next time I went he said, "I'm playing with a band tonight, do you want to come by?" He told me the name and I thought, *That sounds like a dinky cowboy band*—so I didn't go; I wasn't really interested in Steely Dan—that's the band he started with, Steely Dan.

The Les Paul I play now is from Kent Henry, who had his own band called Blues Image, then the band broke up and he got an offer to be a replacement guitar player with Steppenwolf. And sometime in that period, we were on the road and he called me up and said, "June, I really need money. Do you want to buy my guitar?" I wasn't really interested in buying this Les Paul. But I said, "I'll call our accountant and see if you'll sell it to me for five hundred bucks." It's a '57 Les Paul. I still use it. People say I shouldn't even travel with it anymore. But that thing plays me in ways that other guitars can't, you know. I don't even really play, when I play that guitar. It just, like, happens (*laughs*).

SF: I can't carry those Les Paul's. They're too heavy for me.

JM: There was this biker making straps, who I met at McCabe's—you know McCabes, that little place in L.A.? He used to hang out at McCabe's and sell these straps. It's really wide and it's beautiful, and it has this sheepskin on the other side. It really saved my shoulder. So I can play the Les Paul fine.

SF: Did you ever get any problems with your shoulder?

JM: No.

SF: Never?

JM: No. I mean, I'm sore when I haven't practiced, but not problems. Also, I stopped practicing electric excessively when I started to play with Chris Williams and that probably saved my ass, because I don't have problems that other guitar players have, like repetitive tendonitis.

Mostly what I do is if I'm trying to come up with a solo, I come up with it conceptually and I hear it in my head and I try out different things, then I just play it. I don't spend like five hours practicing. You know what I'm saying?

SF: So you're still fascinated with guitar.

JM: With all music, really. I produce records now, so I hear everything in a different way. And I'm deaf in one ear. I've always heard everything differently anyway.

SF: Have you always been deaf in one ear?

JM: Uh-huh. But I didn't know until we moved to the States, when they give those hearing tests. I remember I was in the trailer, they put it in one ear, it was fine, they put it in the other ear, and he kept looking at me funny, turning knobs, and finally he said, "Did you know you're deaf in your left ear?" I said, "No." (*laughs*) I didn't think anything of it. I went home and I mentioned it to my mom. I don't think anyone was surprised. I don't have equilibrium on that side, and it's profound.

SF: Listening to you talking about the '60s, '70s, the whole scene back then—how do you think it compares to now?

JM: I think because there's so many fewer places to play, people don't have the advantage of learning the craft. And the people who really are a direct connection to what I consider to be American music, which is directly from field hollers and gospel to the blues to rock and roll, those people are dying out.

SF: Definitely. I will attest to that.

JM: So you don't have a chance to go to some small club somewhere and hear the real thing. That loss of the direct transmission is profound in terms of musicality, number one. Number two, with the advent of technology the way it is now, people don't even feel they have to learn how to play well. In fact, they don't need to play at all, either. Just sample. It's accepted that you don't even need to be an amazing musician.

To tell you the truth, when girl bands started to, you know, that riot grrrl thing, you know, G-R-R-R-L, I don't know how to pronounce it. I didn't think they were very good, because basically, that's the shit that all the bands sounded like in 1965 before they got their shit together. So I never had that much respect for [riot grrrl] because I've heard this all before. And in fact, they call them garage bands. That's where we rehearsed when we were learning how to play. (*laughs*) I mean, maybe the lyrical content was electric in terms of people's lives, but I couldn't get past the fact that I didn't think that, musically, there was anything going on.

SF: I think you're right. I think, as a craft, there's a lot that's missing now.

JM: You don't have the direct transmission. You don't have the idea that you actually need to play well. And you don't have enough places to play in, to even practice. You know, the band's gotta go out there and play gig after gig after gig. That's how you learn how to do it. And you just can't get the gigs now.

I mean even when Al Green first started up—well shoot, you could just go and see Al Green (*laughs*). You know, first time I saw him I was in London, we were playing, I heard about this guy. During our set break, we had a limo, so I had the limo driver rush me to the club [where Green was playing], I ran upstairs, I caught this guy and—I swear, I'll never forget this—he was wearing shorts and they were made from green velour or leather or something. He looked like a Black guy in a Swiss outfit.

SF: In lederhosen or something (*laughs*).

JM: Yeah. I jump back in the limo, back to the club, did, you know [our] next set. By the time [Green's] album came out, dude, he was in that white suit. Let me tell you, it was completely different. The minute he had a hit, I thought he was gay. There he was in that white suit, looking ultra-chic. But the point is that I could go see him. I could go see Sly and the Family Stone. You know, I could go stand in front of Jimi Hendrix. I could go see Buddy Guy in L.A. at a little place down the street. Jackie Wilson. And you watch these guys do "it," whatever "it" is.

I would go sit right in front of Mavis Staples, because I was just such a huge fan. I knew she was passing something on. It wasn't about what she was singing. It was the music. She wasn't doing gospel singing. She was doing Staples Singers. But, oh my God. What she was passing on was something that I was drinking from. Like I was in the middle of the desert and I hadn't had water in two weeks. I just drank it down; I needed it so bad. I feel sorry now for people who can't get that thing, you know.

SF: They don't even know what they're missing.

JM: They don't know what they're missing. Because I'm teaching here in a girl's rock camp, one of the things that we do is we have the girls, when they come in on orientation day, have them play something that they've written, or that they know how to play, to show us where they're at. Or they play a song off a record that they like. When I put these records on, I mean, the EQ needle goes to zero and it stays flatline. There's no dynamics anymore.

I teach these girls: *this is like a conversation.* Music is a conversation. You take just one thing away and it's quieter, and it's great. Now it's the rhythm section. You know, whatever. I mean, they don't know that. They just think it's every single frequency picking up and you just sit there—that's what music is. And it's so *not* that. It's not. It's profound. I treat these girls as if they need that cool drink of water, and most of them don't know it. Some of them do, of course, because they found their way to our camp.

I did an interview today and the interviewer asked me, "What do you listen to?" And I had to say, "I can't think of one thing. I don't listen." For the most part, if there's not something going on, I'd rather have silence. I'd rather hear what's going on in my head as I work on my autobiography. I really need those moments to kind of go inward, rather than have my mind filled. But if you listen and play for twenty, twenty-five years, how much more do you really need to do?

SF: Probably not. And you heard the best stuff.

JM: We toured with Chicago, played with all the greats, played double bills with the Kinks. Jean hung out with the Who. I mean, we recorded at Abbey Road, how much more do you need? It's very, very difficult to impress me anymore. That's a little bit too bad, because I've seen so much good stuff come down the pipe. One time, after Fanny, I was in New York for whatever reason and I went Max's Kansas City just to see (*sings*) "You're rich girl, and you've gone too far." Who were those guys?

SF: Hall and Oates?

JM: Hall and Oates. We used to do gigs with them all the time. I never could remember their names. It was a real joke: "I know these guys; they're real good. Who are you again?" We did so many gigs, and I couldn't remember who we were playing with, even if they were great. Those guys were really good. Anyway, I went to go see them, and the opening act, oh my God. I wasn't planning on spending the night, but I did, because I loved the opening act so much. It turns out that my attorney was representing this guy as well. He says, "Yeah, yeah, I'll introduce them. You're staying over?"

So the next night I go to Max's and my attorney introduces us, and I'm looking around for this guy, Bruce Springsteen, and he was standing right in front of me. I thought he was, not even the waiter, I thought he was the guy who cleans up the cutlery. He's so diminutive, and so, like, humble. That's the last time I was really impressed, was when I heard that opening act, and I stayed another night in New York just because he's so good. I had no idea who he was.

SF: And which year was that?

JM: Let's see. It was before his first hit. So that was, let me think about this for a second, probably around 1975. Something like that.

SF: What struck me about Fanny is just the whole image of the group: the demeanor, the style of music, the way you played. I hadn't seen another all-chick band do that.

JM: That's exactly right.

SF: Why?

JM: Well, I think everything we just talked about in terms of being lucky enough to be there when the musicians and the musicianship was birthing itself, and we could see the guys who cut the tracks to all the Motown hits, for example, you could actually go see those guys play. I mean, by the time we got to L.A. [in 1969] it was still very exciting, and five years later, basically, it was turning into disco.

SF: To me it seemed like a lot of the later riot grrrl groups [of the '90s] kind of dumbed down the whole thing. Why? I don't understand. Like, it's so weird.

JM: I think it became more of a cultural thing to have an attitude. It was a sort of shortcut, right? Just have an attitude, have a look and sing about certain things, and that culturally meant something, or people were hungrier for that than they were for musical expression. I never felt that whole thing, because I felt like, partly, people didn't see me because I didn't want to put that coat on. I didn't know how to put it on; I didn't even know where the coat was, you know. That color, I didn't even see that color. You know what I'm saying.

SF: You guys were just players.

JM: That's exactly right. There's a plus to that and there's a huge minus, because we weren't looking to play our cards in that way. We thought if we could just be that good, that we would be recognized for it. But it took too long, and by the time we started to get any recognition at all, I was losing it. That's why I left the band.

SF: Why were you losing it? Just too much work?

JM: Well, there were three things. One is that I had no real life. We were always on the road, always working, and had been since my early twenties, and that's when you gotta start getting it together. I learned some things.

SF: You had just done that since you were thirteen. You'd done nothing else.

JM: Right. So, you know, there was that. There was the fact that there was only basically one question the press asked me, which was, "How does it feel like to be a girl playing guitar?" Which, I can't even tell you, drove me insane. Insane!

SF: I know. They still ask it.

JM: I mean, *don't you see what I'm doing?* I understood that they didn't see what I was doing. It was awful to realize. I'm pressing "five" on the elevator and it only goes to the first floor, you know? And then also, I had a spiritual longing and none of my questions were being answered. My interior landscape was just parched, and there was nothing to relieve my pain or my questions, my longing. I knew I needed to get out or I just was not going to grow. I wasn't going to become a human being in the way that I knew.

SF: Being a musician wasn't enough.

JM: It's not that. It was being in Hollywood, caught up in that whole thing. The band got to a place we had worked so hard to get to, and I didn't recognize any of it. It was like being on a bad, existential acid trip. None of it meant anything, and it was like dust in my mouth. I know that sounds biblical, over-the-top, but that's exactly how it felt. It unhinged me. I had no life, I had no girlfriend, because she had left me. I had no home life, no love life, no spiritual life (*laughs*). And I had all these gigs, but it just scared me. I couldn't sit still. I couldn't eat. My mom thought I was going to die; she was so worried. I couldn't figure out how to get out of this ocean of shit. I was stuck and really scared. The only thing I could think of to do was to quit the band and just start over.

SF: Did you guys do a lot of drugs and stuff?

JM: No. Not really. No, I was a vegetarian; I was doing yoga every day.

SF: Didn't drink a lot?

JM: I can't drink because of my equilibrium. I quit smoking pot probably in '68, because—that's not true. In '69, I got into hash with Lowell. That was a lot of fun. Really good hash. But I never really did that much coke. I tried speed. I mean, you know you just do things.

SF: It's such a part of the fabric of everything.

JM: Sure, we did drugs, just like everybody else did. But I was just reading Eric Clapton's autobiography and I was so horrified. Being with his girlfriend for three years, imagine, just doing heroin. All they could think of was their next fix. None of us ever got anywhere close to that. Like I said, we were a hard-working band. Let's say you had to work your way out of this room and all you had was a chisel and a hammer. Well, we were the edge of the chisel. And we were just working so hard, so hard, so hard all the time to where you just were numb. You couldn't even think.

SF: Is that just for acceptance?

JM: Just to make it as a girl band. As the very first, there was nobody to talk to. We'd have these meetings and say to each other, "OK. We gotta stay together at least another year because we know [what] we're doing; there's other girls coming. We gotta do this for them."

I felt like I had a nervous breakdown. I didn't know how to be a human being, and it really scared me. I needed to have that spiritual connection. And I got it. I was reading books on Buddhism. When I left Fanny, I moved to Long Island and then Woodstock and I was reading Shunryu Suzuki's *Zen for the Beginner's Mind*. I met a guru here, a guru there. Really great, amazing teachers.

SF: Were you still playing music, too?

JM: Always.

SF: Just more underground stuff.

JM: I was playing in women's music and I started to produce albums. I produced [jazz pianist] Mary Watkins and a whole bunch of people, and I co-founded the Institute for the Musical Arts in '86.

The IMA really started, for me, as part of the healing around when I went into women's music with an open heart because it coincided with my spiritual needs. Women's music, at its genesis, was about finding our identity as women and expressing a spiritual part of ourselves that women just needed to express. And we needed to find each other. Truly amazing.

SF: Do you think that women, especially, need that little bit of extra encouragement?

JM: Absolutely. Not only that, but women, we need each other's company. I really believe that. A guy doesn't mind if he's just on his own, playing lead guitar in the band and he's just working really hard. Doesn't need to, I don't think, need the company of another the way that women do. We share our stories with each other a lot. I think we're more hurt, I guess. We need each other.

When I encountered women's music—remember when I said I didn't have anyone to talk to? All of a sudden I had all these women to talk to. Everyone was talking and sharing and trying to figure it out. But once you got past all that idealism, then you're four, five years down the line and now you've got a business, which is women's music. It was a business. They couldn't live up to their ideals. That was heartbreaking for me, because I started to encounter the same kind of behavior I had left in L.A. It was a complete shock. After two, three, four years of complaining about it, by that time I had kind of worked myself out of the circle. People thought I was really hard to work with. I probably was.

SF: When you say the same kind of attitudes that you had in L.A., do you mean, being marginalized?

JM: Being ripped off. Business-wise. I had all manner of people lying and stuff like that. It was really bad. I was heartbroken. I don't say that lightly. My heart was broken because I had left everything, all the rock and roll things. I didn't even bring my electric guitar. All I did was play acoustic guitar. I found myself saying the same thing over and over again. You know *The Daughters of Copper Woman*? Have you ever read that?

SF: No.

JM: Yeah, you should. There's a section of it where they say, when you hear somebody complain about the same thing four times, then you have an obligation to say to that person, "Do you know that you've said this four times? I don't want to hear it again. You need to do something about it." I said that to myself. IMA was a part of my own healing, to see whether or not I could walk the walk that I was talking about. Which is hard. It's really hard. One thing that we try to do at IMA is say, *of course we're going* [to] *screw up, because we're human beings*. We're all trying to work it out and we're all trying to be as transparent as possible about everything.

Since Jean and I didn't have any place safe to go and find information, when we were starting out, I realized, "Oh my gosh, we can pass it on!" We have an actual obligation, a responsibility to pass it on. That's what we're doing. We're nesting it so that the next generation has a place from which to pass it on. All these archives, all these equipment, everything, so the next generation can honor it so that they can do it. We're trying to make it as strong as possible, as far-reaching as possible, in terms of vision and everyone understanding what the vision, and responsibilities, and moral, ethical ways to behave. It's a huge, huge goal.

SF: That's a really good goal. So many people get hurt by the business. You can almost bank on it. If you go into this business, you're going to get ripped off.

JM: Now we have girls call us at one in the morning and just talk about what they're going through. In a way, I'm extending a hand back to myself when I was seventeen. It's a great feeling. I can't believe I lived long enough to have enough wisdom to actually be part of it.

You can't be an airy-fairy rock and roller. For so many years, I was just going, just thinking of the next gig. I literally couldn't think three to six months ahead.

SF: So you started that when you were around thirty-eight, or something?

JM: That's right.

SF: That's great. I just turned forty. I found a similar experience with doing this book. It's so easy in this business to be just thinking about yourself all the time. *Where am I going? Where's my gigs? What am I doing? How can I get ahead?* I look at other people and it's all this envy, all these natural or unnatural feelings that we have that we go through. When I started working on this, I started talking to all these other people. It was like this whole bubble just burst. It was like, *Wow, all of a sudden I'm not just, I'm looking outside myself.* It's looking for a community. Coming up, I didn't know any other women guitar players. Everybody I talked to was the same: they didn't know any other women guitar players. They were little freaks. It's so funny to get that perspective and realize there are all these little universes floating around, unaware of each other. Fanny is like that, too. They were a little ball floating around in the world alone, without guidance and without any history for them to tell where they were going and how to deal with this.

JM: It's really useful, what we're doing.

SF: And what about Jean? Is she involved in IMA?

JM: Jean wasn't involved from the beginning in terms of the nuts and bolts of it, but she played, a lot with me at IMA. She's talked, she's come to the camp, she's done work.

SF: And the other ladies in Fanny, do you keep in touch with them?

JM: Yeah. Alice is in Tucson, but I'm not in touch with the keyboard player. Neither is Jean. I actually didn't get along that well with her. It's one of those bad things.

It's been a full life. There's never been a time I haven't been working hard, but I kind of dropped below the surface. Of course, when you're doing Buddha studies you're not exactly not exactly sticking out (*laughs*). I'm a voracious student and I tell people I'm actually a nun cleverly disguised as a rock and roller. I'm happy to just stick to myself and read my books, fiddle around with the guitar and try and do things just to try and keep myself interested.

Do not bore me. *Do not bore me!* That's the fastest way to get someone out of my life, to bore me. If I'm bored after five minutes with them, that's it.

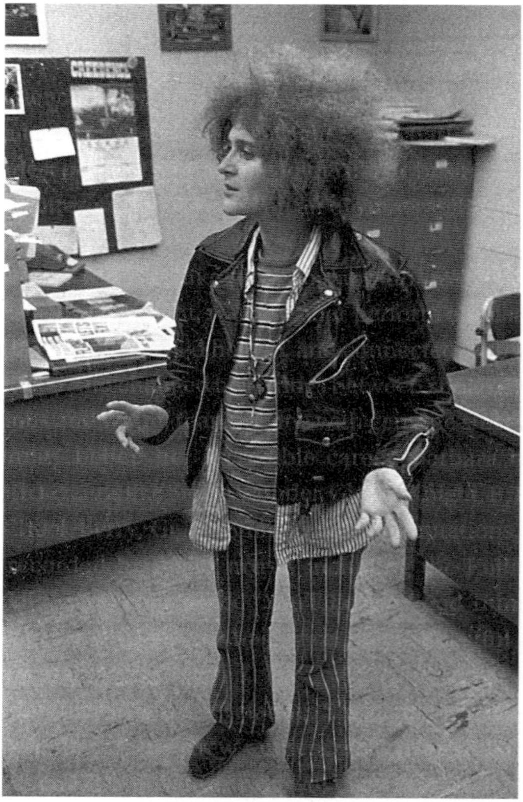

Alice Stuart

ALICE STUART

Alice Stuart is a true foremother of rock and roll. Launching her career in the early 1960s without a road map or role models to follow, Alice became her own inspiration. Judging by the bold choices she made throughout her life, she was a rebel in every sense.

I discovered Alice while researching for this book, after several people brought her name to my attention. I was shocked I'd never heard of her, but after learning her story, I wasn't surprised. Her career has been marked by periods of brilliance followed by long absences from the public eye, a rhythm that mirrors her unconventional life. Starting her journey as a teenager in Washington State, she quickly made a name for herself. By her early twenties, she became the first and only female member of Frank Zappa's Mothers of Invention, one of the most iconic and innovative rock outfits of all time. That fact alone impressed me, but speaking with Alice about her life and choices impressed me even more.

Alice was born in Chelan, Washington, in 1942 and didn't have an easy start. Abandoned by her mother at age three, she was raised by what she calls her "matriarch aunt" and endured a lonely childhood. Music became a channel for her grief, and she immersed herself in early rock and roll. Despite knowing only ten songs from *The Burl Ives Songbook,* she left for Seattle after high school and quickly found her footing in the city's music scene.

Her big break came at the 1964 Berkeley Folk Festival, a pivotal moment that led to tours with folk and blues legends like Joan Baez and Albert King. By the early 1970s, she had relocated to California, where she crossed paths with Frank Zappa and joined the Mothers of Invention for a brief but formative stint. During this time, Alice's career soared. Sporting her notoriously fuzzy hair and cropped top, she appeared as a guest on *The Dick Cavett Show* in 1972 and opened for Van Morrison on his world tour in 1975. She also appeared and recorded with Jerry Garcia of the Grateful Dead, blues musician John Hammond, and others.

Alice's 1964 debut album, *All the Good Times*, on Arhoolie Records, highlights her love for country blues. Her acoustic guitar work honors the traditions of the genre while infusing it with her own spirit. At a time when women in blues were more often vocalists than instrumentalists, Alice carved a unique space for herself as a guitarist with serious chops.

By the late 1970s, Alice faced a crossroads. With young children at home, she made the extraordinary decision to step away from music entirely to focus on raising her family. For the next two decades, she didn't tour or play guitar.

What struck me most after speaking with Alice was the way she let go of her music career for so many years to raise her children. How does someone walk away from something they love so deeply? As a dedicated career woman myself, it's a question I've wrestled with. I barely took a break after having my son and was back on stage within six weeks of giving birth. My identity felt so tied to being a guitar player that I couldn't imagine stepping away.

In the late 1990s, Alice re-emerged with renewed energy, releasing albums like *Crazy with the Blues* (2000), which introduced her to a new generation of fans. Her comeback was about more than just music; it was a testament to resilience and faith. It takes a certain kind of belief to let go of something you love and trust that it will still be there when you're ready to reclaim it. Alice embodied that spirit, showing that stepping away can sometimes be the bravest act of all.

Alice's life challenges us to rethink what it means to be rebellious. The easy path might have been to stay on the road, living the quintessential rock-and-roll lifestyle. But her decision to embrace motherhood and domesticity was, in its own way, a revolutionary act—one that required her to set aside her ego for the bigger picture. Sometimes letting go is the most rebellious act of all.

Alice Stuart passed away in 2023 at the age of eighty-one. She wasn't just a musician; she was a pioneer who paved the way for women in rock and blues. She influenced artists like Bonnie Raitt and many others who followed in her footsteps, proving that the most remarkable stories often belong to those who quietly shape history.

ALICE STUART

— *The Interview* —

[2005]

SF: I can't believe we never met.

AS: I was out of the business for almost twenty years, in a major way. I quit in the late 1970s cause I had a six-year-old boy who I wasn't really giving enough attention to and he was showing signs of needing more attention. I just quit the music business and I went to college for a while. Then I got married and had another daughter, and basically until she was about thirteen I didn't do any music.

SF: I'm most curious how women handle that. Most of the women I talk to choose to not have kids, but I am always fascinated by the ones who do, and how they manage to make it work.

AS: I know that I tried and tried for a long time, and I got tired of my son hanging onto my pant legs when I was trying to leave the house. He needed me. Besides, I was working five or six nights a week and I was barely making it.

SF: Were you a single parent?

AS: Yes, I broke up with his father when he was a year old.

SF: So you raised him yourself.

AS: Yes, but it was good. He's a beautiful man at this point, at thirty-eight. He's got a young son of his own, and my daughter is doing great, too. It was well worth it, and I'm glad I did it.

SF: What did you do to make a living when you took time off?

AS: I got married again and helped put my husband through law school, working as a short-order cook, and then I became a legal secretary.

SF: Are you still married to the same man?

AS: No, I broke up with him when I moved up here.

SF: But you're married again now?

AS: Yes, I've been married now about two years.

SF: So, you've been married two times?

AS: Actually I have been married four times.

SF: How do you keep a relationship together being this kind of woman?

AS: It's very challenging to have a relationship with a man in this business, because lots of times they feel like you're trying to take charge, and they get defensive. The man I'm married to now is totally devoted to my career, and he goes to work every day, which helps me. A lot of people said, "Well, why did you bother to get married?" Partly it was my children. I wanted them to take the relationship seriously, and part of it was the fact that it makes a hell of a lot more sense, tax-wise and health-insurance-wise, if you make it legal. Not that he has any decent health insurance, but you never know (*laughs*).

SF: You once said that while playing with Frank Zappa, your biggest lesson was "how to believe in myself and my music." What about your experience with Zappa helped you gain confidence and that direction?

AS: I was really trying to go in a different direction at that point. He really wanted me to continue playing acoustic guitar, and he wanted to play things around the Delta [blues] stuff that I was playing at the time. Basically at that time he had a blues band; he didn't have what came later. I wanted to start playing electric guitar at that point, so we basically had different ideas. It was a determination, because I was working with him, and he was obviously a go-getter. I just thought maybe I could do whatever I wanted to do.

SF: Was it after that that you started your own recording projects?

AS: Yes, I had already done that Arhoolie album in 1964. I didn't start working on my next album until 1969 and it was released in 1970. I kind of disappeared for a little bit after that, and I got my thoughts together. I have done that a couple of times, where I just drop out for a while.

SF: That shows an amazing amount of faith. I always feel if I take a break, or don't keep up at putting albums out and touring all the time, that I will disappear to my fans and no one will remember me.

AS: Like you'll fall off the radar. The fact is: you do, to some extent. I know when I came back and I started calling these promoters they were all like, "Who are you?" They're all in their twenties and thirties, and when I quit playing I was in my thirties. These people didn't know me, so I had to start all over again and get my promo pack going. I made two independent albums in 1996 and then 2000. Then I did some guitar camp workshops and got some stuff going and one of the reasons I moved back up here is because, having been from Washington originally, I had a fan base up here. I figured it wasn't as spread out as California, and there used to be a great scene in San Francisco, but it didn't seem to be that way anymore. When my husband and I broke up in California, we sold the house and I had a little money to sustain myself.

SF: Were your kids grown by then?

AS: Yes, when I moved up here my daughter was a senior in college.

SF: Did you miss playing when you stopped?

AS: I did miss it a lot, but I didn't miss things like having to do my voice lessons, the repetition and not eating certain foods. Part of me is a real homemaker. I love cooking and being able to devote my time to meal planning and things like that. Some people find that really boring, but I find it stimulating. There were a lot of things that took the place of playing. I got so much satisfaction from being a good mother and driving my kids to events.

SF: Did you still play your guitar at home?

AS: I couldn't, because it's sort of like I either do it or I don't.

SF: You just completely let it go.

AS: Yes, no more calluses.

SF: How did it feel physically when you picked it up again?

AS: It took a little while to get it back. But you know how it is, when you play all the time it comes back quickly. Actually, it was really interesting, because you can build up bad habits in your playing, and all those bad habits were gone. I relearned how to do it right.

SF: Did you ever have any problems from guitar?

AS: No, I've been really lucky.

SF: Did you practice a lot when you were first learning?

AS: I played constantly. I started piano early on, then I played drums, and then when I graduated from high school, I started playing guitar in Seattle. I lived in one of those places that was forty bucks a month. I worked in coffee houses making three or four dollars a night, but we worked every night and we would play all day and then play until two or three in the morning.

SF: Did you have brothers and sisters?

AS: No, I had a first cousin and my aunt. My mother left me there when I was three. I was raised by this matriarch aunt.

SF: Was that not a good situation?

AS: No. A child always wants to know why their mother doesn't want them. Music was my release from all that. I would write songs, silly songs, rock and roll songs.

SF: You must have seen rock and roll as it was invented.

AS: I remember seeing Elvis Presley for the first time on TV. I never saw any live shows because no one came to our town. I didn't see a live show until I saw Chuck Berry when I was nineteen.

SF: How did that affect you?

AS: It was great. I just wanted to do that.

SF: Did you decide to start learning to play heavier guitar after that? Because I know at that time there really were no women players around doing that kind of guitar. It was a folk scene.

AS: Very much, and electric guitar was kind of frowned on.

SF: Who were your electric guitar influences?

AS: Probably my greatest influence on electric guitar is Roy Buchanan. I still listen to his first album, and just marvel at his style.

SF: Is that who inspired you to play Fender Telecasters?

AS: Yes, all that guitar from the '60s, like Buddy Holly and that kind of stuff. The bare-bones kind of stuff. I'm starting to get back to that stuff. I don't think of myself as just a blues player. Instead I see myself more like a roots or Americana guitar player, a bit of country and rock. I seem to fall into the blues category, because most of my stuff is R&B-based.

SF: The first Arhoolie album compared to your most recent is worlds apart. You can still hear the melodic style in your singing—obviously you're seasoned now, and a better guitar player. That song "Beatnik" is so funny.

AS: I still get so many requests for that. God, I can't even remember it.

SF: Did that have any reflection on what your life was like back then?

AS: It definitely did. The place we played was typical of that era. All of the windows were painted black. It took me two or three times to even have the guts to walk in there. It seemed really scary. But I went in and they served little cups of espresso, stuff that you'd never seen before. People would come in looking for beatniks wearing berets with cigarette holders. So we decided to write a song about it.

SF: You mentioned that when you dropped out of the music business you stopped being on some special diet and doing vocal exercises. What does preparing for shows entail for you?

AS: I used to have a lot of allergies. I couldn't eat wheat or mayonnaise. I tried to keep everything really basic. I didn't use anything that would clog me up. I don't worry about it anymore; I seem to have grown out of those allergies. I think I was allergic to my aunt (*laughs*). I don't do the voice lessons anymore, either. I used to do them twice a day, in the morning and then later in the day. I studied with a really good vocal coach before my first album. She told me before I did anything else in the morning, even talking, to sing. It helped me to learn to use my diaphragm and to sing out. I've kind of abandoned that and gotten lazy.

SF: Your voice is really precise and direct. You're a really well-rounded musician. You're obviously a really great guitar player, but you have a great voice and you're a songwriter. Do you think any one thing leads, or are they kind of even?

AS: It's pretty even. I've always wanted to be in a band and just be the guitar player, that's been a dream of mine. But whenever I get into a band, I always end up singing and fronting it. I think I could get really involved in just being a guitar player and enjoy it.

SF: What's the lineup of your touring band now?

AS: I have bass, drums and a rhythm guitar player who is absolutely fabulous. But it's funny, because he's from a completely different musical background than me. His main thing is jazz and African. He's intrigued by what I play, and we play off each other. It's really wonderful.

SF: He just plays rhythm?

AS: He plays rhythm but he plays fabulous leads too. He probably takes four leads a night. It's a real partnership.

SF: What are you listening to now?

AS: I really love Little Feat. I still listen to that first Roy Buchanan album. I listen to country. I listen to a lot of Bob Dylan. My dream is to make an album with Bob Dylan.

SF: Do you think women's places and roles have changed in the music business from when you started until now? Do you think things have gotten better for women and have you seen the rise of stronger women players?

AS: Definitely. It's not so much as an oddity. It used to be you felt like you were in a circus or freak show. I remember stepping up onstage and basically the feeling was, "Oh yeah, right, she's gonna play that?" I always felt like I was being judged as a woman instead of a player, so that's been one of my goals to get that first impression out of people's heads. I must say, though, sometimes it helps, because it is so impressive when you do get up there and really play.

There's been a lot of jealousy among women. When I first started out, there were so few women doing anything except maybe singing and strumming a little soft folk guitar that women weren't helping each other. They weren't giving each other any encouragement. Now I've done a couple of songwriter-type showcases with some younger women in their twenties, and these young women were so respectful and glad to be part of this, and helped each other. This is a new feeling for me, to get encouragement from other women.

I got a lot of encouragement from men throughout my career, but women were like, "Oh no, there's another woman here." You can have eight guitar players who are men, and you don't hear people in the audience going, "Oh, well, Billy and Jim are not as good as Randy." But women—if you get three of four guitar players in the same place, there seems to be some sort of a meter comparing all of us. Why can't we just be players?

SF: When you were growing up did you hang around with groups of women?

AS: No.

SF: I never did either. I always found groups of women kind of toxic. At least I felt that way in high school.

AS: They didn't have the same interests. They always were talking about what kind of jewelry they wanted to buy, or stuff like that, but I was always thinking about music.

SF: Were you a tomboy when you were a young girl?

AS: Yes, absolutely.

SF: Were you aware of Memphis Minnie?

AS: When I started recording for Arhoolie, [label founder] Chris Strachwitz gave me a bunch of Memphis Minnie's stuff and I just went crazy. I recorded her "In My Girlish Days."

SF: She totally changed my life.

AS: She was really respected, won a bunch of guitar contests and stuff. I was really sad when I heard she'd passed away.

SF: Did you ever meet her?

AS: No.

SF: Are you more into subtle guitar playing, or are you into ripping it up?

AS: I definitely love to rip it up a lot.

SF: Do you think there's anything uniquely feminine that women bring to the guitar, or do think music is not gender-related at all?

AS: I have kind of come to the realization that there is a feminine quality that women players usually have. Me in particular, I tend to play the guitar like it's an extension of my voice, as opposed to all those fast, busy guitarists. I don't really like that. I have heard a couple of women who play like that, but it really doesn't work for me. I think of the melody, or if I'm playing backup guitar, I think what's gonna accent what the other players are doing.

SF: I agree that women tend to take that supportive role. That's kind of ingrained in us. I see fewer women involved in cutting contests and things of the sort; however, it does happen. But on the whole, there is something uniquely feminine that women bring to the instrument. The main reason I took this project on was because I felt there was something missing from guitar literature. Guitar magazines focus on gear and technique, and there seems to be this big lack of attention to the philosophies of players and personal lives—things I feel have much more of an impact on your playing. Technique is "what you are," whereas I have always wanted to know "who" a player is.

AS: Have you heard of a book called *Rock and Roll Woman*? I am in it. It came out in 1974. It has me, Bonnie [Raitt], Maria [Muldaur], Linda Ronstadt, Grace Slick, Rita Coolidge, and others. It's one of the only books I've seen of its kind.

SF: In the '70s there were a bunch of women coming up: Bonnie Raitt, Jo Ann Kelly, Rory Block, and Nancy Wilson. I've always wondered if there's something about the guitar and women that rubs people the wrong way, if it's just too strident and individual. Did you ever feel like that?

AS: I played with Albert King and he picked me up off the floor and said, "Honey, you play good guitar." If Albert King says I can play, that's all right with me. I toured a lot in the '70s with my trio, and I always felt that people were glad to see me play like that. I feel that more now than ever. I have young women come up to me all the time now and say things like, "Oh my God, you're my role model. You've shown me that it can be done and that we don't have to go back." So that makes me feel good.

SF: Was it ever difficult to be taken seriously as a player because you're a woman?

AS: Absolutely, early on it really was, but I think a lot of that is belief in yourself. If you think that people are dissing you, I think a lot of that is a reflection of how we feel about ourselves. It's not like you need to think you're better than anyone else, but you do need to feel that you're playing on the level where you are—and not below it. You just have to know that you're really good. No one makes me feel like I am less than I am.

SF: Did that take a while to get to?

AS: It took a while, a long time to sound the way I wanted to sound.

SF: How do you think a player can go about to find his or her own voice?

AS: I remember singing blues when I was nineteen, and I didn't really have any business singing it because I really hadn't been through anything. Now that I am older, I have been through things and have earned the right to sing about it. I have credibility.

SF: So it's a matter of living through the things you're singing about.

AS: I remember hanging out with the Chambers Brothers in the '70s and listening to Willie [Chambers] sing, "We've been together so long to have to separate this way," and he just swooped into those notes. After hanging out with them, it kind of hit me, how actually to sing blues so that you're honest and real. I don't do anything that I can't relate to. Mostly what I do is listen to a song and learn the words and stuff, but then I let it sit for a while so that whoever did it before leaves my consciousness, and I keep fooling with it until finally I get it. That's what I usually do, put the song in my brain and in my heart until it becomes embedded in me and I can play it from my own experience. That's what I did with that Skip James song "Hard Time Killin' Floor." I remembered that from a long time ago and just made it my own over time. I ended up changing it all around from the original, changing the chords and everything.

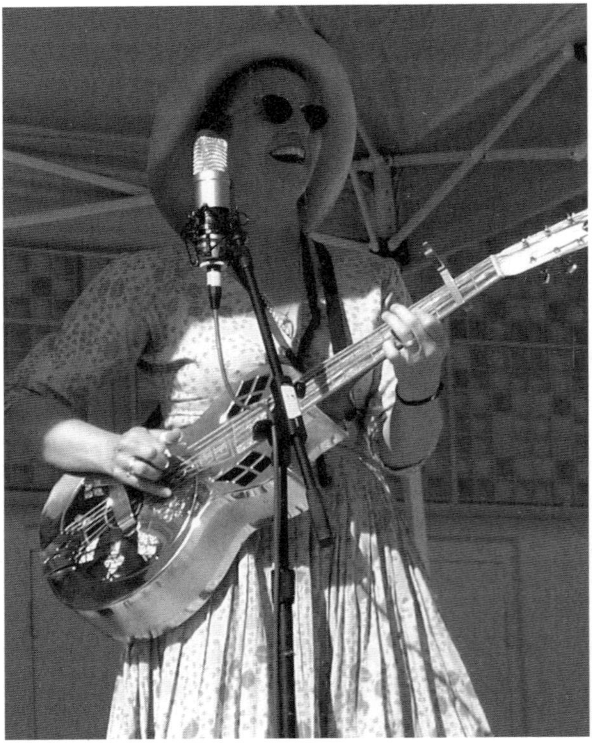

Del Rey

DEL REY

When I first started my interviews in 2001, Del Rey was at the top of my list of players to speak with. She wasn't just a musician I was curious about—she was a living archive of knowledge about women in guitar history. Del (born Della Rey) grew up in Los Angeles but spent much of her early life in San Diego. She picked up the guitar at the age of four, and by her teens, she had already discovered pre-war blues and found herself mentored by legendary Mississippi bluesman Sam Chatmon. Under Chatmon's guidance, Del developed a deep understanding of blues traditions, an appreciation that would shape her entire career.

Over the decades, Del has become adept in many blues guitar styles, seamlessly blending ragtime, country blues, and early jazz into her playing. She is also recognized for her advanced ukulele technique, elevating the small instrument beyond its usual reputation, proving it can be as complex and virtuosic as any guitar. Her work has made her one of the foremost experts on both blues guitar and the historical role of women in American music. When not performing or recording, she conducts lectures, shedding light on pioneering female musicians often overlooked by mainstream narratives.

Del was one of the first people who led me to understand the landscape and evolution of female players in ways I had never considered before. Through our conversation, she instilled in me a desire to pay tribute to these icons, ensuring that their influence would not be forgotten.

One name that comes up frequently in Del's research is Memphis Minnie. As Del passionately argues, Minnie was more influential than many of the men commonly celebrated in blues history. Her bluntness is refreshing, and her frustration is valid. Memphis Minnie was not only a prolific songwriter and performer, but also an electrifying guitarist who outplayed many of her male counterparts—yet she remains relatively unsung compared to the mythologized Robert Johnson.

Beyond historical analysis, Del also has strong opinions about the modern state of blues music. She laments the shift from blues as dance music—designed to uplift and entertain—to its current association with raw, often indulgent, self-expression. She states, "I don't even like to be associated with my genre. There's too much excess." It's a provocative take, but one that makes sense when you consider her perspective. For Del, blues isn't just about emotional catharsis—it's about musicianship, history, and connecting with an audience in a way that brings them joy rather than dwelling in sorrow.

In addition to her solo career, Del has collaborated with numerous musicians, including fellow guitarist and roots music historian, Steve James, who passed away in 2023. I was friends with Steve before I knew about Del, and I was sincerely happy when I heard that they'd teamed up together. They both shared an encyclopedic knowledge of pre-war blues. Their duo performances were a masterclass in old-time blues and ragtime, blending humor, storytelling, and intricate guitar work.

Del believes that understanding the past is key to shaping the future of music, and she's dedicated her life to making sure these stories don't disappear. In many ways, Del Rey is more than just a musician—she's a guardian of a rich, complex musical tradition. She challenges assumptions, demands recognition for overlooked artists, and continues to push the boundaries of what the guitar (and ukulele) can do. Whether she's onstage performing, writing, teaching, or delivering a lecture, she remains unapologetically outspoken, deeply insightful, and fiercely committed to the music she loves.

DEL REY

— *The Interview* —

[2001]

SF: You started playing the guitar at four years old; is there any recollection about that for you?

DR: Yes, I have a pretty good memory from even before that. My mom came home with a Mel Bay book and a guitar and she was going to learn herself. When I showed an interest in it, she went back and got a three-quarter-sized guitar and taught me a bit from the Mel Bay book. Then I started watching that Frederick Noad PBS TV show called *Introduction to the Classical Guitar*. He was on once a week, so we'd go down to the trailer park rec room and watch him on the TV down there. That's how I learned how to read music.

SF: Were you very driven from an early age?

DR: I really didn't like playing until I got into my teens. I really started to play seriously when I was introduced to the music of Memphis Minnie, and I met Sam Chatmon when I was about thirteen.

SF: Where was Sam Chatmon from?

DR: He was living in Hollandale, Mississippi, when I met him and he was in his seventies. He was one of the Mississippi Sheiks. He's from that big Chatmon family that includes Lonnie Chatmon, and Bo Carter is his half-brother. That was a very musical family from Mississippi in the 1920s and '30s.

SF: How did you meet him?

DR: He used to come out to visit his daughter who lived in San Diego, and he would spend a couple of months at a time. There was a record collector who he would stay with, and there was a record store down there called Folk Arts Rare Records that used to put on concerts. A friend of mine and I started hanging around the record store, so when Sam Chatmon came into town he introduced him to us.

SF: You were fourteen, fifteen?

DR: Yeah, around that age, it would have been about 1973 or '74.

SF: You had been playing guitar since the age of four, but at this point you started getting more serious again?

DR: I had been playing the whole time, but had not up to then found any style that had interested me until I heard that. Just before Sam Chatmon came to town, I had been introduced to these Memphis Minnie *Blues Classics Vol. 1 and 2* and I had been listening to that and been learning songs by ear. When I saw him, he played in a style that had a lot of things in common with Memphis Minnie. That kind of same down-home, more songster style rather than the heavy Delta sort of style. Seeing him play, and the chord shapes he used, made the music more accessible to me.

SF: Did you discover the Memphis Minnie stuff on your own?

DR: No, the guy who ran the record store, Lou Curtis, had seen me at an open mic playing some lame '70s cover song like "Stairway to Heaven" or something. He handed me a tape and said, "Maybe you should listen to this." And it was much better.

SF: When I got into the blues, I got so into the whole mythology of it, the fantasy of Mississippi and the '30s and people like Memphis Minnie. Did any of that creep into your psyche?

DR: It was already there. I had been into movies from the 1920s and '30s, so finding about the music of that period just went along with the things that had me enchanted, actors like Myrna Loy, William Powell. The blues was kind of a down-home version of a world I was already inhabiting.

SF: Did you have a happy childhood, or was there something in you that responded to the message of the blues, anything going on your personal life?

DR: My relationship to blues music has never been about serious loss, or the pain of it. I find that's a different strain of the blues. From the first, my connection with Sam Chatmon and most of the musicians and the kinds of blues I've been attracted to, it's mostly the dance music that got me. It's more the songster tradition, rather than the cotton-picking tradition. I've always found the blues to be a very happy kind of music that accompanies all kinds of situations, not just pain and torture or struggle.

SF: That's a new outlook. So many people latch onto the blues because of personal angst, me included. When I first heard it, I thought, *finally, someone understands me!* That was the teenage years. But I also know that this music can be very uplifting.

DR: Especially when someone like Bo Carter or Sam Chatmon played, or even Memphis Minnie. There are lot of personal stories, but the great body of the music is just about life, and not particularly angst-ridden. Especially her autobiographical songs like "Nothing in Rambling," it's told in a very dry, unemotional sort of style. A lot of blues revivalists have gone so overboard into just screaming and making everything so emotional—I mean, get over it already. That's one aspect of blues music, and not what I consider to be the most important one. There's a very dry delivery that people have forgotten about.

SF: What do you think about the situation in the blues today?

DR: Sometimes I don't even like to be associated with my genre. There's too much excess and that seems to be some sort of excuse for self-expression when it should be more like repression. I'm kind of a hard-ass that way.

SF: Do you think there's also an overly reverent attitude in blues? I see so many people in this genre that are so into respect that they don't ever sing their own blues. They're so into doing it just like the record.

DR: My thing is, there are so many incredible songs from between 1920 and 1940. There are so many songs that nobody does. We don't need to hear another version of "Come On in My Kitchen." Even if you can't get it together to write a good song yourself, from your own experience—which is a good thing to do, because I believe this tradition is a living tradition that needs to be worked in now. But even if you can't do that, you can certainly delve a little deeper and come up with covers that no one does. Like Jesse Thomas—who ever covers Jesse Thomas, or Roosevelt Sykes?

SF: I think a lot of students of the blues just get stuck in one era.

DR: Yeah, they're just into an image. A lot of people were turned onto the blues by the Blues Brothers, and they think blues is about sunglasses and a fedora—and that's just a purely commoditized image. It's something that was sold to them because it's cool, and that's not what this music is about. It's not about selling you something; it's about having an experience. If you get suckered into buying an image that you can wallow in, then it's going to be shallow, your blues will be shallow.

SF: So many people don't go back and learn the old stuff. When did you start really studying this?

DR: As soon as I heard Memphis Minnie, because I wanted to know all about her—and at that time there wasn't very much information available. In fact, when did that Paul Garon biography come out, the early 1990s? How long did that take? She's such a major figure and that's how long it took to get a biography out on her?

SF: I found that book really hard to read.

DR: He did some good research and answered some questions that I was dying to know. But, how is it that Memphis Minnie got through all those years without having any kids? Was she infertile? That to me is a very pertinent question of why a woman would have a long career in the blues and another woman would not. The fact that she was childless, was that a decision? It didn't seem to occur to him to ask that question. There are a lot of questions like that, which still need to be answered.

I've been in bands with women, and once I worked with a bass player who had two daughters, and it was pure torture for her to be away from her kids for more than a week. It made it so it was impossible for this very good player to go out and do gigs. She had to choose a different life, finally, because she was too tortured from being away from her kids. A lot of time people haven't been able to be musicians at all, because they had to go home to take care of their kids. Stuff like that is important to know.

SF: Do you think there's any reason there hasn't been more women guitarists?

DR: First of all, I think there's a ton of them that people just ignore, like Mary Osborne: who knows about her? She's a great guitar player. You go through the history of jazz and her name never comes up. Or Mattie Delaney. There are a ton of women guitar players that people don't bring up. That's the main thing. Then, when they do bring them up, a lot of times they're underrepresented and that's just because people didn't take the time to go out and find them, because people didn't consider them important.

SF: Did Mattie Delaney make very many sides?

DR: No, she didn't make very many: maybe two or three, and I think that happens a lot. You know, someone like Louise Johnson, great piano player, but the only reason we got to hear the three sides that she's on is because she was dating Charley Patton at the time when he went in for those sessions. When you do find a great guitar player like Mary

Osborne, they do things like market them as singers. Since they figure a woman playing guitar can't be that interesting, they'll put a dancer in front of her. It's such a mindset, and hard to pinpoint any particular reason why there aren't many women guitar players, but it's basically the whole structure of the system. There was no place for them, they weren't sought out, and when they did get found they tried to market them as singers.

SF: Is there something about the guitar itself that created that? Is the image of the guitar more macho?

DR: No, what, are you kidding—more macho than a trumpet?! Nothing could be more macho than a trumpet (*laughs*).

SF: The electric guitar is a powerful stance.

DR: Have you ever seen Sister Rosetta Tharpe, who invented the windmill play? She's an incredible macho guitar player. I don't think that has anything to with it. I think there are many things in that era. For women to engage in any kinds of activity was either actively discouraged or filled with so many boundaries that they had to consciously overcome, that it was hard for them to continue to leap over those hurdles.

SF: I guess that's what makes Memphis Minnie such an icon.

DR: But look at her alternatives—did she want to be a sharecropper? Did she want to farm or work as a maid? Black women jumped over those hurdles because their alternatives were nonexistent. If they were an independent spirit, which she undoubtedly was, they had no alternatives besides a profession that was looked on with disdain and as "unrespectable"—but what did she care? As a Black woman from that era, she was already disrespected and looked on with disdain. It didn't matter, and that's why it's harder for white women who have this feeling of protection under the system to step outside these boundaries. Think of who does step outside the boundaries: country women, hillbillies, people who are economically disadvantaged. There are a few examples of women who are privileged who move in that world. Like Vahdah Olcott-Bickford, the founder of the American Guitar Society, very influential woman performer who's absolutely forgotten by history. There's a huge archive of her at the University at Northridge, in northern California. There's a doctor at Northridge, Ron Purcell, who has all her papers, and he's a wealth of knowledge about her.

SF: And she lived until the age of ninety-five.

DR: She published one hundred and forty reference books. There were two Martin guitars named after her. She was very well known, all through the 1920s and '30s. She played parlor music, that kind of polite, almost classical stuff. But it's insane that nobody remembers her.

SF: When I started researching this project, I looked through the history of guitar books and websites and there's no mention of most women players. There was a little picture of Bonnie Raitt in a book of a thousand pages, and just very little mention of any women players.

DR: It's weird. People try to make like what we're trying to do is some kind of feminist ideology, but no, we're just trying to get our place in history. We have been systematically excluded. That's why we have to yell so loud about it. Don't let them tell you that none exist, because they do exist and they've been left out. For instance, the history of jazz guitar should include Mary Osborne. A history of guitar in general should include Vahdah Olcott-Bickford. I mean, how can you make a cult figure of Robert Johnson who recorded thirty measly sides and ignore Memphis Minnie who recorded two hundred? Get over it already.

SF: Memphis Minnie also made the big jump from acoustic to electric.

DR: Her style is the perfect historical mirror of what blues music did for African Americans, not for what white people in the 1960s thought about blues music. It was a really good example of what African Americans were listening to from 1929 to 1949, and every stylistic change she made was a little ahead of the curve. She was leading the pack on all of that stuff.

SF: When did you start performing blues live?

DR: I started when I was about fifteen.

SF: Were there any other female role models playing on the scene at the time?

DR: There was a cool Black woman in San Diego named Bonnie Jefferson, who used to play. Except every time she'd go out to do a gig, her husband would get jealous and beat her up, so she had to stop playing for a little while. There was a woman named something like Dorothy Lee, who played piano. There were lots of folksy role models. I also saw Lydia Mendoza at that time, and she made a huge impact on me. There was that great twelve-string style that she had. She was a great muscular, powerful player. She played at the folk festival in 1975. None of the folkies had a guitar amplifier at that time, so she had to borrow mine.

SF: Was she playing solo?

DR: Yes. She was great and beautiful, she looked so great when she played. I had not heard a lot of that kind of music. My dad had some mariachi music, but I hadn't heard that norteña style she had. There were definitely other women I saw play live.

SF: Before Sam Chatmon, were there other people mentoring you, or influencing your style? You picked up dobro, which is a conscious choice to pursue that style.

DR: I've played metal-body guitars since the early '80s. I was playing with Bob Brozman then, and I thought, *this guy is so much louder than me, I can't stand it.* So I got a metal guitar immediately.

SF: Do you ever think that women approach the guitar differently, or express themselves differently on the instrument?

DR: No, when you reach a certain level of musicianship and you're working with really good players, I don't find much difference between working with men and working with women. I find that sometimes when you're playing with beginning students, there's sometimes this thing about how boys approach learning and how girls will approach learning. Maybe a boy will be like, "I only know this one chord, but I'm going to wham the hell out of it," whereas a girl might back off and lay the one chord and try to be sweet. But when you're dealing with people who actually know how to play, those kinds of things disappear.

SF: Did you ever study with anyone?

DR: Not really, I played with Sam Chatmon when I was young, but I haven't had any official teachers. Once I realized that I was obsessed with the music, I stopped listening to guitar players, because I didn't want my brain full of other people. It was my own arrogant, useful approach to it. I listened to piano players for many years.

SF: Do you approach your playing from that perspective?

DR: Yes, I think like a piano player. I also have listened to lots of horns, so I started reviewing for a magazine in 1990 and I wanted to make sure I didn't make any mistakes so I went back and listened to a lot of guitar players and did some research. But up to then I kind of avoided it. After that, I thought I'd been an arrogant fool.

SF: When you play live do you play solo or with a band?

DR: I play metal resonator guitar exclusively, and the new band that I play with mostly I play ukulele, but I work with a band, and I work by myself. Mostly I work by myself, because who can afford a band?

SF: You've been traveling around with your course "Women in American Music."

DR: Yes, I mostly do that in March during women's history month. I just found out about a new guitar player I had never heard about named Josie Bush, and I found another guitar player, Lee Morse, who plays like Eddie Lang. I'm always adding people to the show.

SF: Are they all recorded artists?

DR: Vahdah Olcott-Bickford is mostly transcriptions; I am not sure if she recorded. Josie Bush never recorded, she was famous for a piece called "Riverside Blues." She was married to Willie Brown, and apparently she kicked his ass so bad on the guitar. That's why they would fight.

SF: Is it really a rewarding experience for you to share these stories and your knowledge with people?

DR: The more we learn about our past, the fewer stupid mistakes we will make in the future. The more I know about the 1920s and '30s, the more informed I am about what's going on now. That's what I like about it. When I was a little girl, I didn't know there were any other women guitar players, but my students now know about them. Girls are so much more informed than girls of our generation, or our mother's generation.

SF: They're not necessarily more informed because they know more about the past.

DR: A lot of them are, many of them know about history. What happened in the 1960s probably helped. We're always getting our history rewritten for us. People like women and Black people and poor people get written out of history all the time, so I feel it's part of my job to remind people of what actually happened. What keeps happening if these people get forgotten is you keep getting sold the same bill of goods again and again and again, because no one remembers what happened the last time.

SF: Do you find that there are more female guitarists now coming out?

DR: I think there's an onset of everything female. Girls are just empowered to do whatever they want to do now. If they want to go out and get a job, they do that. If they want to be an artist of whatever kind, they can find a place to be that. It's not like women feel quite so obligated to just shut up and have kids. It's a good thing.

SF: Do you have other aspirations of what you would like to do with your project?

DR: I'm quite happy doing what I'm doing. Talking and drinking are my hobbies (*laughs*).

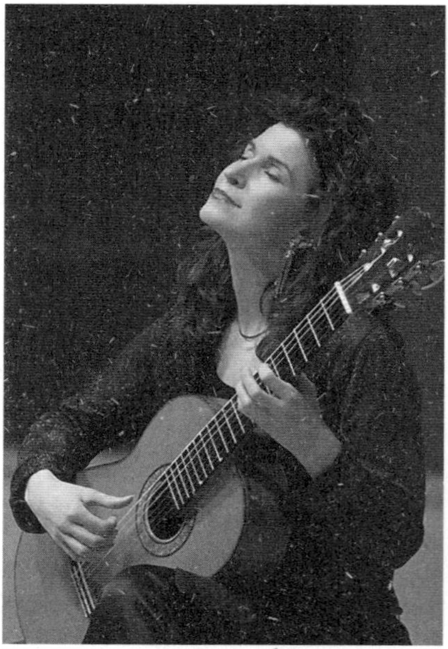

Sharon Isbin

SHARON ISBIN

World-renowned classical guitarist Sharon Isbin was one of my first interviews for this book. I'm not sure what made me reach out to her so soon; I knew nothing about classical music and was almost taken aback when she agreed to speak with me. As it turned out, Sharon's inspirational story and musical philosophy made it easy to find common ground.

The first thing that struck me about her was that she was an adventurer, both musically and in life. Born in Minneapolis, she began traveling the world at a young age. She lived in Italy with her family, where she first studied guitar at age nine, and has toured Europe annually since she was seventeen. From the start, she was a serious musician, beginning her lessons with only the best teachers, including Andrés Segovia. Determined to perfect her technique, she practiced five hours a night by the time she was in high school.

At the time of our interview, Sharon was promoting her album *Dreams of a World: Folk-Inspired Music for Guitar*, in which she explores various folk styles from around the globe. Her music has taken her everywhere—from tours with the Zurich Chamber Orchestra, Austria's Tonkünstler Orchestra, and Belgium's Philharmonique de Liège, to the Amazon rainforest, where she performed with an indigenous tribe. In the summers, she finds peace in Aspen, surrounded by the mountains she loves.

She has collaborated with icons such as Sting and Antonio Carlos Jobim, met with U.S. presidents, and received too many awards to list, including multiple Grammy Awards.

In 1989, Sharon founded Juilliard's guitar department, becoming the school's first guitar instructor in its 115-year history. She still chairs the department today and, in 2020, was named *Musical America's* Worldwide Instrumentalist of the Year, the first guitarist ever to receive the honor in the award's fifty-nine-year history.

Sharon spoke about the influence of science in her life, no doubt inspired by her father, a scientist. This made perfect sense as she explained her musical philosophies, problem-solving skills, and the way she absorbs and studies information with such precision. It would be easy to assume that a scientific mind might make someone mechanical, but Sharon is anything but. She's deeply multifaceted. She discussed faith, spirituality, Transcendental Meditation, and her intuitive approach to teaching. She was ahead of the curve in these practices, having applied them for decades. What stood out most to me was Sharon's unwavering belief in herself and the fearlessness with which she pursued her goals. The fact that she is arguably the most successful classical guitarist in the world speaks volumes.

I met Sharon in person twice after our interview. One occasion was in New York City, where I observed her teaching a small class of advanced classical guitar students at Juilliard. Sitting in the back of the room, I watched as she instructed with a balance of authority and warmth. She even asked my opinion on a few performance tips. Not having much classical music vocabulary, I offered general advice on communicating ideas, principles that apply across all genres. What impressed me most was how down-to-earth she was. She made me feel comfortable and confident, which I believe is the mark of a great teacher. Her encouragement came in such a matter-of-fact, clear-minded, and almost innocent way that it left a lasting impact.

My brief time in Sharon Isbin's presence left an indelible impression. When she told me during our interview that she thought I would write a great book, it gave me a surge of confidence I didn't know I needed. If she believed it, maybe I could start believing it, too. That moment has stayed with me ever since. I've come to think that opening doors for others, encouraging them to dream bigger or to trust their own abilities, is the mark of someone fully at ease in their own power.

SHARON ISBIN

— *The Interview* —

[2001]

SF: I want to profile a lot of the top female players, all over the world and in a variety of musical styles. Your name came up. I am not familiar with a lot of classical. Ida Presti's name came up.

SI: She's been dead for many years. You'd have a hard time interviewing her (*laughs*).

SF: Was she an influence on you?

SI: No, because I never heard her solo music until much later, on someone's bootleg copy because you can't even buy solo recordings of hers. I did know her as a duo with her husband. I never met her and never heard them live, because she was already dead by the time I was starting. I've noticed in France that there are more female students of classical guitar than there are in any country I've been in, even the United States, and I think the reason for that is because Ida Presti was a role model in France. Not in America, not in Germany or other places because she wasn't really as established elsewhere. But in France, she was part of the fabric of the guitar world.

SF: Do you think that's why we don't see more women players in North America?

SI: I think the deal in North America is that when classical guitar started to take off, and the first seeds of it were beginning to sprout in the '60s, the people who would study the guitar were teenage boys who had been playing rock music. Maybe they would hear a Segovia album and think *this is cool*, and so at the age of sixteen they'd switch over to classical. Since most girls weren't playing rock guitar, you didn't have girls entering classical either. In the '60s you could count on one hand the number of universities in the United States that even offered a guitar department, so it was really fledgling at that point.

SF: If we cross the barriers to any style of music do you think it's a matter of role models?

SI: I think it makes a big difference. One of the mystiques attached to classical guitar is its origins from flamenco, and flamenco had traditionally been a male guitarist's domain. They accompany the male and female dancers and the male and female singers. But can you name a famous female flamenco guitarist even today? No.

The origins of Spanish guitar and classical guitar—and certainly Segovia being the one who modernized and legitimized the instrument on the concert stage—comes from a whole Spanish tradition that has its association with flamenco.

SF: See, I didn't really know classical guitar and flamenco guitar were even related.

SI: Related only in the sense that the instrument is very similar and came to its development at the same time in the nineteenth century, with Torres in the 1800s, that's the instrument as we know it today. Our associations of Spain with the six-string classical guitar will naturally also bring us also to the flamenco associations. Those role models have always been men. I am the most established woman today with an international career as a classical guitarist.

SF: How does that feel to you? Do you feel like an icon?

SI: I don't think about it very much, because frankly the prejudice I have faced has been more about the instrument than about being a woman.

SF: Do you mean with composers or orchestras?

SI: With composers who are afraid or resistant to the idea of writing for guitar, or orchestras who are resistant to the idea of bringing in guitar as a soloist. Look at the New York Philharmonic. They've hadn't had a guitar soloist in twenty-six years, until I performed and recorded with them in 2004. I can name some orchestras where the last soloist they had before me was Segovia in the 1950s. So it's definitely an instrument that has had to battle for acceptance in the mainstream of the classical world. Part of it has to do with the music that is programmed.

SF: Is it hard to just pick up a score and play it on guitar?

SI: The sight reading on guitar is tough, because you have to do all kinds of configurations with the left hand to get things to work. Whereas on piano, you've got one pitch for each key, so you know exactly where you're going to hit that note.

SF: Exactly, on the guitar you can go to several places or positions.

SI: On the violin you don't have the level of counterpoint and different voices that you can do on guitar. On the brass instruments you're doing one line. So the only other instrument that is probably as difficult to sight read on as the guitar is the harp, which is confounded with all those pedals.

SF: Do you take scores yourself and adapt them to guitar?

SI: Yes, I've done transcriptions of all the Bach lute suites and worked with a great pianist, Rosalyn Tureck, who devoted her whole life to playing the music of Bach and became the renowned expert of Bach playing on the keyboard. I went to her to get guidance about all the performance practice applications and how that would really make this music work. It's like playing jazz today. You don't pick up a chart and just play the bare chords and the bare notes. You have to improvise in between. That's what baroque players did during Bach's time, except that stuff wasn't written down, so you have to know what to do with it when you see the music now.

SF: Do you feel comfortable improvising?

SI: I prefer to plan out most of the embellishment in Bach, because the multi-voice fingering is so complicated on classical guitar. We only have six strings. On the lute, they have more strings than we do and they're open strings, so the left hand is freer to move around and change according to your whims at the time, if you want to put a trill in here or some other kind of embellishment there. It's harder to do that on a six-string instrument, where it takes a lot of forethought to work out how you're going to get those basses and all the other voices.

SF: As a person who has not listened to a lot of classical music and doesn't always understand it, I am wondering how do you make a personal statement in a classical composition that's already written out?

SI: One of the easiest ways you think about classical guitar is that it performs the role of many people. It's the singer, the troubadour who's singing the upper line. You've got the rhythm section provided by the same player and the harmony again provided by the same player and all the different counterpoint, which means the levels of voicing. If you're looking at a choir, for example, you've got the sopranos, tenors, altos basses playing together. That's what I have to do as a single player, plus be the rhythm section, the harmony, and the melodic voice. So with all of that it becomes much more demanding in terms of the technique.

It's not just strumming or picking a tune; it's much more complicated because you have to carry many threads that are independent at the same time, and preserve their individuality in their interaction, along with providing everything else that goes into making a good musical composition: rhythm, articulation, harmony, phrasing, the works. In terms of a statement, look to some of the greatest composers of our time, like Bach. He wrote his music down and that doesn't in any way diminish its extraordinary nature. He was really masterful at what he was able to do, and by writing it down allowed other people from generations that have succeeded him to be able to play and perform his music.

SF: What is the difference between hearing you perform a piece of Bach's to hearing another guitar player perform the exact same piece?

SI: It's a thousand things. First of all: expression. *What do I have to say?* Which is, *why am I bothering to play?* I have something to say, which is what I communicate—just as what a writer communicates when they're writing poetry or a novel. There's something metaphysical, something intangible that reaches you. Beyond that you can break it down in terms of technique and quality of technique, sound tone—all of which are elements that relate to the personality and presence of the performer, and character of the performer. Your tone is your soul, basically, and the different colors that you can extract. I've heard many guitarists who play monochromatically as if they're a painter painting only in black and white and gray. It's boring, because they don't know how to create colors.

On the classical guitar, because of how you use your fingernails, your flesh, the angle of attack, position on the string in which you strike—you have a variety of sound that is possible. To be able to use that effectively as a painter does—you know, you put a little green in this corner—that's going to affect the whole composition of the canvas. It's the same thing with timbres and colors in a composition, you have to know how to apply them and be able to—whether or not your playing is legato.

Most guitarists have trouble with that, because they think of the instrument as a percussive instrument, whereas it can, in reality, imitate the human voice. There are many tricks you can employ that can give it that kind of lyricism, and to capture the cry in the human voice and the connecting between notes that a singer is able to do. I grew up listening to singers and that's why they have been my models, and that's why my playing is so different from many other guitarists—because it seeks in essence to be the troubadour, to be the singer. It requires not only the ear to do that in the vision in your mind, but also the technique to be able to capture that legato quality. That's a more complicated explanation to go into technically.

SF: This is a very philosophical topic. Do you ever delve into that aspect when you're teaching?

SI: Absolutely, if I'm hearing someone play with no shape, and there are spaces in between the notes, of course I am going to talk about that. I have them sing until they are able to recreate the line with their voice in the way it should sound. Then we work on how to get that on the instrument.

SF: Do you think there's anything that can't be taught?

SI: I don't think there is anything that cannot be taught; I think that some people are going to catch on better than others, and that's the difference, ultimately, between human beings. Also, dynamically, a lot of guitarists have a very small dynamic range because they don't explore the possibilities of great sound versus small intimate sound—and to be exciting you have to be able to communicate a large range. Again, like applying colors, you have to know where and how to do that and how that fits in with what the composer wrote, because very few composers before our time gave much in the way of indication of dynamics and articulation and phrasing. That's for us to figure out.

SF: So you have to listen to the piece and then find your own way through it?

SI: You have to find a way to express what the composer was trying to say by understanding what they were doing or writing, and then make an emotional connection between what's written on the page and the character that you're expressing and the feelings. It's like being an actor. You go to a script, and you have to imagine yourself as the individual that you're playing and what that individual is feeling. Same thing with the music: what is this music saying, and how can I express it?

SF: Do you see a growth of expression in the last years?

SI: Absolutely, the more I've experienced, the more I have to communicate and express to others.

SF: Do you memorize pieces?

SI: Yes, and when I do solo recitals it's all from memory. That allows you to internalize it more, and to really become the music. The ultimate goal is to not think about this as being a guitar recital, just to be immersed and at one, and to experience the music. That is the message the audience will tune into.

SF: I've read that you use Transcendental Meditation (TM) to boost your mental stamina. I was thinking about how much mental stamina it would take to keep memorizing these long pieces.

SI: It's not only that, TM is a form of trance, and when you are at your best performing you are in a trance. You are in the state of flow of that medium. TM has given me a facility to click in and out of trance, and to enter into that altered state—which is ultimately the states I want to be in while performing, meaning not thinking about where my fingers are going, not thinking about who's sitting and listening, but being at one with the music.

SF: Do you think that there's anything innately female or feminine that you bring to your music or to the guitar?

SI: We all bring who we are, and the fact that I'm a woman and I have certain life experiences, absolutely that will be part of the instrument. If an individual is stuck on being in a macho kind of mold without an attunement to sensuality, that's going to be reflected in their playing. It's going to be more acerbic and hard-edged without the beauty that is possible. Is that male and female? Well, people could argue that either way. I think that ultimately these are characteristics that both genders can have. Men can be sensuous too, one would hope. I think that women are perhaps brought up to cultivate certain characteristics more than men are, but really none of that is limited to gender.

So what do I bring to my playing? I bring passion, because I am a passionate person. I bring a lot of feeling, because that's who I am and what I experience. I bring sensuality, because that's part of who I am as well. And what draws me to any form of art is beauty, so that's something I cultivate in music as well.

SF: Is there anyone you'd really love to collaborate with? Have you ever heard Paco De Lucia?

SI: I think Paco is a great player. The project that he did with John McLaughlin and Al Di Meola a few years back was really dynamite. That would be fun. I would also be thrilled to do a duet with Eric Clapton. I think he's a really hot player. I'd love to do a duet with Bonnie Raitt.

SF: I was originally going to just make this book a blues thing, but then, I thought, *this is crazy*.

SI: You're doing exactly what has to be done now, because by doing so you're going to provide young girls with the chance to really see these role models and know that they can do this too if they want. This has for so long been the domain of men, and it need not be that way.

SF: When I think of it, all you need is two hands and some musical talent.

SI: And really the folk music field has been one of the only ones to transcend that. You certainly had Joan Baez as an icon for many years, and subsequent followers. The folk field has never been wanting for women role models. But when you go beyond folk, it's a lot harder to find. Bonnie Raitt certainly broke through in her field.

SF: As a teacher and player, do you see many more female players than you used to twenty years ago?

SI: Odd to report, not really. In the United States, for example, amongst my students at Julliard some of the top students I've had have been women—but none of them have been American. They've all been from foreign countries. In the United States, there still are very few girls picking up the instrument to play classical.

Part of that is that given the realities of the industry, and the chances of making money as a classical guitarist—I mean, you can't play in an orchestra, so you can't fit in that way. Most of the teaching positions are sewn up at this point, unlike in the 1960s when it was a wide-open field. I don't think that many people are really gravitating to study classical guitar in the first place. Therefore, if you're savvy and you want to look toward a bright economic future, it's just not the choice you're going to make. I'm lucky because I am one of the few in the world who can earn a living doing this and thrive from it. But that's not going to be the situation for most people, so why should they study classical guitar as a living? As a hobby, yes.

SF: You seem like you enjoy challenge, and that you're always reaching out to different cultures and different kinds of projects.

SI: I created my own market, because I've made projects that are new and different—and that people will want.

SF: You're innovative in sculpting your own destiny.

SI: Take working with composers for example. By really getting some of the top composers writing today to write concerti for me, works for guitar and orchestra has created demand in the mainstream classical orchestral world that didn't exist before. They want to hear [John] Corigliano because he won the Pulitzer Prize, he won the Academy Award and he's one of the most famous American composers. He wrote one guitar concerto, and I'm the one person who plays it, so something like that gets me a lot of engagements. Same thing with the other composers I'm working with. People want to hear something new and different, and they want to have the freshness associated with a performer that's part of their own time and culture.

SF: Have you always been a person that was easily able to challenge yourself and stretch out?

SI: I guess that really did come from the beginning. Part of it is because I've always had an innate curiosity, and that's kind of crucial to anybody who wants to pursue something that is unusual, and the curiosity is what led me to say yes and to explore things even before I knew what I was talking about. I always had faith that I would be able to meet the demands, and that the will would be there. I had confidence in myself that I would find a way. On a microcosmic level, if I'm asking a composer to write for me, I have no idea what they're going to come up with. I have faith that whatever they create and whatever collaboration I exchange with them will be something that's workable and possible to play and that I'll be able to do.

You have to always have that faith beforehand when you're jumping into the unknown. Starting out as a kid being interested in science, my great passion was model rocketry. I would spend hours and hours a day building and launching model rockets and designing them, working with microscopes, dissecting things, and building cloud chambers. My father was a scientist. I got that from him.

SF: How old were you when you were doing that?

SI: I was ten years old. That taught me very fundamental rules of problem-solving, and that became crucial when I became my own teacher from the age of sixteen on. I'd sit in front of a mirror with a tape recorder and try to figure out how to do all this.

SF: How were your teen years? I spent mine in my room with my guitar.

SI: That's what I did. For hours a day.

SF: Did you have a social life?

SI: I had very little social life when I was in junior high and high school. I think I went out on one date.

SF: Do you have time for a personal life now?

SI: Yes, absolutely. My playing was probably a lot more boring then, because of that. Now I really appreciate life, and I am grateful for music for giving me the ticket to explore it, because I wouldn't have seen half the places that I have if I didn't have the chance to travel for my work.

SF: Traveling seems to be a big part of what you're about.

SI: I also love people. I grew from being a very shy kid that didn't have much of a social life to someone who really is fascinated by people and really intrigued by their individual life stories.

SF: So the guitar basically opened up all those avenues.

SI: Absolutely. Had I gone in the other direction, which seemed much more likely for me to go, that was to be a scientist.

SF: You would have been a lot more cloistered and quiet.

SI: God forbid, I couldn't even imagine what I would be like. I would have been a very different person.

SF: Do you still dabble in or read about science?

SI: I don't have too much time now. But one of the funny things that did happen is a few years ago I got a call from an astronaut, who was planning to take up this rather extraordinary travel guitar that I had come to endorse. It's a really cool instrument. I can take it on vacations with me and not lose my calluses and still keep up the technique and not have anything that's going to get smashed or devoured by termites. It's a great handy thing. So, anyway this guy had decided that he was going to give it as a gift to one of the Russian cosmonauts when they docked with Mir [space station]. This was in November of '95.

I was thrilled because my love of rockets and space from my early years was now something happening in my adult life, in a way I could never have expected. He brought up a CD of mine and this travel guitar and was calling me every day the week of the launch, just to give me a progress report. The day before the launch, he called to say they had approved it. I was thrilled when everything worked out so well. He brought back all these pictures that he had taken of the travel guitar and the CD. Four months later when I was in Houston, he gave me a four-hour tour of [to] the Johnson Space Center and I got to sit at the shuttle simulator. I got work the controls just like the astronauts do when they're practicing, and it was totally fascinating.

SF: In school, were you good in math?

SI: I was good in math and computers, partly because I had a really great teacher in junior high. That changed in high school; I completely shifted over to the humanities. I had a great teacher of philosophy and American history. That just goes to show how important mentors are, and why kids growing up really need to have the stimulation of adults who can provide them with challenges they can run with.

SF: You said after sixteen you were your own guitar teacher.

SI: I had no teacher during the year. During the summer I would get a chance to have master classes. If Segovia came to town, I'd get a lesson with him, he'd give me a few suggestions and that would give me an impetus to go on. But basically I was sitting there analyzing what I'd just taped, sitting in front of the mirror trying to figure out how to make this work better. Again, that's the problem-solving stuff I had learned cutting up bees and worms and building rockets

SF: Do you ever wonder what was driving you to be so great?

SI: I often wonder what was driving me, because I had tremendous drive and ambition. It's always been a part of me. Before I played the guitar, I would spend hours and hours in my room with these science experiments. I was very happy doing that but I don't know where that comes from. When I shifted over to music instead of playing only twenty minutes a day, I was nine and we were living in Italy. I only took up the guitar because my older brother defected from it—because what he had in mind was Elvis Presley and the Beatles, and my parents figured somebody had to study with this teacher since he was a really good player, and it was too good an opportunity to miss. I volunteered, not having a clue what classical guitar was, sort of out of family duty. I liked the fact that it was very personal. I played the piano before, and it really didn't inspire me at all because it felt mechanical. After I finished my lesson, twenty other little kids would pile in and play the same piece.

However, on the guitar, an instrument was built for me, which was my own, and you cradle it almost like another person. I can even remember smelling the wood. There was something very earthy and organic about it and yet I had no professional aspirations. When I say twenty minutes a day, that's all I did for at least a year or two. When I was fourteen, I won a competition and got to play with the Minnesota orchestra in front of ten thousand people. I thought, *this is even more exciting than watching grasshoppers go up into space.*

SF: By what age did you get really serious?

SI: I was fourteen when I really turned the corner and decided to put in five hours a day.

SF: How much do you practice now?

SI: That really varies. It's supply and demand. If I don't need to I won't, and if I need to I will.

SF: If you're getting ready for a big show?

SI: Then I have to put in some hours. Not a lot. I can do two or three hours a day, and that will work. If I have to learn something new and have only a short time to learn it, then I will do what it takes, even ten hours a day.

SF: It must also take a lot of intellectual work.

SI: Yes, I do a lot of mental work too. I do a lot of visualization apart from the instrument, where I am able to see all the right- and left-hand fingerings and hear the music sounding exactly as I want. I do that mental kind of practice like athletes do.

SF: Did you figure out that technique yourself?

SI: I did. One day when I was a kid, my teacher in Aspen took us all on a hike and told us to just go and meditate. I remember suddenly the music started coming to me in this visualized form. I realized that helped to put me in touch with it more, and solidify the memory, so I developed my own system of how I would use that and basically create a foolproof method of memory training. I do this with my students, and they're always amazed because nobody teaches this. It's always been "hope for the best" and that's about it. By having a whole method that is spelled out, kids who have come to me with that insecurity about their performance about memory can leave knowing that it's all going to be there. It gives them a confidence of being able to get through the program without memory slips, and also increases their enjoyment—because instead of worrying they can just immerse themselves in the music.

SF: Have you ever thought of writing a book on your teaching methods?

SI: I actually did write one book. In that book there's a chapter on memory work, and if you follow my methods it'll work. You hear about studies with basketball players. They divide them into three groups. One group was told just to practice shooting baskets. The other group was told to do it mentally, but not with the ball. The other was told to do both. Remarkably, the group that did it mentally and the group that did both were fairly hand in hand, but clearly surpassed the ones who only did the physical shooting.

There's much to be said for involving the mind in this way, because the other thing that happens, musically speaking—forget about just the increased confidence it gives you in mental stamina, but it also allows you to have a vision unencumbered by technique. So if you're going through a piece in your head without your instrument, here you are able to imagine the entire thing in your mind, the virtual reality or the entire performance. By doing so, you give yourself much higher goals and possibilities than if you never did it mentally. You can now aspire to something that you didn't even know was achievable, because you weren't stuck on the instrument and your own physical limitations.

It's how composers work, too. They imagine in their minds what they want. They get their inspiration from the cosmos and then they yield it to paper.

SF: Is there any set of recordings you've done that you're most proud of?

SI: Because everything is so different, each represents a different part of myself. I particularly am proud of *Journey to the New World* [2009], with guests Joan Baez and country fiddler Mark O'Connor, who join me in a folk-inspired journey from the British Isles to America. In that CD, I also premiere Duarte's "Joan Baez Suite" for solo guitar. I'm honored to have recorded three Latin concerti with the New York Philharmonic, their only recording with guitar. I enjoy the lyricism of *Dreams of a World* and am really happy with the uniqueness of *Journey to the Amazon* working with saxophonist Paul Winter, and with percussion in a way that hasn't been done before. On that CD, composer/percussionist Thiago de Mello used his instruments in a melodic fashion, not just beating out rhythms, but also actually imitating the melodic patterns that I'm doing. In a variety of levels and counterpoints, that is very unusual and that changed the way I played.

SF: It definitely throws in some call-and-response kind of stuff.

SI: And having fallen in love with the rainforest and the jungle, to be able to realize this on a musical level was also very unexpected. Just like the rockets, where you have no idea how one little simple facet of your life . . . I love monkeys, so I wanted to go to the rainforest to see them. All of a sudden I am playing with a Mawé Indian from a tribe of the Amazon, and doing his music. I couldn't have envisioned that.

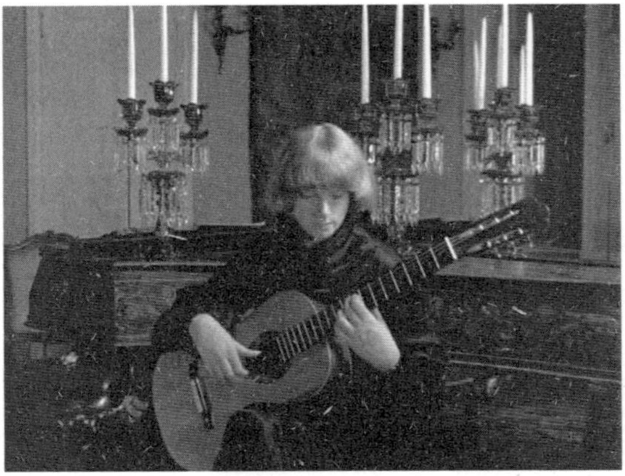

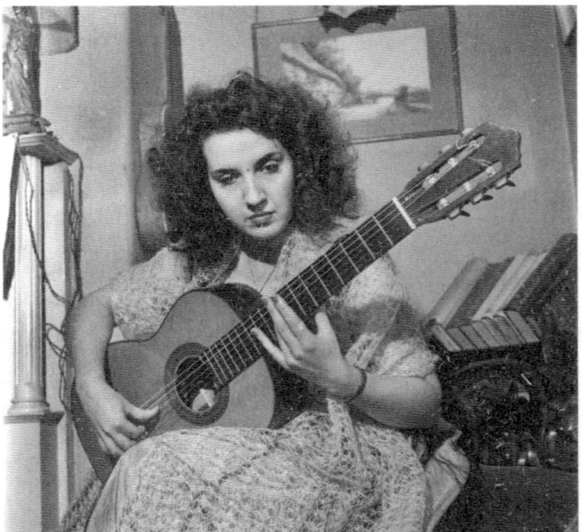

Alice Artzt and Ida Presti

ALICE ARTZT

One of the most intriguing women I researched for this project was the French classical guitarist Ida Presti. Born in 1924, she was affectionately nicknamed "Ida Prestissimo" by Andrés Segovia for her dazzling speed and musicality. I managed to track down the only existing biography on Presti, written by her daughter and translated into English by guitarist Alice Artzt, and after reading it, I was completely captivated.

Unable to interview Presti herself, who died in 1967, I had the privilege of speaking with Artzt, one of her best-known students. Artzt had traveled with Presti and her husband, Alexandre Lagoya, during their American tours, serving as their interpreter. She also studied with the duo in France, where they often took in promising students and gave them private instruction free of charge. Artzt remained close to Presti and shared insights that painted a vivid picture of who Ida was, both as a performer and as a person.

Presti was a child prodigy introduced to the guitar by her father, who idolized Segovia and was determined that his daughter would follow in those footsteps. Legend has it that when Ida was a baby, he would stretch her fingers as she slept so they'd grow long enough to manage the fretboard. She was raised in total musical immersion, somewhat like a captive though a willing one, completely cut off from a conventional childhood. She didn't attend school but instead practiced guitar for hours every day. By ten, she had made her first recording; by thirteen, she was already gaining national acclaim in France for her skill and stage presence.

Presti's story isn't only one of brilliance; it's also one of profound loss. When she was nine, her younger brother died of an infected dog bite he received while protecting her. She often felt that he had sacrificed his life for hers. Only a few years later, she lost her father—her mentor, champion, and closest ally. The emotional weight of those losses was immense, and she took on the burden of financially supporting her family through her performances, all while enduring the poverty and fear that swept France during the World War Two and the German occupation.

Ida met Alexandre Lagoya in Paris after one of his performances. By then, she already had a flourishing solo career, and after they married in 1952, they performed exclusively as a duo until her death in 1967. Guitar duos were still rare at the time, and audiences were drawn to the intimacy of their musical dialogue. Watching them perform was like witnessing a private exchange, fluid, intuitive, and deeply connected. Together they played nearly two thousand concerts, transcribed major works by Bach, Scarlatti, Debussy, Falla, and Granados, and commissioned new pieces from contemporary composers.

Ida had been briefly married once before, during the war, and had a daughter from that union, the same daughter who later wrote her biography. With Lagoya, she had a son, completing the family that would carry on her legacy.

There has long been quiet speculation that Presti may have been the stronger musician in the duo, and that she set aside her solo career to elevate Lagoya's. Alice Artzt speaks candidly about this. Lagoya was a gifted musician and a fine composer in his own right, but it was widely understood that Ida possessed something rare, something that couldn't be taught.

Presti died suddenly at the age of forty-two. The most likely cause was an internal hemorrhage from esophageal or lung cancer, compounded by years of heavy smoking. Her death sent shockwaves through the guitar world. Though she had achieved a great deal, much of her potential was left unrealized.

Presti is often portrayed as a slave to her talent, robbed of a normal childhood and burdened by genius. But many who knew her tell a different story. Despite her hardships, she was remembered as warm, loving, and joyful. Her family has remained largely private, which may be why a proper documentary on her life has yet to materialize.

Technically, Presti was a phenomenon. She employed a distinctive technique of striking the strings from the right side of her nails, producing a fuller, louder tone. Later in life, she could sight-read the most complex music with ease and rarely needed to rehearse. Her skill seemed effortless.

There's still an outdated belief that the guitar favors the strength and physiology of male players, and that women must work harder to keep up. Presti's technical mastery and physical command of the instrument completely disprove that notion. Her story made me realize that talent knows no gender; what matters is dedication, belief, and the will to transcend barriers.

What I find most inspiring is that Presti was raised in a world where she was never told she couldn't do it. She was taught that greatness was her destiny, and she pursued it without hesitation. I love the purity of that. Alice Artzt described her as childlike and sheltered in some ways, yet powerful because she never questioned her place as a virtuoso.

Ida Presti deserves to be remembered as one of the greatest and most influential guitarists the world has ever known.

ALICE ARTZT

— *The Interview* —

[2007]

SF: The reason for the book I'm writing is that I couldn't find any books on women guitar players.

AA: I don't think there have been any. There's just been the one on Presti. I find the beginning part of it fascinating, but I also find there is a strong agenda on the part of the daughter to portray Presti as the suffering, unhappy, miserable slave to her talent. I really do feel very funny about some of the statements in there. Lagoya tended to self-promote quite a lot. In his publicity, he tended to say "I" instead of "we" for anything that the duo did. I realize the situation he was in. I mean, I shouldn't judge, because it would have been terribly difficult to have the whole floor pulled out from under you in that situation.

SF: You mean with Presti dying?

AA: Yeah, but he really didn't seem to work very hard at polishing her star, and did work hard at polishing his own. There's a film company in England that wanted very much to make a documentary on Presti, and he wasn't terribly co-operative. He finally came around to being a little bit co-operative just toward the very end, but by the time they could have interviewed him, he had died. He didn't seem to promote her the way I would think he would have.

SF: It's just unbelievable that she's not a household name.

AA: Absolutely. She was astounding as a musician. Astounding as a performer. She could do absolutely anything at any speed with a beautiful sound, instantly. In some of the footage that this film company did interviewing me, I describe a situation where I had just gotten a copy of a new classical piece. She said, "Oh, wow! A new piece. Oh, that looks nice." Then she sat down and played through the whole solo part at high speed. I mean, it would have done for an LP recording. Gorgeous. Beautiful phrasing. Everything there. And the funny thing was, she was so modest about this kind of thing. I still remember her whipping the pages. Then she stopped after about five or six pages, and looked up with a look kind of a little kid in a candy store or a kid doing something a little bit naughty. She said, "I'm sight reading, you know." And then whiff! On she went, right through to the end of the thing.

I mean, nobody can do stuff like that. And yet, she was such an innocent. She is the closest thing that I ever will know to a saint. She was astonishing, and also just a real person. She was also a very fun person. She loved horror movies. She was amazing. Just so joyous. She made you love her just walking into the room. She was fascinating in that way, and absolutely adorable. Do you know Angelo Gilardino?

SF: No, I don't.

AA: Angelo Gilardino is one of the main guitar people in Italy. He's the person who selects and edits all the [sheet] music that Bèrben puts out for guitar. He has also taught there for years in the conservatory system. He's had festivals. He's a big cheese in Italy.

When he was a little kid, his father gave him five bucks or something, you know: "Go watch a movie or something." So, he sent little Angelo off with a little money to go see a show. Angelo went to a movie theatre, and then he saw a long line next door in another hall. It was a really long line, so he thought, *Well, that looks better than the movie, so I'll get in that line and see whatever that is.* He gets up to the front of the line. It was an Ida Presti concert. She would have been eighteen or something. Angelo went in there and he sat down and he said this beautiful lady came out and played the guitar. He'd never heard anything like that before in his life. He was completely transfixed.

He says to this day, he remembers every single piece and exactly how it was. He didn't know what the pieces were at the time, but he said he since figured out what all the pieces were. It was like the road to Damascus. It transformed his life. He came out of there knowing, *that's what I've gotta do for my life.* That was Presti.

SF: Did you meet Presti and Lagoya abroad?

AA: We heard this wonderful French duo was coming to the United States and gonna play in New York. I don't know if I'd necessarily heard of them before. I went to the concert, and I had a whole pile of questions for them afterward, including, "Where can I study with you?" And they said, "Up in Canada." I went there the next summer and studied with them. That was my first experience studying with them, and it was absolutely transforming. I changed my whole right-hand technique around, and I'm quite sure I would not have had the career I had, had I not done so.

SF: This is the picking with the right side of the nail?

AA: It means you can get away with less strength. It's more stable, solid, and it just made a tremendous difference. I was already playing, and I was a very determined person. I think you probably have to [be] to get into this kind of business, anyway. You just do it one hundred percent. You go for it with everything you've got and hopefully it works. I would have just as soon practiced twenty-four hours a day and not done so much else.

I studied with Presti and Lagoya that summer. The next thing was they were teaching in Nice at the Academy International. I went there the next summer. What I found out from the people who had known them a little longer than me [was] if you go to Paris and you just stay in a hotel and you let Presti and Lagoya know you're there, they will invite you out. Maybe each weekend or whenever they have spare time. And you get a lesson.

That's what I did a couple of different summers. Not only went to the Nice Academy, but also stayed in Paris practicing my head off and waiting for a phone call to say, 'We're free this afternoon. You wanna come out?" They never charged for those lessons. What we did was we'd usually bring a box of candy or we'd bring some flowers. If they liked you and they wanted to teach you, then you got invited out. If they got tired of you or if, I suppose, they didn't think you were worth bothering about, then maybe you didn't get invited out. A pile of us would go there and everybody would play.

SF: What do you think is the best thing Ida Presti taught you?

AA: That every note is important. Even the little notes. Even the fast notes. Even the non-important notes. They were all very, very important and they should all sound gorgeous. That way, if you're playing with that point of view, it should sound exactly the way you want it. You get a real bee in your bonnet and you get some control. Then even if people don't like what you're playing, it still sounds good.

SF: When I interviewed Sharon Isbin, she said it was rumored that Presti was the stronger guitar player in the duo.

AA: It's not a rumor.

SF: It's true?

AA: Oh, sure. Well, they had to wait for Lagoya to die to even write the book at all, which I think is ridiculous. Lagoya was stronger physically, maybe in some ways—though you would never know it from listening to the playing—but the guitar was a piece of her. She could do anything, and she nearly never practiced. She did when she was a kid, of course. A lot. But when I would see the two of them, she would be there with no music, playing the hardest stuff. Talking. Discussing things.

I have a tape, actually, from a friend of mine in Belgium—they must have put a tape recorder under their chair or something while they were getting ready for a concert or rehearsing in their living room. You got Presti talking and just doing whatever—just kind of thinking or something, with the guitar going. Then you hear Lagoya laboriously practicing, carefully and slowly. Doing all the stuff that a normal person would do getting ready for a concert.

The wonderful thing about Lagoya was that he managed to sit up there on stage with this absolutely, incomparably amazing guitarist, and not look like an idiot. That is already more than most people in this world could do, and it was very hard work for him. He worked like a dog at it. He did it, and he pulled it off. If you just listen to records, you can pretty much tell who's who. But seeing them on stage, because she deferred to him a lot, it was not immediately evident that she was just so astronomically better than he. And that is to his amazing credit. When you'd see them practicing, she would make a suggestion and he would snap to it and do it. He was the student for sure.

SF: Is she very well known in France?

AA: Oh, yeah. These days I can't say, but at the time—I mean when she died, her family, do you know how they found out? On the radio. They're listening to the radio, the morning radio program, and they heard about her death before Lagoya even called. He was waiting for a better hour to call them. That can't have been easy on them. It was esophageal cancer. I'm like, 99.99 percent sure. What they say in the book is a lot of nonsense.

SF: They just said she was throwing up blood.

AA: Yeah, she was throwing up blood. They went to the doctor in St. Louis and the doctor took an X-ray and said, "Well, this looks not good. This looks dangerous. You've got to stay here overnight, and we'll keep watching and see what happens." But Presti and Lagoya were saying, "We have a concert in Rochester tomorrow. We can't stick around here." They got on the plane in the early morning to go to Rochester. She was still coughing up blood and spent most of the plane trip in the ladies' room. She was pretty weak and not in good shape by the time they got to Rochester. The plane people knew, and they had an ambulance ready to take her to the hospital the minute they landed. They worked on her pretty much all day, and she died in the very late afternoon.

The book says something like it was all the doctor's fault. I mean, when somebody's been coughing up blood for twelve hours by the bucketful, you prudently wait? You don't do anything? I mean, get real. And that the doctor must have missed a tiny, invisible tumor and this caused her death? Basically, that it's all their fault?

Well, the tiny invisible tumor wasn't a tiny invisible tumor. I've had a doctor who specializes in exactly that here, taking lessons. He says that sounds exactly like esophageal cancer, because the heart is right in front of where the tumor would have been, so you couldn't see it. You could have a very large tumor there, and you still wouldn't see anything. Now, what I don't know is if even Lagoya knew. But she told this close friend of hers in Belgium, who told me, that she had a premonition of her own death and a lot of premonitions of other people's deaths, which I didn't know about.

SF: And her father also predicted her young death.

AA: She predicted she would die when her son would be fourteen years old, which is exactly what happened. She also had been to a specialist in Paris, because she knew she had a condition and that something was wrong. I don't know how much—if any of this—Lagoya knew. She may have kept it a secret from him. Lagoya was always very anti-doctor. I remember when she had a headache one time, he wouldn't let her take an aspirin: "No! The body must heal itself." What I gathered from the friend is that it's very likely that she went secretly to the doctor in Paris and didn't tell him. I can't bring it up with them because they're so set on this idea that the doctors in America took a perfectly healthy person and killed her.

SF: There's a lot of speculation in the book.

AA: Well, there's been all sorts of speculation. There've been websites that have been saying [Andrés] Segovia poisoned her, and she died of this, she died of that, and she died of a heart attack, and she died of cancer, and she died of heaven-knows-what. There's so much speculation, and they won't release the autopsy to anybody but the family, which doesn't help anything.

Another thing that I find interesting is the daughter emphasizing how much Ida was suffering, saying she was hunched over the guitar all the time, and that she was in constant pain and could hardly walk. Well, the last tour or the next-to-the-last tour, I took Presti and Lagoya to the Cloisters [museum in New York] and we walked all over the place—she in five-inch high heels! I couldn't walk in things like that. She was very lively. No problem. She never complained, but that didn't mean anything because she probably wouldn't have complained. But if she'd been in horrible pain all that time you would have noticed something.

SF: Is esophageal cancer caused from smoking?

AA: Probably, which she did a lot—both she and Lagoya. They smoked a lot.

SF: What recordings would you recommend?

AA: Anything of Presti's. Get the solo ones, too. You may not have an easy time finding them. It's all interspersed with Lagoya's records, and they've got Lagoya's name all over them. Another thing you might find interesting would be an excerpt from the material that these English filmmakers got. They got some archival footage of her, including from the [1938] movie *Le Petit Chose* that she was in at age thirteen. There's also some other archival footage of the duo together.

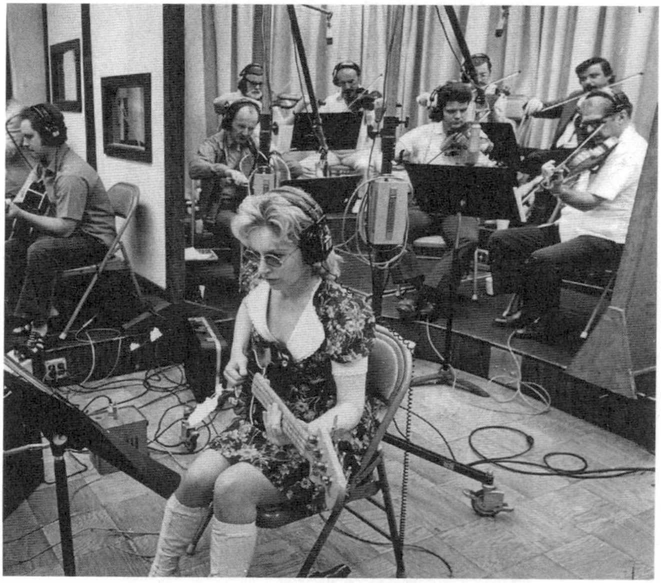

Carol Kaye

CAROL KAYE

Carol Kaye has one of the most impressive biographies of any musician. She is the most recorded bass guitarist in the history of popular music, with more than ten thousand sessions spanning over forty years. During the 1960s and '70s, Carol was the lone woman playing in the Wrecking Crew, a revolving group of Los Angeles studio musicians who recorded for artists such as the Monkees, the Mamas and the Papas, and Simon and Garfunkel. Her bass lines are heard on the Beach Boys' *Pet Sounds*, as well as countless hits including Ritchie Valens's "La Bamba" and Nancy Sinatra's "These Boots Are Made for Walkin'." She also developed one of the most influential and widely emulated bass styles in history, which led to a long and fruitful career as a writer and educator.

I was both awestruck and a little intimidated at the thought of interviewing Carol, and I had good reason to be nervous. She is known to be outspoken, and, let's face it, people over a certain age tend to say exactly what's on their minds. That can be both refreshing and a little daunting. After a few minutes, I realized this was not going to be a typical music interview. Carol took me far beyond the realm of bass guitar.

"Do you know what it's like to be poor?" she asked emphatically, right after we began speaking. She talked about quitting school at fourteen to help support her family, and how she navigated the world of nightclubs as an impressionable adolescent, teaching herself jazz guitar.

She shared strong opinions about what she called the "pornographic" nature of today's entertainment industry, and how women have done themselves a disservice by focusing too much on looks and fame. It was an honest perspective from a woman who built her life on talent and skill. Carol also spoke about her marital struggles, including an abusive husband whose violence left her incapacitated for years.

As a fellow musician, I was awed by her career, but as a woman, I was even more moved by her humanity and vulnerability. It made me wonder how someone so strong could still fall prey to abuse and self-doubt. The answer may lie deep in her past.

Carol was born in Everett, Washington, in 1935, during the Great Depression. Her childhood was marked by hardship. Her father, a World War One veteran, struggled with opium addiction, and the family often lived in poverty. At around nine years old, Carol encouraged her mother to divorce him and began working odd jobs to help make ends meet. Despite their struggles, her mother managed to buy her a guitar. Both parents were musicians, and Carol began teaching and performing by thirteen.

Jazz gigs didn't pay much, so she took day jobs for extra income. After having her first child at sixteen, she pretended to be a widow until she married, but she soon divorced after her second child was born. Later, she remarried but left when her husband objected to her playing with Black musicians. She hired a live-in nanny and kept working, undeterred.

In 1957, producer Robert Blackwell heard her playing jazz and invited her to record on Sam Cooke's "Summertime." Studio work soon became steady income. One day, when the regular bass player didn't show up, Carol picked up the bass and developed her signature pick technique. From then on, her career soared. She became one of the most in-demand bass players in popular music, working with Quincy Jones and earning praise from Frank Sinatra, who called her his favorite bass player.

One of my main takeaways from our conversation was her advice to use anger as fuel. Carol urges people to stand up for themselves and refuse to take any more abuse. Throughout her career, she's been outspoken toward critics who questioned her work on famous Motown sessions. Recently, a character in *The Marvelous Mrs. Maisel* was loosely based on her. Instead of being flattered, she dismissed it as "fluff." What a badass.

I love the freedom that comes with age, and I wish our society valued it more. As a woman in my fifties, I've realized my admiration for aging is mixed with fear. I tell myself it's just a number, but I know the entertainment industry doesn't see it that way. That's why Carol's attitude toward fame and status feels so refreshing. She sees life clearly now and is far beyond worrying about what she can't control.

Now in her mid-eighties, Carol remains active, teaching bass and giving interviews. She still wakes up every morning with purpose. She is an ambassador for the evolution of the Fender bass in popular music—an evolution she personally helped shape through her innovative and distinct style. She stands by her truth and her values. Her story reminds us what can be achieved through talent, perseverance, and drive—and through the wisdom that comes with age.

CAROL KAYE

— *The Interview* —

[2001]

SF: Are you writing a memoir?

CK: I started it about ten years ago. I have to finish it now, because they're going to do a movie. I've got to get it done before they start in on any script. I don't want anybody else writing my life story for me. There have been several people who wanted to do it, but I didn't want just anyone doing it. This company is very big, so I'm going to go with them.

SF: What are they going to call it, do you know?

CK: Honey, I have no idea, I don't even care at this point. I do want the story told right. You have to understand, I live in Hollywood, and it's a business town. I'm not into image. I'm not into stardom. I'm not into any of that stuff. That's for people who want glamor. We made people into stars. With that said, it's just a business. I'm not impressed with anything like that. When you're in the business, you look at it from a business angle. You don't look at it from the public's angle at all. You look at it from the talent point of view—and what appears to be talent to the public might not be talent at all. It's the work of people in the background that makes something sound good or look good.

SF: Do you think in the last ten years women have taken a backward step, as far as their image in the music business?

CK: I think that the pornographic stuff has really hurt women a lot.

SF: Do you mean the videos?

CK: Whatever, they have porn on ads in magazines. It's very debasing. That sort of tabloid stuff is not only using and exploiting women, but it's causing a sick world. It's not just here either; it's happening in Europe. It's happening all over, as people get this narcissistic thing to exploit being stars. It's a stupid thing to do, because they lose track of who really owns this world.

You live and you die. When you get older, you realize that stardom is a very phony viewpoint of the world. Unfortunately, there are so many people in the world who are in love with stardom. They treat people like gods. People are people; we're all prone to making mistakes and doing things wrong like that. It's a very false way to live, but it's affected how top women professionals are looked at. You don't have to be the best in the music business to be a professional, but there are so many poor things who pawn themselves off as image out there just to get gigs. It's a shame that talent takes a back seat to so much that's going on out there.

SF: Is that because everything has become so visual lately?

CK: Yeah, we're looking in the water and seeing ourselves for the first time with videos and movies and all of that. It used to be that only certain people could become stars and those were promoted in the '30s and '40s, in fine films, in the '50s too. But people in the music business in the '60s and '70s became "stars," so now the general public, with their reality shows, now everybody can be a star, they all want their little bit of fame. I think a lot of women are getting in the crossfire here.

SF: When do you think the change started taking place?

CK: It actually started in the '70s with the ego. The pornographic got to be hip sometime; I don't know when that was exactly. Then the esteem of real women went down the toilet. It's hurt women in the business, too. It really has. Even though there are more women today who are serious about their music, and they're out there doing a good job, I think it's tougher for them because of the general attitude toward women. Plus, there are some women out there who are just plain old tough and catty and nasty and stuff like that. Those kinds of women hurt the cause of the good women. It's the same thing with men: there are a lot of nasty men out there hurting the cause for all the good men. I've seen a lot of good men and I've worked with them. I've seen a lot of great men in our business, but I keep hearing about some bad ones.

SF: How active are you in the studio scene now?

CK: Not like I was. I used to do three or four dates a day. Now I'm lucky to do three or four dates a year. And that's just fine with me, because I only take the work I want to do. There are dates that I turned down, because I don't want to play that kind of music, or there's people that I don't quite like, or there's something that I just don't want to do. You get tired of it after you do so many years. I've been playing music since 1949 as a pro, and I'm kind of tired of it. I'm very careful of what I want to do. There's not that much work anyway. I mean, nobody is working.

SF: Do you find after having music as your living for so long that you just don't enjoy the art of music anymore, even listening?

CK: You don't listen as much as you used to. I'm better at it than most people. Most of my group, they don't even have the radio on when you walk in their house. It's dead silent because they're burned out. But I still listen to and play some jazz, and I listen to some classical. Most of the music that's out there I don't listen to. Once in a while I will listen to some Mexican music because some of the Latin music, even the Mexican hillbilly music is good. It's real; it's not a phony put-on music, like "I'm going to play this to make a million bucks."

SF: Back then, you were there to make hits. It wasn't the same kind of attitude as it is now, what you just said about making a million bucks and all that.

CK: That's the attitude I hear, that a lot of people try to do their music, and it comes out phony. That's the attitude I meant. Some of the music we played was very boring, because it was so simple—it was surf rock stuff and it was kind of crappy music, I guess you'd say. But we never would allow that thought to creep in our heads as we were playing it, because we were trying to do the best job we could to try and get the music cut and make it groove. We always played that stuff with the highest amount of integrity.

But we were the hired guns. It didn't matter about our opinions. Every date, we tried to play the best style music, whatever style it was, we were required to do. We tried to get everybody a hit record in spite of themselves, some of them because they didn't know how to get a hit record. And we did, because that's what we did in jazz ever night, we invented every note that we ever played, every night. Once we figured what to do about the format, certain lines here, breaks there and stuff like that—to put the framework around any tune—it didn't matter the tune, it didn't matter the singer.

We used to brag that we could take any singer off the streets and make him into a star. That's not exactly true, but close. They didn't have to have much talent to sing that good, but they did have to have a very strong background. That's why the jazz players dug in and did the most work. There are a few others [in the Wrecking Crew], like Glen Campbell and Leon Russell, who worked from the rock and western music field, and they had some good and inventive lines too. But most of the players on the dates were either from the jazz world or from big bands.

SF: Is that still the world of music you identify with the most?

CK: Of course. I'm not going to sit and listen to simple music when I play the world's greatest music. I listen to really good music.

SF: Do you still play jazz guitar?

CK: I haven't had time lately, because I'm teaching and I'm trying to finish this film. Doing this business, this keeps me going like crazy right now. As soon as I get this film done, then I can go back and play some more.

SF: This film isn't the film of your life.

CK: No, it's a tutor film for guitar. I've written a lot of great stuff for guitar. I've taught on guitar since 1949.

SF: It's funny how everyone just assumes you're Carol Kaye, the bass player.

CK It's funny because the people I work with in jazz often wonder what ever happened to that really fine jazz guitar player Carol Kaye, because they didn't know about all the rock bass I did in the studio.

SF: Who were your favorite jazz guitarists growing up?

CK: I don't have any favorites. I didn't listen to jazz guitar players. I listened to everybody. It didn't matter. Whoever was laying the finest bebop jazz: Sonny Stitt, and all the jazz guys back in the fifties.

SF: Did you get to see Charlie Parker and guys like that?

CK: Honey, I didn't have the money to go see them. I was born poor. I was poor until I was about twenty-six. Raising kids and working day and night, you don't have money to go out and listen to anybody. You are out there working yourself. Everybody thought I played with Bird and I said, "No, Bird died just before I was on the scene in 1956." He died in 1955. But I played with all the rest of the New Yorkers that came out there and they all know me.

SF: Did you know Mary Osborne, the guitar player?

CK: Yes, I met her and I hung out with her a couple of times. She was one of the top players in the studio back in New York. I heard a little bit of her recording, and it was more or less like the Charlie Christian side of jazz, which is like the '40s jazz. Very, very good, a lovely gal. She was one of the guys, and we hung out together and laughed and told jokes and stuff like that, listened to some music back then. We got along fine, just great. She was about fifteen years older than me.

There was another gal named Mary Kaye. I met her brother because my first husband Al Kaye knew of him. I spoke to her nephew, John Kaye was his name. He filled me in on her career: he thinks that she single-handedly started the lounge acts in Las Vegas in the '50s. She was the biggest star back then. She was the only woman who led her group. She was the only one who was a guitar player. She wasn't a bebop jazz guitar player; she couldn't solo. But there were some records that she played on. She was more of a singer star, though.

SF: But she backed herself up on guitar.

CK: Very well. People, men and women, everybody could play well back then. They all got chordal education, which you don't find these days. The present-day teachers were all from the rock days and there weren't very many chords in rock.

SF: I noticed you said that it was all scales now.

CK: Yeah, and that's not the way to learn music. Music functions in chords.

SF: What was the most valuable thing your teacher taught you?

CK: Chords and arpeggios and how to function in chords. If you know your chords, you can pick up anything on stage.

SF: It sounds like a simple concept.

CK: It's not simple if you think about the tunes that we had to play. I had to play "Rose Room," or "Exactly Like You," things that had a million chords to them. It wasn't three-chord rock and roll at all. It was standard songs (*she sings "Blue Skies"*). You had to know all the chords, and if you didn't know the tune—you really didn't know three or four hundred tunes—but with the chords you could hear the anticipated chord changes. And your soloing comes from the notes in the chords.

This ignorant so-called education that these kids out there from the rock days who learned to play in the '60s, that's not how standards function. That's not how songs function at all. Once they got away from rock and roll, they couldn't play music. You have to have chordal notes and you don't get them from those scales and those scales are what they teach because that's the only thing that they know what to teach with. And that's not the way to learn music.

SF: When you were doing your first gigs were you just playing rhythm, or did you just jump right into soloing?

CK: I was playing solos. It was similar to Charlie Christian, because he really innovated the solo guitar. The person who did before him was Django Reinhardt in France. But it was Charlie Christian who influenced everyone in the United States. He played with Benny Goodman. When you listen to that music, it's got a ton of chords to it and you know what to do. I couldn't solo on every tune, but I did enough. With each gig I got better and better and better. At the age of fourteen that meant a lot of money to me, so that I could buy food for my mother and myself.

SF: Was it just you and your mother living together?

CK: My mom was married to a fellow. My mom was a piano player and my dad was a trombonist and they had me late in life. My dad was a lifelong drug user from opium from World War One, when he sailed over to China. He wasn't into it real heavy, but he eventually died of it in the '70s. He wasn't into it heavy, but just heavy enough to drive my mother crazy.

SF: I guess that turned you off drugs forever.

CK: I had no idea why he was so mean. I had no idea why he was so brutal. And then I figured it out later on, because my mom let it slip, how much he was into opium and stuff like that.

Life back in the '30s was very different than life today. You didn't have the public on drugs back then, like you do now. The public was not into drugs. They were into booze drinking, but only the musicians were into drugs. Half of the musicians were into drugs. My dad got into drugs like most people did, in the wars.

SF: When you were young were you a tomboy?

CK: Yeah, kind of. When you're poor you do everything you can to exist. You get very independent.

SF: How did your social life change after you started playing guitar?

CK: I didn't have a social life. You don't have a social life when you're poor.

SF: Did you practice a lot when you started playing?

CK: I was very good at school even though I stuttered, so I could take the time to practice. I used to practice all night long when I was going to school. I'd rather practice than sleep. It was something that I could do, and that I could do well. I knew it at the time.

SF: You just knew it instinctively when you picked it up.

CK: You know if you're good at something or not. I only took lessons for three months and then I could play gigs.

SF: When you were playing gigs you must have been playing with people a lot older than yourself.

CK: Yes, they didn't know how old I was because I was playing in places where drinking was allowed.

SF: Was that against the law?

CK: Yeah, but I'm not the only one, there are a lot of musicians who were all working at the age of fourteen, fifteen too. Life was struggle back then. It was a struggle just to put food on the table.

SF: So you were responsible for bringing your money home and helping the family?

CK: Of course, have you ever been poor?

SF: I didn't grow up with money either, and I started gigging professionally at sixteen. So they didn't know how old you were, and they didn't care that you were a woman?

CK: I was born in 1935, and World War Two made you grow up quick, when you think that you could be bombed any night. By the time you're fourteen, you're really, like, twenty-five in your age, from the struggle. You grew up quick. I looked older than I was, and I acted older than I was.

SF: How old were you when you got married?

CK: I don't care to talk about that.

SF: I was interested in how people were raising kids while being in the music business, do you care to talk about that?

CK: I had a child when I was sixteen, then another child when I was twenty, then I had another child when I was twenty-seven.

SF: Did you raise them all yourself?

CK: I was married twice, and the marriages didn't work out. I threw the men out and I kept the kids.

SF: I read that you were working all day in the studio and having a housekeeper to help with the kids.

CK: Eventually I did have to have a housekeeper, because my mother was too old to take care of children, and I had to help her, too. She helped me with my first two, but she worked hard all her life and she put up with my dad. It was tough for her, and I wanted for her to at least have a nicer old age. I contributed to her support, but I had to have a woman in the house to clean the house and to take care of the kids so there was a stable life for the kids when they came home from school. That took money. Even then, that took a lot of money. I had to go out and work hard, because $75 support from the second husband didn't get it, when my nut was two thousand a month.

SF: Two thousand a month! What year was that?

CK: In the mid-'60s, with the house, with childcare and with the kids. I did take over the house payments.

SF: That's a lot of money even back then. That's about my nut right now.

CK: It's tough these days. I don't see how people do it. It's very tough to raise kids, especially when you got all these pressures of the drugs. The drugs are everywhere. It's just ridiculous. Plus, the kids in school think it's cool to use drugs because all the musicians use drugs. What I'm saying is we didn't. We're the ones who played on all those hits in the '60s, and you didn't see any drugs at all on any of us in the studios. You saw a little bit in the '70s. You saw what it did to the younger musicians, and some of our group got into drugs in the '70s, but never in the '60s. We could sit and cut a hit album in six hours in the '60s. That's how good we were.

We would just live on coffee. The guys smoked. I never smoked, but the guys all smoked. Because you're sitting there waiting to do take and then Phil Spector and all these guys are in the booth trying to figure out how to do this and do that. I mean, they really didn't know their crap there in the booth at all either, they were just trying to figure it out. Phil sometimes would do a take thirty times, just because he's a showman type of guy. There's no reason for that because he probably took take two. The guys all smoked waiting to record, because when you record you play about four or five times harder than you do when you're playing live. You want to make sure that that record really gets the powerhouse feel on it. We knew that the business could fail any year, and we tried to keep it going by playing strong on every date.

SF: Did you always play with a pick?

CK: I always played with a pick. I am guitar player and they never asked me to play with my fingers.

SF: You break these misconceptions I have about guitar players who turn to bass. Usually I think it's a disaster. You can always tell a bass player who's a guitar player.

CK: It has to be with the right technique. You can't put your wrist up in the air and expect to get a good sound. What has happened is that people today think that bass is only played with the fingers. Back in the '60s, most of the recordings were cut with people playing with a pick. Most of those records of the '60s were cut by myself or by Joe Osborn. Bob West also used a pick.

SF: Was it a hard pick or a soft pick?

CK: You have to have a hard pick to get a good sound.

SF: You guys got a really warm sound. Usually when I hear guys playing bass with a pick, it's that brittle sound.

CK: They don't know how to mute their strings. They probably don't know what kind of strings to use. You have to get flat-wound strings. You have to get close to the end of the neck. You never pick next to the bridges. You have to use a certain kind of muting to get the strings to sound good, or else you're going to have trouble with your sound. There's a craft in recording. And it works well playing live, too.

On top of that, you have string bass players who don't want to play with a pick. They'll say, "That's not the way to play bass, you can't play bass with a pick"—simply because they don't want to do it, they don't want to even try to do it. I taught string bass players. I just had Jim Hughart over here to play, and he's one of the greatest jazz bass players in the world. He was a fine string bass player before I taught him on electric bass. From 1969 on, after I taught him with a pick and everything, he had a mountain of hit records. There's a whole flock of people that I taught the pick style to, and some of them have gone on and created a lot of hit records and some of them are still doing it today.

You don't hear pick players talk bad about string bass players. All string bass players really talk terrible about people who play bass with a pick. They're totally wrong, because they don't know the history. They don't know the recorded history of bass in the 1960s music. It doesn't matter today if you play with a pick or with fingers, but teaching in the first part of the '70s; everybody was required to play with a pick then. I had my hands full trying to teach everybody the pick.

SF: Your rudiments for bass were basically pop music and rock and roll.

CK: I I had been a guitar player in the studio for five years up to that point. I had a feeling of what was missing. I could feel a lot of bass parts that should've been played but weren't played. I'm not putting the bass players down. They had two or three bass players on a date at one time, but they were playing very simple parts. I heard different kinds of rhythms in my head that should've been on bass.

I got playing bass one day at Capitol when a bass player didn't show up. That would've been mid-1960s. I sat down and started playing and I said, "This is kind of fun, I think I can do it." Every time I played bass it was a hit record, and I got better and better at it. [Drummer] Earl Palmer took me aside after a date one time, and he said, "You know, you're sounding good." I said, "Oh, thanks," and he said, "But you're rushing." I said, "No, I'm not." I was kind of feisty. Then I listened to the playback and by golly, he was right. He was absolutely right, so I went home and practiced getting my time together. I wasn't thinking that the time might be off, especially drinking a lot of coffee. I would go home and practice with my metronome and finally got my time sense in.

SF: You had to put the note in a different place than when you were on guitar.

CK: It's an entirely different technique. The strings are bigger. It's not a string bass and it's not a guitar, and so many people try to put it in those categories. One thing is very important: when you play bass, you have to have your time thing together, because you're responsible for that time groove, between yourself and the rest of the band and the drummer. Sometimes you have to keep the drummer in line, too.

SF: How do you teach that?

CK: You put them with an electric metronome leaning on the two and four. If they're off a little bit, I show them where they're off. I tell them when the electric metronome sounds like it's playing in good time, that means you're in good time. When it sounds like the electric metronome is grooving, that means you're playing in good time, not until then. You can get close to it, but close is not getting into time. Playing bass you have to lead just a hair, you have to be just a bit on top of the beat—but not so much that it's going to rush.

SF: You were making up your own bass lines for those hit songs.

CK: They didn't know how to write bass lines, and the arrangers didn't know how to write rock and roll arrangements. When we first started in the 1960s we all had to write out our own chord charts a lot of the time, which was easy to do because we come from the era where we played chords. If we heard chords, we could write it down just fine. One or two times through and we had it, then we figured out the arrangement from there. Arrangers were hired to do chord charts at first and then they would write a few little licks, then they write more and more licks—but they still relied on us to come up with most of the lines. It got to be more reading and more reading.

SF: Some of those bass lines define the whole song as well.

CK: With the bass lines, any arranger can tell you that "Carol Kaye can play a better line than I could ever write." But there were a few arrangers, especially with Motown, they could write darn good arrangements. Gene Page was one of them. He's a piano player, so he was more on the beat. You would be reading the part and at the same time having to invent your parts to make it sound good.

SF: In your email to me before we spoke, you wrote, "There are more dire issues being a top woman professional in the business that I want to tell you for your book, very important things that I think the public should know. It's not about minor hassles or discrimination . . ."

CK: That's some stuff that I don't feel comfortable talking about right now. I'm going to put it in my book. I have to be careful, because there is a danger. There's a physical danger and I don't feel right talking about a certain record company.

SF: I thought maybe it was about you supplying hook lines and bass lines.

CK: It's nothing that simple. Some of it is a publishing company, too, because I've run up against some pretty bad crooks in the publishing company. The music business: most of it is good if you play your instrument and just watch your p's and q's. But be careful, too. I will say there are a lot of men who love to steal credits from women. I've had it happen to me, especially when I was crippled up and out of sight. There were about three men that jumped in and tried to grab all the credits of mine that they could. They thought they could get away with it, but surprise! I've had a second surgery and I'm back in action and playing again. It all kind of died down. Two of them are still trying to claim a few credits because they're too lazy to take it off their websites.

Tell the women out there: watch the men, they can sweet talk and be as nice as they can, but let something happen and you're out of sight, they will steal your credits and feel like they should because they're men. *You're nothing but a lowly woman,* that's their attitude.

Women play on records like the new Tommy Newsom CD. He's the guy that used to substitute for Doc Severinson on the Johnny Carson show. I know Tommy, he's a fabulous arranger. He put out a CD recently with a bunch of seriously great band charts and great playing. I looked at the CD and thought, *who's that drummer? They're fabulous.* And it's a woman. *Who's the bass player*? It was a woman. *Who's the sax lead on that?* It's a woman. I said, "God bless you, Tommy, for taking these New York women and putting them on a CD." You know that Wynton Marsalis doesn't have one woman in his Lincoln Center band, not one? [Note: this finally changed in 2024.]

SF: Do you think maybe men just don't like to be shown up by women?

CK: Well, maybe some of them. I have taught men who think I'm great and it doesn't matter to them. They admire you for the playing. It's better out here in California. I think there's a lot of prejudice in New York. Take the bass player of the *Letterman* show, Will Lee. He's the first one who says, "I love women that can play."

SF: They have a great woman guitar player on that show.

CK: Will Lee will stand there and encourage women to play, so I think it depends upon the person. I think that women stand a better chance out here.

SF: Do you teach many women players?

CK: I've taught a lot of women. There are some who are very serious about playing and there are some who are very sick, too. They cry if anything goes wrong. I say, "Honey, you're trying to use music to heal your soul. You need to go to a therapist." I try to be nice about something like that, but you know how it is. I think some of them see the image and they fall in love with it and they see the power that it implies, but I've taught a lot of women who are very serious and who have done very well.

SF: Do you think the ratio is still way more men?

CK: My teaching is about one woman to every ten men. For players out there, I don't know what the percentages are. Around here you see a lot of women who can really play and are very serious.

SF: Do you ever wonder why there are not more?

CK: I think that some women dig being women. They dig the power that their body has: the boobs, the pink nails, and that stuff. That's the opposite of being a really fine musician. Who knows if that's right or wrong, because if you're trying to get the right husband, you can get a rich guy by looking like a movie actress. You can't get it with your instrument.

SF: You draw a different kind of man, probably.

CK: Yes, you draw all kinds of men who love to be your guy and be there for you. But some of those men will turn around and say, "OK, now do it my way." That kind of thing, they want to pull the strings.

SF: That's hard to do with a woman who's already made her own way.

CK: But some will try, because that's power. They're drawn by power just like women are drawn to powerful men and rich men. It's a power trip with them.

SF: Do you think the guitar is a very powerful role, or stance?

CK: If you're a singer, that's more power than anything, because it's the lead and you're in the front. But bass is kind of in the back. You and I know how powerful it is, but the general public doesn't.

SF: You're keeping a very vibrant career and you're very active. What's your secret to being so healthy?

CK: Herbs and diet, and stay away from the cow, anything by the cow. Goat milk, goat cheese, all that stuff is good, some chicken, too. You have to [be] careful about how foods are processed. You have to stay healthy; you have to keep bad thoughts out of your mind. You have to pray to whoever or whatever god that you think that you have. You have to stay in touch, because there are a lot of things that can be resolved. You don't have to see a shrink. Phil Spector used to go to a shrink every day, so that's not good when you see what happened. I think that there are a lot of things that you can do. You don't have to take drugs, or drink booze. I tell all the women, I say, "Don't smoke, don't drink, and don't do drugs."

SF: Do you still drink coffee?

CK: Once in a while. That's not great either because when you stimulate your gall bladder and your liver with a lot of coffee, that eventually turns out to be bad because they don't work well anymore. I try to rely on healthy thing like herbs and alternative medicine. And stay out of other people's problems, because other people can drag you down real fast. A lot of times they just want to use you. There are a lot of people who need help and all kinds of people that run up and help them, so sometimes you have to let them sit against the wall

I learned a lot around [bassist] Joe Pass, he said the only time he stopped doing drugs was when his mother wouldn't bail him out of jail for the thirteenth time. When one of my own kids got into drugs, I joined a program with him. I learned a lot about drugs. Don't get involved with people that have drugs. Let the experts take care of that. Because other people will try to drag you down with their problems. I'm not saying to be cold, but just be aloof from other people's problems.

SF: You said you had a debilitating illness for a while. Did that have anything to do with your playing?

CK: I couldn't play. I had rheumatoid arthritis because I got attacked by my ex-husband—who I sued, by the way. He attacked me after I said we needed to talk about something. I was going to talk about the music and he almost killed me. He broke my jaw, he broke my teeth, broke bones in my face, in my shoulders, my hips. It took me about seventeen years to rebuild my life after that. I made it. I divorced him quick, had him thrown out of the house. He got served with papers, that was enough satisfaction. I didn't want our problems aired out to the public, because I've seen more Black men hurt and dragged to death and things like that. I suffered the injuries and I finally got well. I had rheumatoid arthritis, which I cured up by having my teeth pulled and going into the herbs.

Anybody can do it. You can always put your life back. You just can't keep looking backward, you have to look forward. Use your anger as the engine. Use that anger as the power to keep going. You get your anger out that way, in constructive ways. If you can do that, then you're doing a world of good at the same time. There are a lot of angry women out there, and I understand. The men simply don't know all the little things that they do to make them feel bad. Women carry that around because our memories are as good as an elephant. If something happened thirty years ago, we remember it.

SF: Anger is something a lot of women have to deal with.

CK: You can do it. Get the anger out of you and then all of a sudden you're not depressed anymore, because you're acting on that anger. You're using the anger as energy.

SF: Music is a good place to start too.

CK: Music is a good place to start, but start by dealing with whoever you deal with in a very straightforward honest way. That's power. Use your anger as a power to honestly deal with it. Don't ever say something you'd expect that other people want you to say. Speak your mind.

SF: So you're feeling good these days.

CK: Pretty much so, yeah. The trip is to get enough sleep and rest. That's the main thing.

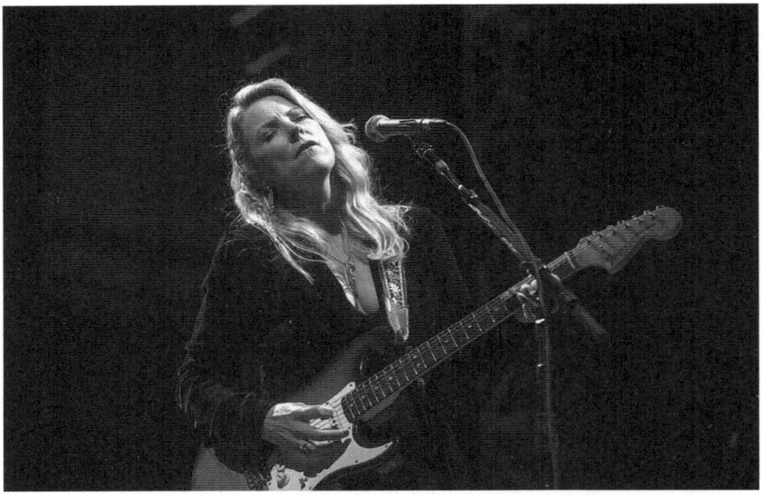

Susan Tedeschi

SUSAN TEDESCHI

When I caught up with Susan Tedeschi in 2006, we were both on tour. At the time, we each had young children at home; my son was about eight, and hers were even younger. Parenthood had changed our perspectives in ways we hadn't expected. As we reconnected, we realized we had far more in common than we ever knew.

Susan and I came up around the same time in the blues scene. I remember playing a show in Boston early in my touring days and seeing her in the audience. She was sitting at a booth with guitarist Ronnie Earl, whom we both admired. After the show, I went over to say hello. She was full of enthusiasm and praise—warm, open, and incredibly genuine. It was clear she loved the blues and was excited by our show.

I was so consumed by the grind of the road that I wasn't always present. The cycle of traveling, performing, and recovering from exhaustion blurred everything else. I started to notice how that lifestyle wore me down, not just physically, but emotionally. I saw older musicians who had been on the road forever, many of them burnt out, bitter, or battling addiction. I knew I didn't want that path for myself. So when I got pregnant, I welcomed the change. I stepped off the circuit and returned to Canada to raise my son and find the kind of love and stability I hadn't felt in years. It was the right decision, and one I've never regretted.

Around that time, Susan's career started soaring. Her album, *Just Won't Burn* (1998), had become a blues phenomenon, earning her a Grammy nomination and introducing her to a global audience. I'd hear her name all the time, see her on festival posters, and read glowing reviews. Then she married Derek Trucks, one of the most gifted guitarists of our generation, and together they became a true power couple in the roots music world. I'd be lying if I said I didn't feel a pang of envy. While I was doing laundry and going to playgroups, she was making records and performing with my heroes. The comparison game is a dangerous one, and I fell right into it.

When I saw she was touring in France in 2006, I reached out for an interview. By then, I was fully committed to documenting the stories of my fellow female guitarists, and I was eager to reconnect. Our conversation turned out to be one of the most cathartic and eye-opening interviews I'd ever done. It shattered so many of the illusions I'd built up in my mind.

Susan was just as I remembered: smiling, grounded, and humble despite all she had accomplished. She seemed genuinely happy to reconnect and was candid about the challenges of touring, motherhood, and the insecurities that come with balancing both. Even though she had reached a higher profile, I realized we were still walking similar paths, and managing similar struggles. I began to understand that the idea of someone "having more" is often just that, an idea. Everyone carries burdens, no matter how polished their life appears from the outside.

Susan's story began just outside Boston, where she grew up in a deeply musical household. She fell early for the gospel, blues, and R&B sounds that would shape her voice. She earned a degree from Berklee College of Music at just twenty years old, a remarkable accomplishment that reflected both her talent and her discipline. Early on, she performed with local musicians, refining her voice and guitar chops. With *Just Won't Burn*, she became one of the first female blues artists in decades to earn a gold record. The album's success was a turning point, not just for Susan, but for the visibility of women in modern blues.

In 2010, four years after our conversation, Susan and Derek Trucks formed the Tedeschi Trucks Band, a sprawling, genre-blending ensemble known for its soulful arrangements, impeccable musicianship, and electrifying live shows. Their debut album, *Revelator* (2011), won the Grammy for Best Blues Album. Since then, the band has released several acclaimed records and become one of the most beloved touring acts in the world. Through it all, Susan has remained a commanding vocalist, expressive guitarist, and a leader with heart.

As we wrapped up our interview in Paris, we talked about collaborating someday. Who knows, maybe it will still happen. What I do know is that our meeting reminded me of something essential: this business is full of illusions. We are all more alike than we often admit, and sometimes the best way to reconnect with our own story is to listen—really listen—to someone else's.

Despite the pressures of touring and recording, Susan continues to balance life as a musician, wife, and mother with remarkable grace. Looking back, I'm grateful for that conversation, not just for what it revealed about her, but for the clarity it brought to my own journey.

SUSAN TEDESCHI

— *The Interview* —

[2006]

SF: One of the most fascinating parts of this project is discovering how everybody balances kids and a career. It changes your life so much.

ST: I think about you all the time because I know you've gone through so many similar types of experiences like being on the road, touring with the child.

SF: And leaving him.

ST: Yeah, which is heartbreaking because they're like, "Mommy, where are you, why aren't you home?"

SF: Do you bring them on tour with you?

ST: I do, I have my mother-in-law and the two kids. They have their own bunks, and we all go on the bus together.

SF: How do you feel with your conflicting tours with your husband? Do you feel like you're under a lot of pressure?

ST: I feel really lucky because I'm in a position where I can sort of work my schedule around his. I find out when he's touring and with whom. For example, this year he's touring with three different groups: Derek Trucks Band, the Allman Brothers, and Eric Clapton. He's starting with Clapton this spring. They start rehearsing in the south of France and then they go out on a worldwide tour, a month on, a month off. So, on his month off he's working with his band or the Allman Brothers.

SF: He's working all the time. Do you have to chase him around?

ST: There are a couple of times this year when he'll be home, so I have taken time off for that time as well. Just to make sure that we're all home as a family together. But it's pretty ridiculous that only three times a year you're all home together as a family. We usually take December off, even though we end up doing a couple of fly-in dates here and there. It's hard on him, because he wants a wife who's around to help take care of him while he's on the road, because he's working so much. And I feel like I'm under a lot of pressure because I get stressed that I can't be there for him, and if I'm not with the kids enough I get stressed, and if I'm not doing my career, there's stress. There's always something. At the same time, I just try to keep cool and realize that I'm really lucky and blessed to do all three. As long as I can manage it, I will.

SF: How do you find that place of peace?

ST: Probably onstage, just playing, that's my release. Writing. And taking a shower away from the kids. But it's hard, because even the situation with my mother-in-law—who's really helpful and is around a lot—well, she's got kids of her own. Derek is her son, but she has kids who are younger, sixteen and thirteen, so they're still in school. I have to work around their schedules, too. I can't have her help me unless she's available. I should have a nanny, but I feel at this time it's really important for the kids to be around family.

SF: I think for the first couple of years it's very important that it's family.

ST: Maybe when they get older, I can expand out more, but Sofia is still a baby. Charlie would probably be all right by now, but Sofia is still so little and clingy.

SF: Up till about two years old they need to be with family. I kept Joe with me the whole time because I was nursing. I nursed him until he was two and a half (*laughs*).

ST: Two and a half!

SF: I just didn't know how to stop.

ST: I had to force myself to stop at eighteen months with him.

SF: I was wasting away too, because they eat you up.

ST: They take all your boobs away, too.

SF: It's quite a trip. We took him everywhere and he was like a little gypsy baby. After two-and-a-half he was fine, but still he has always stayed with my mom when I have to leave. My marriage didn't work out, so I never had the option of having his father around to pick up the slack.

ST: I'm so afraid of our relationship not lasting, because it is so tough. Because we never see each other.

SF: And then when you get together, there's all this pressure.

ST: Yeah, to make it incredible and have this moment.

SF: You're preaching to the choir.

ST: It's sure not easy.

SF: No, it's not, but I'm fascinated by it.

ST: Me too. But I do look up to you, because you're a very talented woman. I've always thought so, and I think it's great that you have Joe. That you didn't let it hold you back. I'm sorry, I feel like I'm going to cry now.

SF: Thanks, likewise.

ST: I don't know what people think. They think it's so glamorous doing what we do. But we do it just because we love it. Thank God we do.

SF: I'm really happy for your success, too. At first, I was very envious. I had this thing like a lot of people do, like, thinking, *Why her and not me? Why is she getting all the attention? Blah, blah, blah.* After a while you have to realize that we are all on our own paths and also, it's not necessarily any easier when you get singled out. Did you ever feel like that? The extra pressure, especially from blues musicians, because everybody's on about the same level and then when one person gets lifted up—

ST: I could say that I felt the same way about you for a while. Because everybody was talking about Sue Foley and I was envious of you a lot. I could see you were doing so great and you were getting to play with so many great people and at festivals and you're also so talented. I always thought that you were, to me, the best female guitar player I'd ever seen. Not to take anything away from anyone else, but I always thought that you really were even more true to your roots than them and you were reinventing a lot of stuff that I love, that people take for granted.

Then I heard you were pregnant and had a baby and I thought, *Wow, I want a family too*, because I didn't think it was going to happen. With Derek it was kind of an accident. It was a good accident, but at the same time, I didn't take advantage of my opportunities, like when I got the Grammy nomination.

For whatever neuroses I have, I think I do better when I have tons of stuff going on, when there's a lot of pressure. At the same time, I wasn't as comfortable with who I was, and I had a lot of pressure from other people who wanted me to do their songs. They wanted me to be more of a rock player, which I wasn't really into. It was a weird time, and I didn't take advantage of a lot of the opportunities I had at the time. In a way I am glad that I'm doing a slow build. I've had some success, but I don't feel like I've had huge success. You know, there are artists who have sold millions of records, and you don't even know who they are. For me I feel my success has been just having a family and being able to play with B. B. [King] or John Lee Hooker or whoever.

SF: To be able to just play with great musicians.

ST: Exactly. That's my gift, being lucky to be doing what I'm doing.

SF: It's funny, because when your career took off, that's when I first had Joe, and I was stuck at home with this baby, nursing, and hearing all about you. It was like, *whaaa, I'm stuck here with this baby*. But it's all turned out really good for both of us.

ST: I always hear from people that I need another guitar player in my band. My husband is like, "No, you do it yourself; you have your own style. I like how you sound like an old blues guy." So I always just tough it out. But I have thought if I was ever going to hire another guitar player, I've thought about calling you up and saying, "Hey, you wanna come out on tour?"

SF: You should do that sometime. That would be fun. I'm into collaborations right now. I'm doing a lot around this women guitar player thing.

ST: That's wonderful. It's amazing how many guitar women there are. It just eats me up when people are like, "You don't ever hear of women guitar players." I mean, I never heard of a Black guitar player until I was in college. I never knew Muddy [Waters] was a guitar player until later. I knew about John Lee Hooker, Muddy, and B. B. King but no one else. I never knew about Albert King. I never knew about Freddy King. I never knew about Otis Rush or Magic Sam. For me it was like finding a whole hockey team of all these Black guys who just kicked ass. It's the same thing with women guitar players: people don't realize they're out there. Maybe they don't sell millions of records.

SF: I think also we have not even been aware of each other. We've all been growing up side by side, playing and living these parallel lives. I was out there playing, and totally unaware that Joanna Connor and Debbie Davies were out there, and they were doing the same thing as me.

ST: It's true. The editors of these magazines and journalists have not even done enough research.

SF: Are you inspired by Derek?

ST: Oh yeah, he's incredibly innovative. The problem with Derek's playing is that he plays everything in open E. He doesn't play anything in standard tuning.

SF: But he's not always playing slide, is he?

ST: No, but even when he plays regular, he's in open E tuning. Even if he shows me something in open tuning, I don't play that way and I don't even think that way. Also, especially when he's playing slide, to me he sounds like a female gospel singer, on his guitar. Then he can play like Duane Allman, too. He's more of a world musician. He plays Pakistani music, he plays Latin music, and he plays John Coltrane. He's not afraid to tackle the masters. I would be petrified, but he's like, "Oh, here's a John Coltrane tune. Here's a Nusrat Fateh Ali Khan tune."

SF: Is he younger than you?

ST: Yeah, eight-and-a-half years younger.

SF: Do you feel it makes a difference? Or are you guys about on the same wavelength?

ST: On a lot of levels we are, but on some levels it's difficult. Because he has all the young hot women chasing him all the time. Sometimes I feel so inadequate, because I'm a mom with two kids. I have to work a lot harder at it, I guess.

SF: I can understand when you'd be feeling out of sorts about that. The way guy guitar players are perceived onstage and the way we get perceived is totally different. We don't get young guys chasing after us. I get fifty-five-year-old men.

ST: It's true. I get like, Buddy Guy, or Little Milton hitting on me. There's no one even in our age group.

I'm starting to get some of Derek's crowd because I'm married to him. I'm getting the hippie crossover crowd, which is cool. But really, it's still mostly fifty-five to seventy-five-year-old men hitting on me.

SF: Did you play much guitar on your new album [2005's *Hope and Desire*]?

ST: I didn't play any on it.

SF: Was that a bone of contention? Was it something you thought about or worried about?

ST: I was pregnant with Sofia when I signed the deal, and I needed to make the record within so many months. I was working on all this original material, and I was supposed to record with my band. I thought of Joe Henry because I liked his work with Solomon Burke, and Derek thought he'd be good too. Joe has really great sensitivity about soul music and blues, and it was really a pleasure to work with him, but he really insisted on having his guys in the studio. All the records that you hear by him have all the same guys on them.

They have a really nice ability for old soul records: old Stax and Muscle Shoals and stuff like that. Of course, we all like that stuff. Most musicians do.

We all like each other, except they were all dressed better than me. They'd all show up in their Prada shoes and bad-ass jeans, funky and cool, and cute. I was like, "You all look like a fashion magazine." This is only a few months after having Sofia, so I was trying to get my figure back. The record went really great, we did it in five days and basically cut everything live.

SF: How long have you been playing?

ST: I've been playing since 1994.

SF: At Berklee, were you studying singing?

ST: I studied classical voice. I was also in a gospel choir. I would study everything they gave me, all styles basically.

SF: Did you graduate?

ST: Yes, when I was twenty; I was really young. I started playing guitar when I was twenty-two or twenty-three.

SF: Did you take lessons?

ST: No, I had a boyfriend at the time, and I learned my basics through him. We listened to a lot of Jimmy Reed records and I would just build on it. Then Magic Sam or something like that. I was just trying to expand all the time. I'm still learning. I still feel like an amateur.

SF: So do I. I still take lessons.

ST: See, I've never really taken lessons. I would like to. I feel like my lessons are being on the road and doing it and being around great musicians and listening and soaking it all in.

SF: For me, sometimes my playing gets in a rut, so I was taking flamenco lessons. Because I was losing direction on the instrument, and I would play everything in the same three boxes, so it shook me out of a musical rut. I just started learning to play in open tuning because I want to learn some Jessie Mae Hemphill stuff. I've never played slide, and I've never played in open tuning.

ST: I used to play in open tuning. I played acoustic. One day I realized I was outside of first position. Then one day I woke up and realized I could play in every key, that was a big step. I got into playing in every key using the major scale and the minor pentatonic scale. That's pretty much all I use. It's fairly limited, but when I approach a solo, I sort of sing it.

SF: That's a good way to approach guitar soloing.

ST: I never think of it as just a bunch of notes. When I'm singing, I can't see the guitar but sometime, I look down and see shapes, certain shapes of chords or scales. I guess I use a lot of geometry. Like you said, you get into three boxes. I feel like sometimes I get in a rut and then other times

I surprise myself and play something I never expected, and it's like *hey, what was that?* I try not to focus on it too much.

SF: Who were your favorite guitar players early on?

ST: Ronnie Earl, Duke Robillard, Tim Gearen, Paul Rishell. I had a few lessons with Paul. He taught me to play in some open tunings. My song "Looking for Answers" is in open tuning. That's why when I met Derek, he really wanted to play that song, because it's in open tuning. That's so natural for him. I can play the chords, but when it comes to soloing, that's another thing altogether.

SF: Yeah, it screws my mind up. Do you find since you've had kids that it's harder to concentrate? I find it gets harder for the creativity to flow.

ST: It's hard to have time to yourself, as you know. Especially now with two kids. I want to be there for Charlie, and I want to be there for Sofia, I want to be there for Derek. It's hard to divide your time and to focus.

SF: You get an hour to write or something.

ST: Then, when you do that, you just want to take a nap.

SF: Do you think women guitar players and men guitar players play differently?

ST: Probably. I haven't really listened for the differences, maybe dynamically and emotionally. But then again it depends on the person. If you take Joanna Connor, she plays very aggressively, kind of like a guy. I think some women can play real pretty, and some don't. Maybe they don't play differently. It depends on the person.

SF: I think a lot of guys play with their sensitive, feminine sides too, like Ronnie [Earl], he can play really pretty and sweet.

ST: And dynamic. He was someone who I always thought was an underrated player. He's big in Boston but here, people hardly know him.

SF: I was changed after the first time I saw him.

ST: I was, too. I had never heard a guitar player like that. I had never seen someone do all those things at once. He was doing the Magic Sam rhythm and bad-assed leads at the same time, and he'd bring it way down and just build and build and build. He has so much versatility. Stylistically there was a lot of blues, but he played other things too.

SF: What do you think about women's roles in popular music today?

ST: Norah Jones is not the most normal popular star, I think it's a good thing that she's there. She has a very distinct voice and has some good songs, but she's not the norm. I feel like so much pop is just based on tits and ass, non-singing, and over-singing.

SF: Do you think women guitar players and men guitar players play differently?

ST: Probably. I haven't really listened for the differences but just because maybe dynamically and emotionally. If you take Joanna Connor, she plays very aggressively, kind of like a guy. I think some women can play really pretty and some don't. Maybe they don't play differently. It depends on the person.

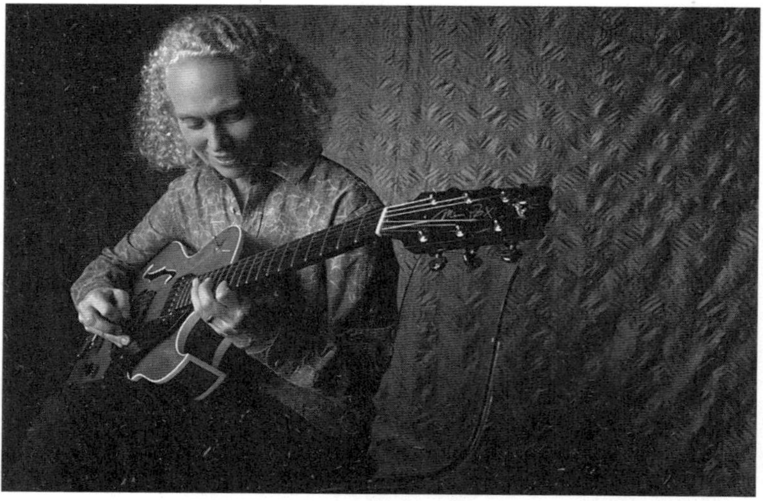

Mimi Fox

MIMI FOX

Mimi Fox comes across as grounded, honest, and straightforward. These qualities are reflected not only in her words, but in her approach to music. A jazz guitarist with decades of experience, she has built a career on her own terms, rooted in dedication, integrity, and an unwavering commitment to the craft.

Born in New York City and raised in a working-class, Italian-Jewish family in Queens, Fox first picked up the drums as a child before switching to guitar at the age of ten. Early on, she was captivated by both folk and jazz, sharpening her skills by listening to artists as varied as Wes Montgomery and Joni Mitchell. In her twenties, she headed west and eventually settled in the San Francisco Bay Area, where she became a central figure in the local jazz scene. Over the years, she has toured internationally, released more than a dozen albums, and performed alongside legends such as Joey DeFrancesco, Branford Marsalis, and Diana Krall. She is also a respected educator, having taught at institutions including the California Jazz Conservatory and Berklee College of Music.

When we spoke by phone, I was immediately struck by Mimi's warmth and sincerity. Her voice carried a calm confidence, thoughtful pauses, and the rhythm of someone who has spent a lifetime listening as deeply as she plays. She was generous with her insights and unafraid to speak plainly about both the beauty and the difficulty of her chosen path.

What stood out most in our conversation was her unflinching candor about what it really means to live as a jazz musician. Hers isn't a story of glamour or easy success, but one of grit, love, and endurance. We spoke about the underrepresentation of women in jazz guitar, and she pointed to the culture around jam sessions as a major factor. But Fox didn't let that stop her.

At the time of our interview, she had just finished the *La Guitara* tour, a collaboration with singer-songwriter Patty Larkin and several other female guitarists. For Fox, the experience wasn't about headlining or competition, but about community—about mutual respect and shared creativity. That attitude mirrors her approach to the instrument itself: she views music as conversation, not contest.

Fox describes jazz as a language, something that immediately resonated with me as a blues guitarist. Instead of relying on scales, she emphasizes phrasing and melodic expression, thinking in arpeggios, intervals, and shapes. It's a way of playing that speaks, rather than just sounds. "When you play," she told me, "you have to say something. Otherwise, it's just notes."

Her insight extends beyond technique. Fox is equally candid about the realities of a life in jazz—the long hours, the financial uncertainty, and the constant need for reinvention. She spoke about teaching as both a livelihood and a way to stay connected to younger musicians. "You learn as much from them as they do from you," she said. "It keeps you humble, and it keeps you growing."

For Fox, the heart of her artistry lies in perseverance. Jazz, she said, is "not about perfection, but about honesty." She sees her role as both musician and mentor, helping others find their own voices while continuing to refine her own. Her playing reflects that philosophy: lyrical, articulate, and deeply expressive.

She also spoke passionately about her influences—players like Joe Pass and Pat Martino, as well as great horn players whose phrasing she often tries to emulate. Her curiosity and reverence for the lineage of jazz are evident in everything she does. Yet, despite her technical mastery, she has no interest in flash or ego. For her, the purpose of music is connection.

Listening to her talk, I was reminded of the parallels between jazz and life itself: both require improvisation, listening, and trust. Fox's approach reflects a deep belief in intuition and communication—the idea that every performance is a dialogue, both with the audience and with oneself.

After decades in the business, she continues to balance performance, recording, and teaching with an unwavering sense of purpose. She has weathered the changing tides of the industry without ever compromising her artistic integrity. In an era when image and spectacle often eclipse substance, Mimi Fox remains refreshingly authentic.

Our conversation reaffirmed something I've learned from so many of the women I've interviewed: greatness isn't always loud or self-promoting. Sometimes it's quiet and steady, built day by day through patience and love for the craft. Mimi Fox has lived her entire career by that principle.

Her story is one of persistence, artistry, and faith in the music itself. She stands as a reminder that the guitar, like jazz, is a lifelong teacher, and that the truest players are the ones who never stop listening.

MIMI FOX

— *The Interview* —

[2005]

SF: You grew up in New York City. Is that where you formed your love of jazz?

MF: It's funny. Obviously, I'm a jazz musician, but I think of myself as more of a folk musician because I am very acoustic-oriented. I missed rock. I went folk, funk, blues, jazz, and classical, too. I studied classical guitar for a few years in my early twenties. I mainly plug in because I have to play with my band, but I really think of myself more acoustically. And I think of jazz as actually folk music. Not that folk music is jazz, but jazz is folk music, if you catch my drift.

SF: What kind of guitar are you playing if you're plugging in, like a hollow body?

MF: I have several really beautiful arch tops. I'm a Heritage Guitars endorser, so they have made me four or five really beautiful guitars over the years. I also have a custom by this builder out here in California that made me this really nice arch top with antique cello wood. It's just gorgeous. I usually use one of the Heritage, because it has more appropriate sounds, more bluesy, and more Wes Montgomery-ish, more standard jazz sound.

SF: You play with a really clean tone.

MF: That's what I'm saying. I'm a real natural player. I don't use any effects. I wouldn't know what to do with them.

SF: What kind of amp are you using?

MF: Well, it depends. Sometimes I don't even use an amp. Sometimes I go direct. For live shows, I just use a DI and go right into the house system a lot of times. That's usually when I'm playing solo. When I play with a group, I usually use either a Fender Deluxe—I love the old Deluxe Reverbs—or I also have had nice experiences with the Roland JC-120. I use both of those. But again, no, absolutely no effects.

SF: You have a little reverb.

MF: Yeah, a reverb set at a half.

SF: A half of one?

MF: A half of one, exactly.

SF: Oh, my. Wow. That's a brave way to play guitar.

MF: I don't know if it's brave. If you're saying that you can't hide behind any distortion units, I suppose so, and I've had students over the years that when I unplug all their paraphernalia, and I just hand them a little acoustic guitar, I say, "Now play the same thing." It's hard for them to play cleanly. If that's what you mean, yes. I think that that's true.

SF: Well, there's nothing to hide behind, right?

MF: Yeah. But, on the other hand, for me, I am such an idiot with effects, and pedals, and all that other shit. I tried it once, because I was doing some project, and I needed to do it, and I don't know what I'm doing. And I suppose if you don't dig the sound of something, you're not going to apply yourself and make it sound good. It works both ways. I don't like effects and they don't like me.

SF: I'm the same way. I don't get along with pedals, and I've been able to use a reverb pedal. That's about it.

MF: Well, everyone has their thing, but yeah, that's what I'm saying. I tend to hear things with a very clean sound, whether it's electric or acoustic. My ideas aren't old school, but my sound is. My approach and sound that way is more traditional.

SF: Did you never go into the fusion area?

MF: No, it's not my bag. I have friends who are wonderful who have done that fusion thing. I don't really relate to it. It doesn't really move me. It feels more cerebral to me. It's not that I don't respect the players or don't respect the music, but it's just not my bag.

SF: Just before I got ready for this interview, I listed the women jazz guitar players that I could name. Mary Osborne—do you know her?

MF: I did know her. I don't think she's alive anymore. And Emily Remler.

SF: Yeah. And Sheryl Bailey.

MF: I know Sheryl, yeah.

SF: Leni Stern, but Leni again is not traditional jazz.

MF: Oh, no, no. She's certainly not straight ahead. It's a different thing.

SF: Am I missing people here?

MF: No, you're hitting pretty much everybody I know. There was also a woman named Monnette Sudler. But, yeah, there's really not a lot. There's Jane Getter, a good player, but definitely not jazz. A little more on the rock end of the fusion thing. Good musician.

SF: How come there's so few?

MF: Jazz is a very male-dominated field, obviously. Women have been allowed to be singers. That was a medium that was open to them without them facing a gauntlet of all kinds of bullshit. I'd say vocalists and pianists, because those were instruments that women were allowed to play without being seen as a freak. Going down through the years, I'm sure there have been great women players on all instruments throughout the years, but when you're young, and you're first going to jam sessions, you're always going to be the only woman, other than vocalists, getting up and playing. It's a very nerve-wracking thing when you're young, to go to jam sessions, to play with more experienced players, to handle the tempos, and all that other stuff. A lot of young women—because of all sorts of issues, whether it's personal or sociological, and I think they tend to overlap—young women often don't feel like they have the confidence. And plus, there's the issues of getting mentoring where you're not either getting hit on, or all kinds of other stuff. So I think it's very difficult.

I was lucky to find a few good teachers over the years that were really supportive, without me having to go through all kinds of harassment or other extraneous stuff. But even those guys, in a situation with other men, would become—I don't know, sort of when guys get together. And they're very hard on each other too, so don't get me wrong, it's not like I'm saying jazz is easy for anybody. It isn't.

For women, you have the added burden of just being a woman. I used to buddy up with different women players, horn players, sax, trumpet, and we'd go out together, when we had the luxury of doing that. It would give us the opportunity to be together and not feel like we were quite so isolated. These different issues, I'm sure they affect women in other fields, too. If you're one of a very small amount of women in the field, you're going to have to contend with a lot of stuff.

I think it's a very uncomfortable environment for a lot of young women, and they just simply make the choice. *Who needs it?* Look at it this way, I'm a smart person. If someone had told me years ago, "Look, you're going to practice six to seven hours a day for twenty years, you're going to make shit for money. You're going to have to endure all kinds of bullshit from guys, sometimes jealousy from other women. Let's be honest. You're going to have to endure all this kind of shit. And the music that people dig in this country is not jazz." Jazz has now fallen below classical music in terms of what people buy, at least in the States. I think classical music is like 3.2 percent, and 1.7 percent of the people buy jazz. If someone had told me that years ago, that's pretty daunting.

I should have listened to my high school guidance counselor, and become a lawyer. He's like, "Mimi, you like to argue. You should be a lawyer." Whatever. I am glad I didn't, because it's worked out well for me. But man, I have paid some fucking dues, all the smoky bars and all the stupid shit I've had to do over the years just to make things happen.

Anyway, with all those things, I can see a lot of young women just saying, "Jesus, who the hell needs this?"

SF: Yeah. How badly do you want this?

MF: It's daunting to most *guys*. If you are good at what you do, and you're persistent, there are opportunities. But it's still very competitive and it's cutthroat. It's not for everybody. You have to have a certain disposition. I, fortunately, am the type of person that when adversity hits, I am tenacious, and I'm stubborn, and I just hang in there. And there's not really anything else in my life that I love this way, so I made this choice to hang with it.

SF: I grew up in the blues, and I don't know what percentage of record buyers buy blues records, but it's got to be down there with jazz.

MF: It's probably above jazz. I think blues is a little more accessible to some people, but still, blues also suffers like jazz from the fact that the roots of it are Black. There's still the stigma of the music not being taken seriously, because of the roots of the music, which jazz has, too. I get tired with the rockers calling me dude: "Dude, you shred." It's like, *Oh, okay. Is that what I do? Great. Okay.*

SF: When was the point when you thought your career was coming around until it's a little more easy to do now? Or is it easier?

MF: Obviously, you don't just wake up one day and have everything click. It's an ongoing process. In the past ten years, I've had a very active recording career, and that has really helped. I've been through a lot with the different record companies. I happen to like the one that I'm with now, Favored Nations, they've been really good to me. And Steve Vai has really been very supportive of me, not just as a player, but personally. That's meant a lot.

Having an active recording career, getting a lot of publicity because of that, and the nonstop touring has made a big difference. It's enabled me. Also, my teaching has helped, for instance, with my book, and I'm writing another book for Mel Bay.

All of these things are other sources of income that enable me to turn down gigs that I would've actually needed to do years ago, and now I don't need to. I have been able to be much more selective, and just go to the festivals, and concerts, and clubs that I want to play, and turn down some of the stuff I don't want to do. I also have a manager who's worked his ass off for me for over ten years.

I've been doing this *La Guitara* thing with Patty Larkin. The tour that I was on was Patty Larkin, Kaki King, and Muriel Anderson. We did some of Muriel's stuff, some of mine, some of Patty's.

That's been tons of fun. For all of us, it's enabled us to reach different audiences, because the agent was very creative where he booked us. We played jazz clubs, we played folk festivals, we played concert halls, we played performing arts things. And I loved all the women. We really hit it off and had a lot of fun.

SF: Did you collaborate too?

MF: We did a lot of collaboration, yeah.

SF: Patty thought of that idea, and I heard about *La Guitara* just as I was thinking about doing a similar tour.

MF: Did she beat you to the punch?

SF: On the touring front, for sure. I've done some dates up here with other women guitar players. I've been approached by other groups of women who wanted me to play. I'm thinking, what is going on right now that all this is coming out now at the same time?

MF: Oh, yeah, something gets going. When Patty approached me, I had just gotten back from New York and done a few dates at Sweet Rhythm, this club in the Village. It was a lot of fun with Jane Getter, this fusion player. And Leni Stern was supposed to do it, but Leni had to go out of town suddenly, so she couldn't do it. Sheryl Bailey couldn't do it, because she was out of town. But Jane and I talked about the idea of touring as three or four women, and we were just going to do jazz. We all had slightly different—actually very different—approaches to jazz. But we thought maybe people would dig it.

Next thing you know, I get a thing from my manager saying he had gotten a letter from Patty's promoter. It all came at the same time. Maybe we just feel the world has come to a point where they'll be really turned on and excited about it, including men.

Throughout the years, when I do clinics at colleges and stuff, a lot of young women will ask me, "Well, Mimi, what advice can you give us?" And it's find the people—not find the *women*, but find the *people* who will support you. Yes, I've had to deal with all kinds of sexist schmucks, but I have also dealt with a lot of men who have been really, really supportive. I always say to young women: find the people who will support you to be the best of who you are. And if someone has a bad attitude, lose them immediately. Just lose them. Don't spend time worrying if they're right about, *oh, you shouldn't play*, or, *you should take up knitting*, or whatever the fuck they say to you. Just hold your ground. Anyway, it was neat to see all these guys coming up and saying, "Wow, this really blew my mind. This was great." I think that's cool.

SF: I found the same situation when we did some shows up here. I did it with Ellen McIlwaine and—

MF: Oh, I love Ellen.

SF: Yeah, and another young player named Rachelle van Zanten, slide player, really good. I found the men were really supportive, and it brought more women out to the shows as well. Often at guitar shows, you don't see as many women in the audience. I think it's just taking time for the instrument to become acceptable for them that they could actually get off on it. But, to actually see another chick playing, they're going, *wow*. And now, I'm seeing little girls coming out, like twelve-year-old girls, and even younger, and they're all like, "I'm going to be a guitar player." I'm like, "Wow, this is awesome." Ten years ago, I didn't see that, and I didn't notice that there was a community of women players. But we're all out here, and we didn't really know

about each other. I knew maybe a few historical figures and a couple of women that were in the blues scene, but I couldn't name anybody else.

MF: Oh, I know.

SF: And you always thought you were the only one.

MF: One of the great things about hanging together is realizing, first of all, to be on a tour, and again, not have to deal with some of the BS that I've had to deal with guys. Touring is hard. We did a grueling tour, did like eighteen cities in twenty-one days. It was really tough. And the two days that we had quote-unquote off, we were flying, so that's hardly an off day, as you know. And we did a lot of interviews and stuff. But to be with a bunch of pals, it was really a nice experience for me.

And I've never been one of these jazz musicians that's just in this jazz box. I've always listened to a lot of different kinds of music. I love a lot of different kinds of music. I loved each night hearing Patty do her folk stuff. She's a beautiful songwriter. We did some collaborating together, and she played on some of my stuff. Muriel, each night, I didn't know what she was going to do, and same with Kaki. It was really fun. I enjoyed it a lot.

SF: How did you grow up? Did you have siblings? Were you inspired by your family?

MF: I was lucky. We moved a lot, and my life was hard growing up. There were a lot of different personal problems my parents had, a lot of different things going on in the house. But one thing that was good is that my mom was a singer, and sang jazz up until the time I was about twelve, semi-professionally. I heard Ella Fitzgerald, Billie Holiday, Sarah Vaughan, all of the greats, Dinah Washington. I heard a lot of the great jazz singers. And my dad had all these old jazz recordings, Dixieland recordings, so I heard that. My mom also loved classical music, so I had a great musical education from the two of them. My brother and sister were into rock, and pop stuff, and Motown, and Aretha.

SF: Are you the youngest?

MF: Yeah, I'm the youngest. Growing up, I really heard everything in the house. From the time I was five or six, I was picking out things on the piano. Then, when I was about nine, I had really been taking my mom's soup pots, and I would take some spoons, and just bang along to my dad's Dixieland recordings. Finally, my mom got me a little snare drum when I was about nine, and I love that.

When I was ten, I really liked the Monkees, which was really silly when I think about it now. It was just this thrown-together band to imitate the Beatles. I didn't know that at the time. I was watching their TV show, and asked my mom if I could get a guitar. And man, that was it. I pretty much stopped playing with my friends. I basically just sat with all my brother and sister's records and would play along until I got it.

SF: Nobody talked you into it?

MF: I had an older cousin who showed me a few chords, but literally he gave me two lessons. He was twenty. He came back a month later and he was like, "Wow, I don't really have anything else to show you." I got a little book, and I taught myself bar chords and stuff. I really picked it up fast. I slept with my guitar. My brother and sister always teased me. I really think it was a way that I dealt with some of the chaos that was going on around me, was that I had this instrument. It really did become a friend. Certainly, that was my relationship that I established. And I still feel like I have this ongoing other relationship.

SF: It's true, isn't it? For other relationships with your partners or whatever, that's hard for them to understand sometimes.

MF: My girlfriend's pretty understanding about it. But it's definitely having another relationship. I wouldn't fault anyone if they had a problem with it, but I couldn't be with someone that did, you know what I mean? It's a very big part of my life, and I've been playing for a really long time.

For many years, I was self-taught. I went from learning folk stuff, and some Beatles, to then getting into blues and funk. When I was a teenager, I did play in a funk band, I even played in a bluegrass band. I did a lot of different things.

Meanwhile, in different schools I was at, they didn't have guitar in the orchestra, but they had drum, so I was playing drums in junior high and high school jazz band, and also played tympani. I had five or six bands. I was playing music all the time as my thing. I'm glad that I've had a lot of listening in a lot of different types of music, because I think it's made me a more earthy player.

SF: Is jazz something you just gravitate to when you become really good?

MF: I was playing in a top-forty band before I moved to California, and I was just getting so bored with stuff. I still love a lot of the early music that I played when I was younger. But, harmonically speaking and melodically and rhythmically, well, I always loved jazz. But jazz guitar seemed really hard. I was playing drums in jazz groups, I had that feeling for jazz. Because my parents, that was their generation, I definitely grew up with a sense of what that was all about.

When I came to California in 1980, I met Bruce Forman, who's a great bebop player. He was also mixing in the blues and all kinds of stuff in his playing. I thought, man, that's what I want. I'm never going to be a singer. I just don't happen to have that vocal gift. If I could express myself the way Bruce did, then it's like I'm singing with my guitar. That has really been my goal all along: to find a way to communicate emotionally and musically. But it's not easy. It's definitely not playing a bar chord. It's hard.

SF: No, jazz is an intellectual exercise.

MF: There's a lot of studying that goes into it. I studied classical guitar for a few years, and I love it, I have a lot of respect and admiration for the music. But I found that having to play the piece the same way each time, with only maybe a few ornamentations here and there—again, I got bored. I'm a restless person. One of the things I love about jazz is that it gives me the freedom, even if I'm playing a song that I may have played a million times, I'm not going to play it the same way. I get to improvise on it, and do different things on it. And I love the connection to the blues. I love the blues, and I feel like that's the essence of jazz, that was the foundation of jazz.

I think many roads do lead to jazz. Just the study of the harmony, if you study Duke Ellington or Billy Strayhorn, or even Rodgers and Hart, and Gershwin, and Irving Berlin, you're going to be playing some beautiful pieces of music. All of my favorite songwriters in the pop thing have studied jazz, and they have internalized it: Sting, Paul Simon, Joni Mitchell, Bonnie Raitt, James Taylor, all these people love jazz. You can hear it in some of their best songs. You can hear the influence of some of these other composers.

It's something that is part of our history. I'm going to give you my political commentary, but it's one of the few things we can be proud of as Americans right now is the blues and jazz. It's one of our few Indigenous art forms.

SF: You put out one book called the *Guitar Arpeggios Studies*. I was talking to Carol Kaye, because she teaches jazz guitar as well. She said that to learn proper soloing in jazz, you need to work on arpeggios, not on scales. Is that right?

MF: Well, obviously, you're using both, but what a lot of people do is they learn all these scales. I've had a lot of rock guys come to study with me. The problem is they have all these scales and all these chops, but they don't know how to apply it. When they play, they may not be playing the wrong notes, but they're not playing any real musical lines—because they make these run-on sentences with the scales. The arpeggios are basically just the notes in the chord, right? If you can outline that as you're playing through song, then when you go to add the scale tones, you actually have some control over the sound that you're creating. Otherwise, people just keep playing notes until they land on a right note. Oftentimes, this gives their playing this rambling, ambiguous quality, whereas if you actually learn your arpeggios, you start making lines. You actually start making music.

The arpeggios are pretty important, but if you only played arpeggios, it would be boring, because you'd be playing exactly what the chordal person is playing.

SF: When Carol mentioned it, I was like, "Oh, of course." Because everybody's so intimidated by jazz, and you think you've got to learn a million scales. It's like oh, who can learn them?

MF: Jazz is a lot of work, and it isn't like sitting and picking up a Beatles song from the record, that's for sure. However, people hear a lot of notes being played, and they hear fast tempos and stuff, but that's not all of what jazz is about. First of all, it's about the rhythm, and it's about the swing, and it's about being into the groove, because every style of music has a pocket. For me, regardless of genre, if you go out and hear a group and they're really tight, and they're happening, it's all about the rhythm being there. It's all about the bass player, and the drummer, and hopefully the guitar player, and whoever else is in the group. Everybody's locked in together, and you have this great pocket, and that's really what makes music happen. With jazz, I think it is learning a language. It's a deep language. People get intimidated, because you can't just take a few lessons and say, *oh, gee, now I can play jazz*. You know what I mean?

But you can't do that with any other style of music either. And the fact of the matter is, I have a lot of friends in jazz, they make fun of rock players, and think they're idiots, and yadda, yadda. But I'll tell you something, if I were going to play rock and really get into it, I don't even know how to fucking bend a note, Sue. There are stylistic things, and there's a language for every music. I have absorbed the blues very well, and that comes out in my jazz playing. I've immersed myself in it. But if I wanted to go on the road and play with Eddie Van Halen, it's going to take me a long time to absorb that language. And you can't absorb the language by taking a few lessons or just reading a book. It's like, if I want to learn Spanish, I can play tapes in my car, or I can go to Mexico for two years. You know what I mean?

Jazz is hard, but it's something that you can learn. Unfortunately with jazz, and to some extent with blues, you don't hear it as often. When you turn on the radio, or you listen to the soundtrack to the movie, most of the time it's pop and rock that you're hearing. It's something people aren't as used to hearing.

SF: Who are the blues players you like?

MF: Oh, I go back a million years. I like going back and hearing Robert Johnson, and Josh White, and Big Mama Thornton. I like the real early, Ida Cox. I like the early, real early stuff. That's what gets me off.

Every one of my albums always has some blues on it. Part of the reason I just don't get the fusion thing is because, for me sometimes, it's not referencing the blues. Again, this is not everybody; there are some players that do. If you're going to be a jazz musician and you never reference the blues, it's losing an essential part of the vocabulary of the music.

SF: Do you find you get more from listening to other guitar players? I know a lot of jazz players, and a lot of guitar players pick stuff off from horns.

MF: Yeah, I have more of the latter. Obviously, of the guitar players that I like, of course for solo stuff was Joe Pass. And like I said, I had the opportunity to study with him a little when I was younger. But I love Pat Martino, Wes Montgomery, Grant Green are three of my favorites, and they're very rooted in the blues.

SF: Charlie Christian?

MF: Oh, sure. He's the great granddaddy of the music, for jazz guitar. But, yeah, I do listen more to horn players. And as I was mentioning to you earlier, I also listen to a lot of vocalists, because when I play, a lot of times I mouth the notes that I'm playing. Even when I play very fast phrases, I'm hearing the notes go by in my head.

SF: Right. Do you think being a woman has allowed you to express things that maybe guy players have more difficulty?

MF: A lot of guys I admire who now have become friends, and have been real supporters of my music, and fans of my music, one of the things they've said that they're really struck by is the emotionalism, if that's a word, of my playing. There may be a way that, as a woman, I'm less fearful of being, letting it all hang out. That's who I am as a player. I live close to the edge in that way, I go for things. I've had people say I'm a very soulful, very passionate player. That's what I'm striving for, because that's who I am as a person, and that's a way to express myself.

I think a lot of men become musicians because they're trying to express things that perhaps within constraints of certain cultures, men aren't as free, or don't feel they're as free to express. A guy may sing a ballad about someone that he loves, that may be hard for him to express in another way. For all of us in different cultures, obviously, music is a medium, and it is a weight of expression.

I teach also, so I certainly have my academic side. But when I'm playing, I try to get away from that. I try to connect with the heart of the music. There's a real tendency, especially for jazz players, that people think it's too cerebral, and they think there's too much thinking going on, and too much stuff. No one should have to be thinking of all the hip polytonal ideas I'm using. They should be just digging the story. You know what I mean?

Steve Vai said to me, "I love your technique, and I love the notes you're playing. But more than anything, I love the way you're playing your notes." And that means a lot to me, because that's someone who's not a jazz aficionado, but someone who's an intelligent, obviously gifted musician, and that's what's connecting with him.

That's how I am. When I listen to other people, not just jazz artists, that's what I'm listening for. I'm not worried about, are they having a flawless performance? I'm not worried about, is their three-part harmony tight as can be? I'm listening for the story. I want to be moved.

SF: Do you still practice for that long? Six hours a day?

MF: No, I haven't practiced that long for a long time. I'm playing so much that I don't need to. I have to monitor things, because I want to be able to keep doing this for the rest of my life and not burn out, or have tendonitis, or arthritis, or all kinds of other problems that people get.

SF: Do you have any problems right now?

MF: I have had problems over the years, but I've managed. I've been very careful. Obviously, I'm careful with my hands, and my arms, and my shoulder. I am real healthy, and I am very active, and I do yoga, and I've got a whole series of things that I do to take care of myself. That's made a big difference. I'm also extremely careful, and I don't mess around. I don't do what I used to do, which is practice hours and hours without a break.

What I've discovered is the trick to keep switching positions, right? Sometimes I play with a pick. Sometimes I play finger style. Sometimes I stand, sometimes I sit. Sometimes I play like a little yogi: I sit cross-legged, and just hold the guitar. What happens is when people find a new position they like, then they only use that position, and then that position becomes an overused position, and then they get new injury. It's good to change up, is what I've discovered.

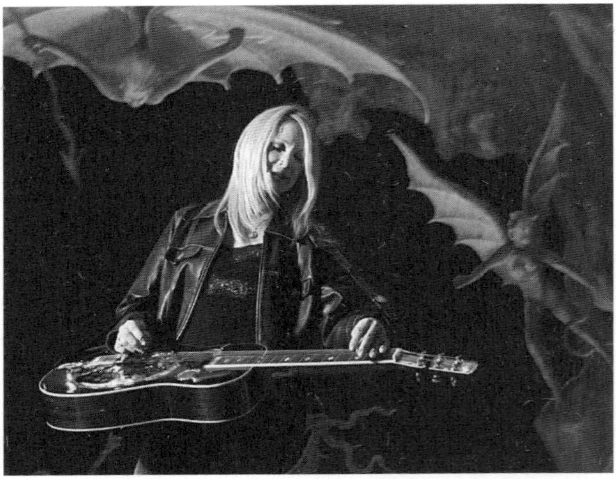

Cindy Cashdollar

CINDY CASHDOLLAR

I'm happy to call Cindy Cashdollar my friend. We've played many shows together, and I can personally attest to her exceptional talent.

We met in the early 1990s, when she had just moved to Austin to join the legendary Western swing band Asleep at the Wheel. After getting to know her, I realized I had actually seen her years earlier as she had a long-standing gig with trad-jazz icon Leon Redbone. I remembered watching Leon perform in Kansas City and being struck by the presence of a female steel guitarist in his band. I was mesmerized by her grace and quiet authority on stage.

Cindy is incredibly down-to-earth, and she exudes confidence, especially when she's performing. She's strikingly beautiful, with long blonde hair, and now, in her sixties, she commands immense respect from her musical peers. Over the years, she has toured with Van Morrison, recorded with Bob Dylan, and has shared the stage with some of the most influential voices in roots and Americana music. She remains deeply involved in her music community, regularly appearing at guitar festivals, workshops, and residencies.

For a time, I was part of a group with Cindy and a powerhouse lineup of female musicians called *Texas Guitar Women*. We played shows throughout Texas, and Louisiana. Sharing the stage with her was always a joy. She's poised, prepared, and a consumate professional. Cindy arrives early, knows her parts inside and out, and has the best tone in the world. When it's time for her to solo, she owns the stage.

The guitar world has traditionally been a challenging space for women to break into, but Cindy never seemed to struggle for acceptance. She didn't demand special treatment; she simply earned her place through excellence. The way to gain respect in this business is to show up, be prepared, and stand shoulder to shoulder with everyone musically. You don't ask for favors, and you don't act like you don't belong. You just show up and deliver. Cindy does that, every single time.

Born in Woodstock, New York, Cindy grew up surrounded by a rich musical environment. She gravitated naturally toward the guitar, and her love for roots music led her to become one of the most sought-after steel players in the world. When we did our interview for this book, she was living in Austin and freelancing. She has since re-married and moved back to Woodstock with her husband, renowned luthier Harvey S. Citron.

Our conversation felt less like an interview and more like two friends talking shop. I focused on her upbringing, her musical path, and what it takes to sustain a lifelong career in music. She spoke with clarity and insight about balancing relationships with the demands of touring. Everything about our talk was easy and natural, just like Cindy herself.

Cindy Cashdollar embodies quiet strength, great musicianship, and professionalism. She continues to raise the bar for all of us who play.

CINDY CASHDOLLAR

— *The Interview* —

[2008]

SF: Is Cashdollar your real name?

CC: Yes.

SF: Is it Dutch or something?

CC: Mohawk Indian. But I'm not sure which strain we are. I met another Cashdollar a while ago, Robert Cashdollar, who grew up on the Mohawk reservation not far from Woodstock. And then someone else had met another Native American with Cashdollar as his name. When I used to travel I used to try and find other Cashdollars in the phonebook, and I did. A lot of them were older people who had no internet; they went down to the local courthouse and tried to trace records back. It's more prevalent in the northeast than anywhere, like Tennessee and Pennsylvania. Yeah, I did not make it up.

SF: How'd you get into the guitar? Was there somebody in the family that brought it to you?

CC: No, I think it was just the times. Growing up in Woodstock, where at that time—that was before the festival, and so it wasn't a commercialized town at that point—there were so many artists, real artists, like a sandal-maker's shop. It was just a tiny little village which was half farmers and locals, and half artists and craftsmen. There was a village center, and you would hear people just sitting on the village green playing guitar. Then of course folk music was very popular then, and I would see people on TV like Joan Baez. I figured that would be really fun to do, and it was, but I never had any designs on doing it for a living.

My mom found me a guitar teacher, and she would take me into Woodstock and see a lot of music. I saw Odetta when I was thirteen. She made such an impression on me, as did all of them. There were these mini music festivals called sound-outs, that you could go to on this woman's farm outside of Woodstock. I was going to those. My girlfriend's father would drop us off at the entrance, and there would be Paul Butterfield Blues Band.

SF: So you just grew up around that environment, that's cool.

CC: Yeah, with a lot of folk musicians that are very well known. People don't really think of many singers from the northern states. You always think it's New York City, but there was a lot of bluegrass, country, and folk, just all kinds of music. I'm going back in a couple of weeks.

SF: To see your guy?

CC: Yeah, yeah.

SF: How's that working out?

CC: Well, it's working out great, he just showed up on my doorstep last Thursday. I was sitting home practicing, and heard a knock on the door and there he was.

SF: Cool.

CC: I know. Cause we were not able to see each other until I get up to Woodstock towards the end of the month. But you know how it is, when you're far away.

SF: How long were you married?

CC: Fourteen years. It was really hard, especially being gone so much with Asleep at the Wheel. Then his father got very ill and passed away, and then right after that my father got very ill and passed away. There was that constant crisis in between both of us working really hard, and instead of kinda pulling together, we just pulled apart. The whole thing came crashing down. It's really tough in this business, as you know, to keep a relationship together. It's hard to find somebody who's understanding, who's willing to let you have your space to be social when you have to be social, and be in the background. They come to the gigs and they're just kind of there, and you're working. I mean, you're still working when you're talking to people before and after the show. They have to be aware of what you do, every aspect. It's very difficult to find people who understand that. Male or female.

SF: I agree.

CC: You and I have both worked with men most of our lives. You see the wives, most of them are just like "Stand by Your Man," steadfast. They pick up all the slack when the men are on the road. It's hard to find good partner material. If you're single, it's very difficult when you're meeting people, like, well, do they like me just because I'm out there playing?

SF: I'm on stage, but who are they really seeing here? Exactly, you get a lot of that.

CC: They all think it's great in the beginning, and then it all comes crashing down. It's like, "We were supposed to go away that weekend. You were supposed to come with me to my brother's wedding." *Well, sorry, you know, I gotta tour.* It's really tough.

SF: Yeah, my God. Tough, if not impossible it seems, just to find people who relate. And then if you go with another musician, that poses other problems, because there's competition, and there's jealousy, or whatever.

CC: It's hard to juggle everything. It's like, *oh yeah, I'm supposed to be playing music, too?*

SF: I noticed your first band was an all-woman band, Whiskey Before Breakfast.

CC: Yeah, that was really fun.

SF: Was it easy for you to make the transition of just playing and hanging with guys? Were you always comfortable in the company of men?

CC: I moved from Woodstock to Florida when I graduated high school. I lived in Fort Lauderdale for a while, and Key West, and hooked up with these guys who played some really cool acoustic. I was playing guitar, kind of like country blues, finger-picking-style guitar and so I hooked up with them. That was my very first legitimate gig, just this wretched little happy-hour bar right on the beach in Fort Lauderdale. We worked quite a bit, and so it was pretty comfortable to work with them, especially being my first band and being around bars. It was good to have guys around—then you didn't get all the idiots hitting on you, because they couldn't figure out why you were playing guitar.

I always got along with men, so the transition from that to the all-women band didn't really feel like a transition in that way, and going from an all-female band to working with the John Herald Band, there was another woman in John Herald's band who played the fiddle. Then after that started the all-male thing. There were times where it was really tough. I think Asleep at the Wheel, they hadn't had a female musician. And so, that was really tough—there was one guy that was really pissed off, that there was this chick in the band. *Can't swear, can't screw around, can't*—you know, that kind of thing. When I joined the Wheel there was a little trepidation there, too, it was like I crashed the party on the bus. After a while if you're comfortable they're comfortable, and it works to their advantage. The guys who are married or have girlfriends, if they're on the road and they have to get a Valentine's Day present or a birthday present, I was there shopping with them, trying on clothes, suggesting things.

SF: Were there ever like times where you ended up having romance unexpectedly?

CC: Yeah, but that just doesn't work.

SF: No?

CC: It never works, yeah. These things backfire. They're just so political. And then if you're with somebody in the band, you're with them all the time, so—

SF: It's a drag. I made that mistake several times.

CC: It's so easy [to do], because there are people there that understand what you do, and then [you] have that support with you all the time on the road. But it does get ugly when things get ugly.

SF: Do you know any other female slide players or guitar players that you really like?

CC: Well, you, of course. I've always admired your style of playing, a definite style. There's a lot of blues-oriented guitar players, but you definitely have your own style. Carolyn Wonderland's the same way. Bonnie Raitt, I really admire her playing, and her tone. Rory Block. Are you talking about female guitar players or slide players?

SF: Either.

CC: I mean, there's not a whole bunch that come to mind, really. There's the great rhythm players, like Chris O'Connell who plays rhythm guitar in Asleep at the Wheel, she was a wonderful rhythm player, she was just a kick-ass, in-your-face solid rhythm guitar. Even Shawn Colvin is a wonderful guitar player; I love the way she accompanies herself. And Patty Griffin, she's wonderful. You hear it right away, you know who it is. They have honed their guitar chops to accompany themselves. I think they all started out as a solo act, so that's why their sound so identifiable.

And I know Ellen McIlwaine. I haven't heard her in a long time. When I was really young, she played near Woodstock, I think she lived up there. I started hearing about her when I was thirteen or fourteen. I was maybe twenty when I heard Rory. I took a couple of guitar lessons from her, because I really loved that style of playing.

It's very rare that I will see a female slide player, let alone steel player—that's even more of an anomaly.

SF: Are you in touch with Marian Hall?

CC: All the time. Yeah, she was a phenomenal steel player. Barbara Mandrell was a wonderful steel player, and it was Marian Hall that influenced her. You remember Barbara from being on the national network shows. There are Hawaiian players, strictly Hawaiian, that were wonderful steel guitar players. But Marian was the first steel player that I'm aware of that was playing all that cool Western swing rockabilly. She was contracted with a couple record companies, but she's on countless recordings.

Marian had a family, she had kids and a husband. He was never very supportive, but she nailed every gig she auditioned for. I still think it's a little tough gaining acceptance in the business, in a lot of instances.

SF: You've just stuck to your guns and been good at your craft.

CC: If you're serious about what you do, then that comes through with anything. I think Marian has told me, "I always showed up on time, I was always in tune, and I always played to the singer." Those were her three rules. If you're a professional about what you do, then it's not as hard, after a while.

SF: That's what Carol Kaye said, too. She said in the '40s there wasn't as much sexism as later on, like the '70s and '80s.

CC: That's an interesting comment. How come?

SF: She was a bebop player and all the beboppers didn't make any comments at all about the woman thing. It was always about the level of musicianship. Because she was, like you say, she was a pro, and showed up on time, was never drunk, and she worked hard and she was good. She said she noticed sexism more in the '70s, and especially more lately, as video changed the perspective on music, away from the playing and singing to a more visual context.

CC: Definitely, definitely.

SF: Yeah, but it seems now it's like we've gone back in time, or gone back to where women are focusing more on their looks. What you see on videos and what kids are exposed to now is just so different.

CC: I often wonder, is it harder for a woman as she ages to keep playing live, than it is for a man. You know?

SF: I think it depends what style of music you're in, for one thing.

CC: They're out there: Emmylou [Harris], Bonnie [Raitt], Marcia Ball, Koko Taylor. I mean, everybody's out there doing it.

SF: But you're citing roots artists. What happens to the pop stars when they're in their '50s and '60s?

CC: I don't think they're gonna worry, because they made so much money. Where with roots music, it is probably true to what Carol Kaye said about the genre of music—but she was so good, I mean bebop, that's serious. They know a poser when they see one. You have to have your shit together.

In Asleep at the Wheel, I certainly wasn't a steel player when I joined that band. Although when Ray Benson heard my demo tape, he said, "Well, I can tell you're a dobro player but you're not a steel player, but I'll give you six months." He saw that I was trying so hard, and working my ass off. I think the rest of the band did, too, and so you gotta be serious, you know?

SF: Oh yeah, you woulda went fast in that, for sure.

CC: Would have been left out on some highway somewhere.

SF: How did you take care of yourself on the road when you were out there so much? Did you have any special regimen you follow?

CC: No, nothing. I wish I was one of those who get up and jog, go to the exercise room in the hotel. But I didn't. I was going out to the bus blurry eyed at 5:00 a.m., seeing all these executive women working out on the treadmill, they've had eight hours sleep. But I was never one to eat a truck-stop cheeseburger at two in the morning. I didn't indulge in too much.

SF: You don't drink that much.

CC: I would drink but not get drunk. I was one of those people that couldn't smoke pot because I would get so hypnotized; I couldn't move one foot in front of the other. I'm an insomniac; I don't sleep very good. And sleep is what you need, bottom line. I think because of that, I realized I had to watch everything else. If we were in a town and we had the day off, I would try walking around, do something outside, whenever I could.

SF: Nothing too strict, just common sense.

CC: I think it took the pressure off. There was enough pressure.

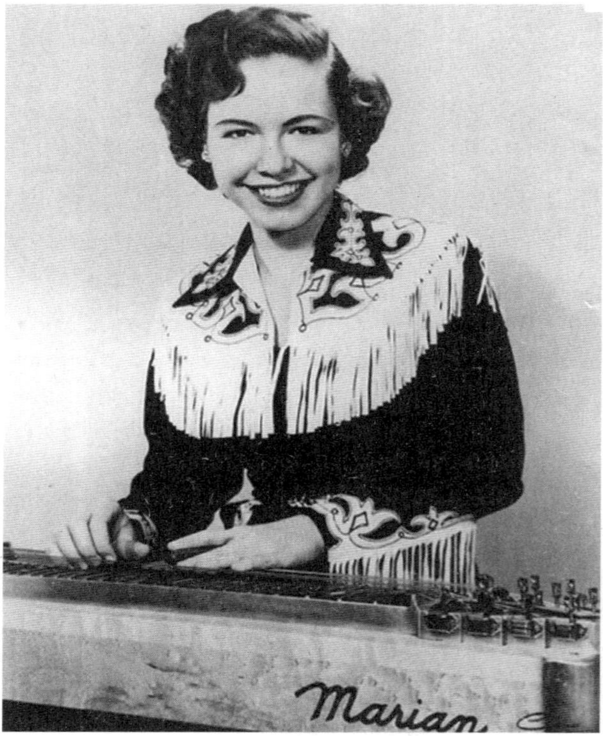

Marian Hall

MARIAN HALL

I first learned about Marian Hall through Cindy Cashdollar, who was close with her until Marian's passing in 2006. Born and raised in Los Angeles, Marian was a trailblazer in 1950s and 1960s country music, playing steel guitar alongside some of the most legendary names in the genre.

Her musical journey began early. By the time she and her sister Joanie were preteens, they had formed their own act, the Saddle Sweethearts. Marian played steel guitar, while Joanie handled rhythm guitar and harmony vocals. Marian's first big break came at seventeen when she headed to Alaska with a fake ID to join an all-female big band. The intense experience sharpened her skills and gave her the confidence to return home ready to pursue music full-time. Despite marrying the first time at fifteen—a union that didn't last—she remarried at twenty and managed to raise two children while maintaining a remarkable career in music.

Marian became a pioneer of televised music in the 1950s. From 1954 to 1958, she played in the house bands for *Town Hall Party* and *Ranch Party*, television programs that featured the era's biggest country and rockabilly stars, including Patsy Cline and Johnny Cash. In the late 1950s, she joined Spade Cooley's all-female orchestra before becoming part of his regular band. Later, she worked with Tex Williams and contributed to *Country Style USA*, a radio show produced for U.S. troops.

By the 1970s, her career shifted again when she joined a western revue that performed at fairs and rodeos. The show featured stars from classic TV westerns such as *Gunsmoke* and *Bonanza*, who appeared as their on-screen characters. She also took on the role of bandleader at Disneyland for a time. Her career, which spanned more than thirty years, was eventually curtailed by rheumatoid arthritis, which affected her ability to play. Her final performance was in 1985 with the Frontiersman Family, alongside her sister.

Marian often spoke of balancing her personal life with her career. She was not a "cookie-baking mom," as she put it, but credited her husband for supporting her as she navigated motherhood and the demands of performing. Their relationship, which she described as "unusual," was built on mutual respect and friendship. Marian always maintained her identity as a musician first and foremost yet managed to have a full and loving home life beyond the stage.

What stood out to me most was Marian's confidence as a player. She never felt the need to act like one of the guys; her talent spoke for itself. She didn't recall encountering sexism in her career, which is remarkable given the era she worked in. Marian simply played her instrument with skill, grace, and professionalism, carving out her space through sheer talent and work ethic.

Hearing her describe the pace of work in her early years was inspiring. In the 1940s and '50s, it wasn't uncommon for musicians to play up to ten sets a day. Marian emphasized that playing constantly was the key to becoming great, a sentiment that resonated deeply with me. Early in my own career, I played three-hour-long sets six nights a week, plus Saturday matinees, which helped me develop my hands and voice at a professional level. Even so, that still pales in comparison to the grueling schedules of Marian's era.

Her commitment to mastering the *Great American Songbook* and navigating complex chord structures reminded me my interview with Carol Kaye. Back then, musicians were expected to carry their weight on the bandstand, both technically and creatively. That level of accountability made them exceptional players.

Marian's foresight in securing financial stability was another lesson in wisdom. When arthritis forced her to stop performing, she was able to live comfortably thanks to rental property investments, a strategy inspired by her grandparents, who had owned fruit trees when she was young. Her practicality and discipline ensured she could enjoy a secure retirement despite her early exit from the stage.

Talking with Marian gave me invaluable insight into what it takes to excel as a musician, to navigate a male-dominated industry, and to maintain balance in life. She showed that it's possible to have a fulfilling career, a stable home, and the foresight to plan for the future. Marian Hall's story is a reminder that true pioneers don't always make noise about their achievements; they simply do the work and let their legacy speak for itself.

MARIAN HALL

— The Interview —

[2005]

SF: I'm particularly fascinated with women who started out in the music business a long time ago.

MH: It was a lot different then. Nowadays, when you look around, there's at least one female in every band on TV or whatever, if not two. In my day, it was really an oddity.

SF: Did you find you were treated differently because of that?

MH: No, not so much. I didn't have very much trouble. I know a lot of gals who did, but I just tried to play as well as the guys as much as possible and carry my own weight—my own equipment and things like that. I didn't get involved in any gossip or any stuff like that. That's the kind of thing guys think is very female.

SF: When you were working with that many men, were you the only woman in those big bands?

MH: Yes.

SF: Did they kid-glove you at all?

MH: No, not at all.

SF: What was the year you started playing out?

MH: 1952 was my very first job. Two times in my life I worked with women. One was my very first job on my own.

SF: That was in Alaska?

MH: Right. And the second time was with Spade Cooley. He had an all-girl orchestra, which was huge. But that's the only other time. I went from about 1952 to 1985. Before that, I was playing a little lap steel with my sister. She played standard guitar and we sang, and we were called the Saddle Sweethearts.

SF: Was it just the two of you growing up? You and your sister?

MH: Yeah.

SF: And how did you get into guitar?

MH: It was my mother's idea. She always wanted us to be in show business one way or another. When I was three, I took tap dancing and my sister took concert piano. Then at some point, about eight or nine I guess, she got the idea that we should take music lessons at a little store that was down the street. The teacher was Hawaiian, and he taught me how to play a little six-string lap guitar, and we put together a little act and sang. My sister is very good at singing harmony.

SF: So, it was just by coincidence that you got into the steel? Because your teacher was a steel player?

MH: I'm not certain about that, truthfully. My mother really enjoyed country music and had it on when we would come home from school for lunch—on the radio. But I honestly don't remember. Now that you ask me, I have a picture of myself with a standard guitar laying down on my lap that had obviously been rigged to play steel. But later, I know I had a little Oahu six-string with the fake mother-of-pearl on it and the little bitty, tiny amp to match.

SF: Did you ever play the standard guitar?

MH: No, my sister played the standard guitar.

SF: You weren't interested in that?

MH: I never got involved in it, somehow. At one point, I decided I was going to play the five-string banjo, but by then arthritis had started trickling in and it was hard enough to play steel.

SF: Do you play any more now?

MH: No, I can't play at all. My hands are very distorted. I got rheumatoid arthritis at about thirty-five, and I kept playing after that, but it got less and less viable. I would just play chords and things like that.

SF: What are the symptoms of that? What happens to your hands?

MH: Well, they twist and get very odd looking—your hands and your feet, primarily. Then it began to creep around and get all of my other joints. I have two mechanical hips, two mechanical knees, rods in my back, two mechanical shoulders.

SF: You're like the bionic woman.

MH: Exactly. Rheumatoid is different than osteoarthritis. Osteoarthritis is from wear and tear. With rheumatoid, it's systemic. It travels around your body. One day your foot will hurt, and the next day your elbow will. It's like a little mouse that's chewing on your joints. My hands are in a condition now where I wouldn't be able to even hold a bar, much less a pick. I was still able to play for quite a while, but it was painful.

SF: This didn't happen because of the guitar?

MH: No. This is just something that jumps on you from nowhere.

SF: Well, I'm sorry about that.

MH: That's okay, sweetheart. I've managed to kind of adapt, as time goes by.

SF: At what age did you finally give up the guitar?

MH: Pretty close to fifty, I guess.

SF: When you were growing up and first started playing, it was you and your sister. Were there any other women that you knew that played guitar? Or anybody in your family?

MH: No, nobody in the family played. You can't imagine at your age that there was no television, originally. But we actually got on TV and did some things. Then eventually we decided to go on our own. Then I got my big break and got my first job on my own.

SF: Right, and that was the one in Alaska? How was that? Was that a fun thing for you?

MH: It was a great learning experience, but I got to tell you, it was not a fun experience because I was so green. I was just terrible. I guess it was the intensity of it. There was no relief. I was far away from home, fifteen years old. It was all about trying to play in this group. But by the time that I finished that two weeks, I was viable. Not great, but a viable steel guitar player. And they couldn't fire me, because there wasn't anybody to take my place, and they had paid my airfare up to Alaska. They were gritting their teeth the two weeks, I'm sure.

SF: Did you stay with that group after that show?

MH: Oh, no. I came back and then I had agreed to go to work for a guy named Tex Wallace. But it was going to take a couple of weeks to do that, so I went to work for Wayne West in a little bar. He liked my playing so much that he offered me thirteen dollars a night. Scale was twelve in those days, so that was a big thing. I mean, it doesn't sound like much now, but to be offered that much more to stay!

SF: Were you still living at home when you were starting to play professionally? Still living with your parents?

MH: Yes.

SF: Did you have to help out with the family?

MH: Not really. It was by choice. My folks didn't have very much money at all, but I don't recall some regular thing [where] you give your mom so much money each week, or something like that. You'll have to forgive me, because it's hard for me to remember. It's been a while.

SF: I bet. I'm sorry.

MH: No, the questions are very interesting because I realize I hadn't ever thought about that. You know, *did I contribute?*

SF: Did you quit school early? Or did you finish high school?

MH: No, I quit school early. I quit in the lower half of the eleventh grade and got married at fifteen. That lasted about three months of being actually married. He went away to the Korean War, and by the time he came back I had gone to Alaska. I came back from that and got a divorce. It wasn't really a marriage. In later years, I took college entrance exams and got three-quarters of a degree in psychology, but I never actually finished high school.

SF: Did you just know that's what you wanted to do? Just play the guitar and see where it would take you at that young age?

MH: I was very single-minded. I may have been very naive, but it worked in my favor. I didn't know you *couldn't* do it—which is an advantage.

SF: You didn't know there was any stigma around being a woman in a man's game?

MH: I wasn't really paying attention to that, if you know what I mean. Being ignorant of something is sometimes a great advantage, because you just bop along and go ahead and do the things, instead of saying, *Well, they won't pay any attention to me because I'm a girl.*

SF: Did you find any attitude about that with the male musicians? I'm asking this because I spoke with Carol Kaye, who came up about the same time as you, but in a different field. She was a jazz guitar player, also from California. We were talking about how people respond to female musicians. She said back then there was really no sexism, as far as the playing went. She said that it was all music, and the guys didn't really even look at you any different, as long as you could hold your own on stage.

MH: That seemed to be the case for me. I have often wondered whether I never noticed it because I wasn't looking for it. There is that phenomenon: If you're looking for an attitude, you can sometimes find it, you know? I honestly wasn't looking for it. I was very fortunate in that I worked with a lot of guys who were infinitely better musicians than I was, and they were very gracious about explaining and teaching me things. I don't know if that would have been true of another steel player, but I learned a lot from all the guys that I worked with.

SF: Did you have any mentors on the steel?

MH: I had guys that I admired a lot, but none that taught me directly. What I learned, I learned from other types of musicians.

SF: Because you were probably the only steel player in the band?

MH: Oh, yes.

SF: What advice would you give to a young person, especially a young woman, going into the music business or the guitar business?

MH: You've got to want to be a musician. If you could do something else and be just as happy at it, I recommend that you do it. You gotta really wanna do this thing and love it, and do it for the love of it. Then learn everything that you can learn and enjoy absorbing all of the knowledge that you can. And from the female standpoint, don't be a girl.

SF: Don't be a girly girl?

MH: That may not sound very nice in print, but you know what I mean. Don't be high maintenance. It isn't fair to the guys, anyway. Just be a musician. If you're gonna be a musician, carry your weight. Musically and otherwise.

SF: I think Cindy Cashdollar is a great role model that way.

MH: Yeah, she's terrific. I love her. Have you ever seen any of the videotapes that seem to be circulating in Austin from *Town Home Party*, the show that I was on from '54 to '58? It was Tex Ritter and all the cast from the regular live *Town Home Party* show. They did it on film, so that's the only reason it survived. Somebody made a video copy of these shows and the tapes began circulating around Austin, particularly. Cindy saw one of them and decided she was going to find me. She started digging around until they found my sister, and then she found me and just called me up. It was the most amazing thing, and one of the most fortuitous things because she sort of resurrected me. God, love her little heart.

I went down there and they were all very gracious and acknowledged me and all that good stuff, because I worked with some of the guys who are legends, like Merle Travis and stuff like that. That's the first time I met her face to face. When she called me, we talked for hours on the phone and just laughed and had a wonderful time because we can identify so well with each other—you know, about all the little nonsense that goes on. About trying to play steel and how they never give you any camera time, you know?

SF: Did you feel like up until then, your whole music career was just kind of over and forgotten?

MH: Pretty much. Many of the people I had worked with had died. They were gone. So, when Cindy showed up, and then these tapes showed up, it brought it all back to life. I'm not sure whether anybody would remember if I lived or died if it weren't for Cindy and those tapes.

SF: Who were the most impressive people you backed up? The ones who left the biggest impression on you? Patsy Cline?

MH: Well, yeah, that was nice. But the things that probably meant the most to me were when I worked for Tex Williams. Billy Armstrong was a bandleader and a very fine musician, and Tex was a really elegant guy. We got to do anything we were big enough to do. In some situations, you're limited. They want you to play within a certain parameter. But with Tex, any bright idea we got, we could do. I also loved working with Merle Travis just because I respected him so much. The man was brilliant and besides, he was a pioneer. I have a lot of respect for the first guy who does anything.

SF: What was the all-woman orchestra like?

MH: It was interesting, but when you have an orchestra that size you don't have that much to do.

SF: When you played in clubs back then, what was it like? How many sets a night?

MH: Oh, dear God. Salt mines! It was five sets a night. For a while there, I would work a double shift on Sunday. Sometimes I would work both shifts, that would mean—

SF: Ten sets!

MH: Yes, eleven-hour days. Looking back on that, I can't even figure how I did it. The ideal to me is about three sets. First one to warm up, and the second two to really play. After that, you start fading a little bit. Unless it's just something really inspiring.

SF: Did you have time for a personal life, or were you just a career girl?

MH: Well, I actually got married and had two children.

SF: And what age did you get married at? Your second marriage, I guess?

MH: Twenty.

SF: Is that the same husband you have now?

MH: We're still married. We have a very unusual arrangement. We don't live together, but there's nobody I admire more than him. We get along like two peas in a pod, and our kids like it this way. When it's Christmas and Thanksgiving and stuff, we're all together. He's an engineer. He used to work for the space program when we first got married. Most people have a hard time understanding us, but that's how it works.

SF: So, you like living by yourself?

MH: Yeah, for the most part. My children are grown, and I have grandchildren. My son doesn't have any children out here in California. My daughter is in Michigan and my four grandchildren are back there, unfortunately. That's not a good thing. But I wasn't the typical, "cookie baking" mother. I was very devoted to my career. I really loved it.

SF: Did you have your kids right around your early twenties?

MH: Yeah, in my mid-twenties. My husband was wonderful. He was a very hands-on sort of father. He would take care of the kids while I was out picking and grinning.

SF: Did you spend a long time away from home?

MH: I didn't go on the road a lot. In later years, in the '70s, I would go on the road when it was fashionable to have western shows on TV. They all decided that they were going to appear at fairs and rodeos as their characters, so they needed an act. I traveled a lot with Hal Southern, and he had put together a group. We made them look good and gave them an act. We would fly out on Thursday and come back on Sunday every other week. That was very doable.

SF: Your kids weren't little by then?

MH: No. I was very fortunate in that I got a lot of TV and some recordings and things like that, so I was able to stay home.

SF: It's always interesting to find out how other musicians balance their professional careers and having kids. A lot of the guitar players I talked to don't have kids. Only a couple of them were mothers.

MH: I can appreciate that. I wouldn't have been able to do it had I not been married to the man I was married to. I had the best of both worlds. Maybe it would have been more ideal for my kids if I had been a "cookie baking" mother, but I think there is something you can contribute by having ambition.

SF: Do they remember back then when you played?

MH: I don't know. I worked for Disneyland. I was the bandleader, and they would have these events. If you were the bandleader, you could bring in as many people as you wanted as your guests. I would take my kids and a couple of their friends in. When my show was on, they would go and get on the rides, because the lines were shorter. So you see how much I was revered.

SF: But it must have been nice just to see their mom.

MH: They didn't, though. They were on the rides. But in later years, my son decided he wanted to play the drums and he really liked the drummer I had, so he roadied for a little while. Then he started playing drums, and he was really good, so I put him in the band. And my daughter, one day, just started singing. Six weeks after she opened her mouth, she had a job singing at the Quiet Cannon, which is a very lovely restaurant in Dana Point. Just knocked us flat out.

SF: Were there musicians in your family before you?

MH: No. Not at all.

SF: Your mom just got you into it because she wanted to put you in show business?

MH: We went to a private school, my sister and I. It was called Hollywood Professional School. A lot of actors went there from kindergarten through high school. It was just half a day, and all they did was the academics. You know, reading, writing, and arithmetic. They didn't have extracurricular activities like football. But in the afternoon, they had things like dancing lessons and etiquette lessons. It was a very unusual place. If you had a job, like on a movie set or something, they totally accommodated you. I don't know whether it warped me from being able to function in the real world or not.

SF: Well, California is its own world, right?

MH: Yes, it is. I was born in Los Angeles. I've never lived anywhere else. I just love California, because anything goes. I wouldn't want to live someplace where you gotta be this way or that way. Where I am, one person is a millionaire and the next guy is a starving painter, which works for me. I kind of like that kind of thing.

SF: Are you completely retired? Do you do any work now in any way?

MH: Well, I was very fortunate. I bought some property in the '70s, just before the run-up of property values, so I am a landlord by profession.

I have enough rentals to keep me going, and that's something that I can do even when I'm incapacitated. When I was a kid, my grandparents were the symbol of stability in my life and they had two things: they owned their home outright, and they had fruit trees. Believe it or not, those two things were symbols of security. That's why I bought property, and I had to take my wages and support the property for a long time. But when the run-up in value came, that set me up perfectly for being able to survive not playing the guitar.

SF: Do you miss playing? Do you listen to music around the house or anything?

MH: I don't identify with a lot of the stuff that's out there now. That doesn't do it to me. It's noisy, and rap is just obscene to me. Some of it, there's so much production involved—like they're shooting off rockets and light changes and all that stuff, and I just want to hear some music, you know.

SF: Have you noticed how women's roles have changed in music? Any difference or transition over the years?

MH: I'm sort of out of the loop. But if I were going to make an observation, it seems like it's very split. The singers are getting fewer and fewer clothes, and more bumps and grinds. And the musicians are not the people who are in the bands that back up all these singers. There does seem to be more and more females in bands. You know, you watch [late-night talk shows], all these bands have one or two females in them. Usually it's the bass player, for some reason. I don't know why. And fiddlers or violin players are usually female. I'm sure it's much simpler now for them to get recognized, accepted just as well.

SF: I was struck by your comment about going into this whole thing ignorantly, before the women's movement. It's like people are looking for sexism more now.

MH: The other way around is that guys were more resentful once the female movement came along. It created some antagonism that didn't exist before. I didn't personally experience any antagonism.

SF: Most of the women I've talked to who are older just say, "No, it never even occurred to me." However, women that came up in the '70s and '80s, they're like, "oh yeah."

MH: It never occurred to me that it was a problem.

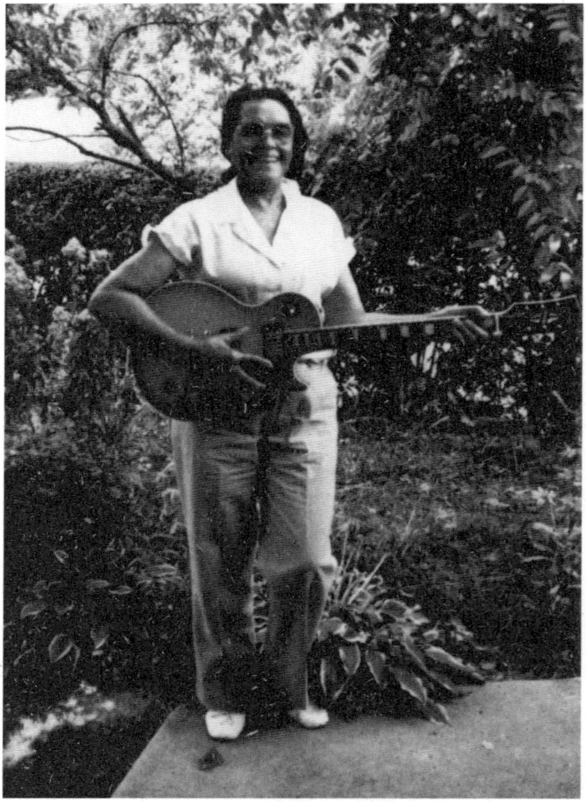

Etta Baker

ETTA BAKER

When Music Maker Relief Foundation founder Tim Duffy and I arrived at Etta Baker's house in November 2003, she had just woken from an afternoon nap. She met us at the door looking rested, content, and sincerely happy to have visitors. Etta was ninety-one at the time, dressed casually in loose pants and a man's shirt. Though petite in stature, what immediately struck me were her hands—large, rough, and calloused from decades of hard work and guitar playing. They seemed out of place on her small frame. Her sweet, high-pitched Southern drawl and easy smile put me at ease right away.

Etta was born in 1913 in Caldwell County, North Carolina, into a family of mill workers and farmers. She began playing guitar at the age of three, inspired by her father, Boone Reid, a skilled musician who played various instruments. While most of her siblings and cousins also played, Etta had a special gift. She described her heritage as a blend of African, European, and Indigenous ancestry, which shaped her music, a distinctive fusion of Piedmont blues, Appalachian folk, and English fiddle tunes.

Despite her exceptional talent, Etta was never encouraged to pursue music professionally. Her husband, Lee Baker Sr., discouraged her from performing publicly. Only after his passing did she begin her professional career, well into her seventies.

Tim and I spent that afternoon in Etta's cozy one-bedroom cottage in Morganton, North Carolina. After chatting for a while, Tim brought in the guitars, and we began tuning up. I was nervous; this was Etta Baker, a legendary Piedmont-style fingerpicker. What could I possibly play for her? I was content just to listen, but Etta encouraged me gently, "You play one." Her kindness helped me relax, and soon we were playing together. Her delicate touch and effortless phrasing were mesmerizing. The music seemed to flow out of her as naturally as breathing. I felt like a child in the presence of a master.

Etta's music had been circulating long before her official debut. In 1956, folklorist Paul Clayton heard her play at Cone Manor in North Carolina and recorded her and her father at their home the next day. Those recordings appeared on *Instrumental Music from the Southern Appalachians*, a Folkways release that introduced her to a wider audience. The album influenced a young Bob Dylan, who later credited her style as inspiration for "Don't Think Twice, It's All Right." Yet, like many African-American artists of the time, Etta received no compensation for her contributions.

Her professional music career began decades later, in the early 1980s. In 1989, she appeared in *The North Carolina Banjo Collection*, and in 1992, she released her first solo album, *One-Dime Blues*. Tim Duffy once compared her musical genius to that of Andrés Segovia, a master in her own right.

Etta's contributions to the Piedmont blues earned her numerous accolades, including the *North Carolina Folk Heritage Award* in 1989, the *National Endowment for the Arts National Heritage Fellowship* in 1991, and the *North Carolina Award* in 2003. She continued performing into her nineties, enchanting audiences with her signature blend of sweetness and virtuosity.

Her life was deeply rooted in family. Etta raised nine children, including two sets of twins and maintained a lush garden she tended daily, often starting before sunrise. Family portraits lined her walls, along with a striking photo from the 1930s, Etta with her guitar, radiating youthful beauty and confidence. Despite the hardships she endured, including the loss of her husband and one of her sons within a month of each other, she remained modest and resilient. When I asked how she managed to raise such a large family, she brushed it off with a humble, "It wasn't too bad." I told her she must be incredibly strong, and in her soft voice, she simply replied, "I had to be."

Etta's humility extended to her music. She never sought fame or glory; she played because it was who she was. Her guitar carried the story of Piedmont blues, a style rooted in intricate fingerpicking and heartfelt storytelling. Her music embodied the richness of her heritage, blending tradition with her own unique voice.

As we left her house that day, Etta said, "I sure hope you come back to see me." I promised I would, or at least call. To my eternal regret, I never did. Etta passed away in September 2006.

Meeting Etta Baker was a magical experience, one that I'll carry with me forever. Her music, her resilience, and her quiet strength remain a testament to the power of art, humility, and the enduring human spirit. In Etta's music, I heard the voice of America itself, echoing straight from the source.

ETTA BAKER

— *The Interview* —

[2003]

SF: Who showed you to play?

EB: My dad taught me, and his daddy taught him. My granddaddy played, too.

SF: Was it all the same kind of music?

EB: Yes. I love other people's music, but I just stick with the way my dad and granddad played.

SF: What did they call that style of music when you were growing up?

EB: They called it country music. My daddy never played any blues until I was three years old and we moved to Chase City, Virginia. Down there, the people had parties and played blues and they taught daddy. That's how blues got into daddy's family.

SF: Was blues not a popular kind of music to play around the house back then?

EB: In places like square dances and entertainments, and just whatever.

SF: When did you start writing your own songs?

EB: "The Knoxville Rag." I dreamed the chords for that.

SF: Did you play it in the middle of the night?

EB: Yes, it was quarter to three. I went out on the porch. This was in Knoxville. Everybody in the building was fast asleep. I got up and stole my sister's guitar from under her bed, and went out on the porch by myself, just putting my dream together. I was in my early fifties then.

SF: How long were you married for?

EB: I was twenty-three when I got married. He passed away in 1967.

SF: I was told your husband didn't want you playing out.

EB: He didn't like to travel, so I just played here at home and worked at the textile place. I worked at Buster Brown's for over twenty-five years. I would play at night.

SF: And you were raising the kids?

EB: Yes.

SF: Did you want to go out and play?

EB: Yeah, I wanted to go, but Lee would say no and I would just settle down. When he passed away, [a friend] asked me why I was working so hard. He told me I ought to just pick up my guitar. That was on a Wednesday and on Friday I quit my job. I went to Winston-Salem and I played with James "Guitar Slim" [Stephens] from Greensboro. That was my first trip away from home. I played guitar and Slim played the piano.

SF: How many children did you have?

EB: Nine. Little David was seventeen when I lost him in the Vietnam War. He hadn't been in but just a little while.

SF: Isn't that too young to go to war?

EB: No. They took him in at sixteen and he was seventeen when he died. That was the eighth of October, and then the seventeenth of November I lost Lee.

SF: What did Lee die from?

EB: He had a stroke. He was an invalid for three years.

SF: And you looked after him too?

EB: Yes.

SF: You're a strong woman.

EB: I had to be. My daddy said if you tell yourself you can't do something, you make yourself believe it and then you really can't. He said as long as you keep telling yourself, "I can do that," you're going to try a little harder. I think of that a whole lot. I had a good daddy. He had to be to put up with me.

SF: Were you close to your daddy?

EB: I loved my mother, but she'd whoop me too much. Daddy wouldn't whoop me. I'd run to him for protection.

SF: What number child are you?

EB: I was the youngest. And all of my family—all of my daddy's family and all of his brothers' family—they're all passed away. I am the only one from that generation that's living.

SF: And you're in fine health. Do you work every day still?

EB: Oh Lord, yes. I have been raking leaves ever since last August. It don't sound true, but the apple trees started turning yellow and shedding in August. I kept them cleaned up. I had the yard all pretty and clean before this last hard rain and there were leaves all over the yard again. It didn't take me too long to get them up. I had seven bags of leaves down there for the men to pick up.

SF: What time do you get up every morning?

EB: I don't sleep after four o'clock.

SF: What do you do in the evening? Do you still play guitar?

EB: Yes. This little cop comes by occasionally. We sat here and played until after eleven o'clock on Saturday night.

SF: Were there any other women players around when you were growing up?

EB: All my cousins played, but they've all passed away.

SF: Was it the same style of music?

EB: Yes, and my sister played great. She's been gone four years now. She was ninety-three.

SF: Was she as good as you?

EB: Yes. My oldest sister played guitar, too. She was living in Wyco, West Virginia, when she passed away, but that child could really play a guitar.

SF: There were actually a lot of women guitar players around. We just never hear about them.

EB: Did you ever know where "One Dime Blues" came from? I had a real good friend years ago. He went to West Virginia and he was so lazy, but he was nice-looking and his music was sweet. He got out there in Virginia and got broke and couldn't get back home, but he learned this "One Dime Blues." When he come home, he taught me [*laughs*]. He was so lazy; he's might near too lazy to tune the guitar.

SF: Did your father show you and all your sisters to play?

EB: Yes.

SF: Did you have a radio?

EB: Not back in my dad's days, we didn't have. Just our music. He had a neighbor who had a radio, and we would start to learn some of the pieces we would hear.

SF: Did you have a favorite singer back then that you liked to listen to?

EB: No one special. Go get your guitar.

I got to get my guitar and when I come back I play my song "Train to Memphis." I am nervous and really don't want to play, but there's no turning back. She wants to hear me. The guitar is out of tune but it sounds alright.

EB: That's pretty (*she claps*).

SF: Do you play every day?

EB: If I get too tired from working outdoors, I can start making a racket and forget being tired.

SF: You have beautiful fingers. Big strong guitar hands.

Etta's hands are huge, especially contrasted to her tiny frame. She picks gracefully at her guitar as we continue to talk.

SF: When you were a little girl were you a tomboy?

EB: That's what they called me all the time. I could go up a tree like a kitten.

SF: Did you like fishing and stuff?

EB: Lord, yes. Anything to do outside.

Tim and I jam on some more blues.

EB: That's purty. What is that?

SF: Just fooling around.

EB: You know, when I played with Slim, the look he had on his face. I asked myself why in the world they asked me to play with him. Lord, he was so out of humor. He looked around at me with this look that said, *who is she to think she can play with me?* I made a poem about that. I said:

I played in Winston, I played in Statesville
The guy I played with, he acted mighty hateful

He looked around as if to say
Who is that, think she can play with me?
I hit a note high and sweet
He said, "You know, that makes me want to get on my feet."
On down toward the show's end
I couldn't have met a nicer friend

SF: So he was all right after?

EB: Yeah, he was so nice after. He got to telling me about his pretty home. He got in a good humor then. But at first, he had the awfullest look on his face when he looked around at me. Like he couldn't believe it.

SF: Then you showed him.

EB: Yes, now I like playing with Slim. We played together at Merlefest.

SF: Etta, do you have any boyfriends?

EB: Oh, I've got a lot of friends, but it's all hello goodbye. I always said one time was all right, but I wouldn't try it no more.

SF: You like being on your own.

EB: It suits me better. I try to be happy with just whatever. Lee was good, and I said the next one might not be good. Then I'd be wearing a striped suit. That wouldn't be too good.

SF: You never had no men coming around looking to be your boyfriend?

EB: No, they come around. But just as good friends. Come in and then go, and that's all right (*laughs*). I love your music. It's pretty.

SF: Still learning. Do you want to play another song?

(*Etta picks up her guitar and plays.*)

EB: Maybe now that I've got my yard work done, I can put more time in on music.

Acknowledgments

With gratitude to those who helped
bring Guitar Women *to life.*

Because this book was started so long ago, I have what feels like an army to thank. Over the years, I've leaned on so many people, not only for inspiration but for the fortitude to keep going. It would take another book entirely to acknowledge everyone, so here I'll focus on a few whose presence and belief were truly instrumental in making *Guitar Women* possible.

First and foremost, my gratitude goes to Don Wilcock, who sparked the idea for this book. If not for our casual conversation back in 2001, I might never have thought about it. Don's curiosity and enthusiasm are boundless. Now in his eighties, he's still out catching shows each week and runs *American Blues Scene* almost single-handedly. His dedication to music and his creative output continue to amaze me.

Phil Alain, visual artist and promoter from Edmonton, was one of this project's early angels. Phil championed *Guitar Women* from the start, promoting shows, designing visuals and logos, and always reminding me to keep going. He's a pillar of his artistic community, creating spaces where others can shine, and his belief in me meant more than he knows.

Phil Cousineau's work deeply influenced me early on. I had read several of his books before attending one of his creative workshops, drawn to his connection with Joseph Campbell's legacy. Phil embodies the hero's journey. He's an inspired soul walking the path he writes about. We became pen pals after that workshop, and his ongoing wisdom and encouragement have stayed with me through every stage of this process.

My thanks also go to Tim Duffy and the Music Maker Relief Foundation, which he founded and continues to run. Tim generously drove me across North Carolina to meet Etta Baker, one of the most unforgettable experiences of my journey. Spending time with Etta was magical, and it was only possible through Tim's kindness and dedication to preserving American folk and blues traditions.

I'm grateful to Editor-in-Chief Christopher Scapelliti of *Guitar Player* magazine, who published excerpts from my interviews in a running column called *The Foley Files*. Seeing those stories in print breathed new life into this long-dormant project and inspired me to finally finish what I had started.

Throughout this process, I've been blessed with editors and assistants who helped shape this book. My heartfelt thanks to Dana Foley, my niece, who researched biographical details for many of the chapters, edited early drafts, and offered thoughtful insight into the subject matter, all while beginning her own journey as a poet and writer. Watching her creative voice emerge alongside this project has been a joy. Thanks also to Christine Lyon, one of my first assistants, for coordinating interviews and logistics, and to Elizabeth Howell, who painstakingly handled early transcriptions the old-fashioned way, before digital tools were available.

Through Phil Cousineau, I met Janet Hubbard, a Vermont-based author who became my editorial guide for several years. Janet helped me discover my voice within these pages, urging me to dig deeper and write without fear. Our long Zoom sessions were filled with laughter, insight, and energy. She was in her seventies but carried the effervescent spirit of a teenager. I was heartbroken to learn of her passing in 2024, just as I was ready to tell her the book had finally found a publisher. Janet was a brilliant teacher and a bright light, and I miss her deeply.

My gratitude also goes to Michael Barclay, who served as the final editor on this manuscript, catching small details, asking sharp questions, and keeping me on track. And to Deirdre Kelly, who introduced me to Ken Whyte at Sutherland House and helped me secure this book deal, I can't thank you enough. Without that connection, *Guitar Women* might still be sitting on my desk in perpetual draft form. Deep gratitude as well to Ken Whyte and to my literary agent, Michael Levine at Westwood Creative Artists, for championing this work and helping bring it to publication.

Thanks to Michael Coghlan, Rob Bowman, and all my professors at York University. I never set out to be an academic, and I'm still figuring out what to do with my degree, but the process of researching and writing my doctorate gave me invaluable tools and confidence. Finishing that project taught me that I could take on something monumental and see it through, and that lesson has guided me through every stage of this book.

To Michele Gare, who keeps the day-to-day business of *Guitar Woman LLC* humming and has been part of this journey for nearly a decade. Michele came in during the final stages to edit text and assist with read-throughs, and she will be immeasurably instrumental as we move forward to share this book with the world. Thank you for the many, many tasks you do so well. You keep our wheels turning . . . and from falling off!

My deepest and most heartfelt thanks to my son, Joseph, for his sheer presence in my life and in the world. You are the catalyst who led me to seek new avenues of creation and helped me imagine myself in roles I might never have reached for. Without a doubt, my greatest role has been as your mother.

Over the past two decades, I've had the honor of speaking with more than a hundred women guitarists from all corners of the musical world. Though not all could be featured in this volume, every one of them left her mark on me and on this work. Each offered her time, wisdom, and truth, and I'm profoundly grateful for their generosity and trust. Having so many great interviews still in the vault leaves room, I hope, for another volume (or two).

And finally, I want to acknowledge the twenty-five women featured here, who have each shaped the language of the guitar in her own voice and her own way.

Charo, Liona Boyd, Nancy Wilson, Suzi Quatro, Bonnie Raitt, Ellen McIlwaine, Lita Ford, Joan Armatrading, Kathy Valentine, Vicki Peterson, Jennifer Batten, Felicia Collins, Rory Block, Barbara Lynn, June Millington, Alice Stuart, Del Rey, Sharon Isbin, Alice Artzt, Carol Kaye, Susan Tedeschi, Mimi Fox, Cindy Cashdollar, Marian Hall, and Etta Baker.

Your music, courage, and individuality continue to inspire me every day. You are the reason this book exists.

SF

Notes

— CHARO —

Berman, Janice. "Ageless Charo Keeps the Cuchi Cuchi Flame Burning." *SF Gate*, August 6, 2005.

Kerr, Jolie. "Thank Heaven for Charo." *The New York Times*, June 22, 2019.

Charo (official website). https://www.charo.com.

— LIONA BOYD —

Green, Richard, Betty Nygard King, and Barbara Norman. "Liona Boyd." *The Canadian Encyclopedia*, March 4, 2015. https://www.thecanadianencyclopedia.ca/en/article/liona-boyd-emc.

Tubiana, Raoul. "Musician's Focal Dystonia." *ScienceDirect* (abstract), May 2003. https://www.sciencedirect.com/science/article/abs/pii/S0749071202000999.

Liona Boyd (official website). https://www.lionaboyd.com.

— NANCY WILSON —

"Ann and Nancy Wilson: Four Decades of Heartfelt Music." *International Musician*, October 5, 2015. https://internationalmusician.org/ann-and-nancy-wilson/.

Hopper, Jessica. "Juicy Tales from Heart's Ann and Nancy Wilson." *Rolling Stone*, September 11, 2012. https://www.rollingstone.com/music/music-news/juicy-tales-from-hearts-ann-and-nancy-wilson-58099/.

Wilson, Ann, and Nancy Wilson, with Charles R. Cross. *Kicking & Dreaming: A Story of Heart, Soul and Rock & Roll* (New York: It Books, 2013).

Nancy Wilson (official website). https://www.nancywilsonofheart.com.

— SUZI QUATRO —

Callwood, Brett. "Glycerine Queen, Forever!" *Metro Times,* April 25, 2012. https://www.metrotimes.com/music/glycerine-queen-forever-2148449.

Suzi Q, directed by Liam Firmager (2019; Acme Film Production Company).

"Suzi Quatro Facts: Glam Icon's Songs, Acting Career, Marriages and Groundbreaking Influence." *Gold Radio,* March 7, 2023. https://www.goldradio.com/hall-of-fame/suzi-quatro-facts-songs-husband-age/.

Foley, Sue. "'I Gave Women a Voice in Rock and Roll': Suzi Quatro Talks Becoming the 'First Rock Chick.'" *GuitarPlayer.com,* April 13, 2023. https://www.guitarplayer.com/players/suzi-quatro-sue-foley.

Suzi Quatro (official website). https://www.suziquatro.com.

— BONNIE RAITT —

"Bonnie's Story." *BonnieRaitt.com.* Accessed December 23, 2019. https://www.bonnieraitt.com/bio/bonnies-story/.

Sweet, Brian. *Nick of Time: The Triumph of Bonnie Raitt* (New York: Da Capo Press, 1995).

Bonnie Raitt (artist website). https://www.bonnieraitt.com.

— ELLEN MCILWANE —

Corby, Paul. "Ellen McIlwaine Is Still Playing the Blues—with a Feeling." *Roots Music Canada*, April 11, 2019. https://www.rootsmusic.ca/2019/04/11/ellen-mcilwaine-is-still-playing-the-blues-with-a-feeling/.

"Ellen's Last Official Bio." *Goddess of Slide*. Accessed October 20, 2025. https://goddessofslide.com/ellens-last-official-bio/.

Goddess of Slide, directed by Alfonso Maiorana (2024; Soul Flicker Films).

Jennings, Nicholas. "Ellen McIlwaine—Goddess of Slide." *Nicholas Jennings.com*, June 30, 2021. https://www.nicholasjennings.com/ellen-mcilwaine-goddess-of-slide.

Smith, Harrison. "Ellen McIlwaine, Fiery Slide Guitarist and Blues Singer, Dies at 75." *The Washington Post*, June 26, 2021. https://www.washingtonpost.com/local/obituaries/ellen-mcilwaine-dead/2021/06/25/21ba9254-d4f8-11eb-ae54-515e2f63d37d_story.html.

— LITA FORD —

Bosso, Joe. "Lita Ford: 'I Had a 45-Minute Window to Escape.'" *MusicRadar*, November 9, 2011.

Ford, Lita. *Living Like a Runaway: A Memoir* (New York: Dey Street Books, 2016).

Lita Ford (official website). https://www.litaford.com.

— JOAN ARMATRADING —

"About." *JoanArmatrading.com*. Accessed October 10, 2020. https://www.joanarmatrading.com/specific-item/about-joan.

Schofield, Blanca. "Joan Armatrading: 'Like Barbra Streisand, I Was Told to Change My Name.'" *The Times*. https://www.thetimes.com/culture/

music/article/joan-armatrading-musician-like-barbra-streisand-i-was-told-to-change-my-name-wvvzcp59m.

Joan Armatrading (official website). https://www.joanarmatrading.com.

— KATHY VALENTINE —

Chang, Ailsa. "The Go-Go's Documentary Offers a Look at the All-Female Band's Journey to Stardom." *NPR*, June 30, 2020. https://www.npr.org/2020/07/30/897345084/the-go-gos-documentary-offers-a-look-at-the-all-female-bands-journey-to-stardom.

Corcoran, Michael. "Beat Goes on for Kathy Valentine." *Austin American-Statesman*, October 12, 2013 https://www.statesman.com/story/news/2013/10/21/beat-goes-on-for-kathy/6721052007/.

"'How Did I Get Here?' with Frenchie Smith, Kathy Valentine, and Louis Black." *Austin Music Foundation*, January 31, 2019. https://austinmusicfoundation.org/how-did-i-get-here-with-frenchie-smith-kathy-valentine-louis-black/.

Foley, Sue. "Kathy Valentine Talks Reconnecting with the Guitar After the Go-Go's." *GuitarPlayer.com*, August 27, 2021. https://www.guitarplayer.com/players/kathy-valentine-talks-reconnecting-with-the-guitar-after-the-go-gos.

Larsen, Peter. "The Go-Go's Kathy Valentine Shares Her Wild Life in All I Ever Wanted." *Los Angeles Daily News*, April 6, 2020. https://www.dailynews.com/2020/04/06/the-go-gos-kathy-valentine-shares-her-wild-life-in-all-i-ever-wanted/.

Roberts, Randall. "Kathy Valentine's Hair-Raising Memoir All I Ever Wanted Recounts the Go-Go's Wild Ride." *Los Angeles Times*, April 2, 2020. https://www.latimes.com/entertainment-arts/music/story/2020-04-02/kathy-valentine-go-gos-all-i-ever-wanted.

Seida, Linda. "The Delphines." *AllMusic*. Accessed September 27, 2020. https://www.allmusic.com/artist/the-delphines-mn0000122658/biography.

Kathy Valentine (official website). https://www.kathyvalentine.com.

— VICKI PETERSON —

Avila, Daniela. "The Bangles' Vicki Peterson & John Cowsill on Finally Working Together and the Secret to Their 22-Year Marriage (Exclusive)." *People*, August 14, 2024. https://people.com/the-bangles-vicki-peterson-john-cowsill-on-22-year-marriage-working-together-exclusive-8695485.

Bender, Abbey. "Bangles Guitarist Vicki Peterson Dishes on the '80s Music Scene and Her New Collaboration With Her Husband." *Woman's World*, August 7, 2024. https://www.womansworld.com/entertainment/celebrities/vicki-peterson-bangles-guitarist-talks-80s-music-and-new-project.

Whitmore, Laura B. "Vicki Peterson Goes Psycho—Exclusive Interview." *Guitar World*, January 23, 2014. https://www.guitarworld.com/acoustic-nation/vicki-peterson-goes-psycho-exclusive-interview.

Vicki Peterson & John Cowsill (official website). https://www.vickipetersonandjohncowsill.com.

— JENNIFER BATTEN —

Amendola, Drew. "Jennifer Batten: The High Priestess of Shred Talks Shop." *Guitar Girl Magazine*, June 29, 2013. https://guitargirlmag.com/interviews/jennifer-batten-the-high-priestess-of-shred-talks-shop/.

Rigg, Paul. "Talking with Jennifer Batten." *Guitars Exchange*. Accessed April 16, 2020. https://guitarsexchange.com/en/unplugged/363/jennifer-batten/.

Varga, George. "Jennifer Batten: A Pioneering Guitarist Reflects." *San Diego Union-Tribune*, January 5, 2017. https://www.sandiegouniontribune.com/2016/03/05/jennifer-batten-a-pioneering-guitarist-reflects/.

Jennifer Batten (official website). https://www.jenniferbatten.com.

— FELICIA COLLINS —

"Felicia Collins Interview." *Guitarhoo!* September 27, 2004. https://guitarhoo.com/interviews/felicia-collins/.

"Felicia Collins—2023 Capital Region Thomas Edison Music Hall of Fame Inductee." *YouTube,* March 23, 2023. https://www.youtube.com/watch?v=-HU1T25GmUQ.

Grondahl, Paul. "How an Albany Girl and Self-Taught Guitarist Landed Letterman Gig." *Times Union,* January 23, 2015. https://www.timesunion.com/tuplus-local/article/How-an-Albany-girl-and-self-taught-guitarist-6032885.php.

— RORY BLOCK —

Harris, George W. "Rory Block Interview." *Jazz Weekly,* March 5, 2023. https://www.jazzweekly.com/2023/03/rory-block-interview/.

"Making a Scene Presents an Interview with Rory Block." *Making a Scene,* September 9, 2018. https://www.makingascene.org.

Schlank, Anita. "Featured Interview: Rory Block—Faithfully Honoring Country Blues." *Blues Blast Magazine,* April 24, 2023. https://www.bluesblastmagazine.com/featured-interview-rory-block-faithfully-honoring-country-blues/.

Weber, Bruce. "Allan Block, Whose Sandal Shop Was Folk Music Hub, Dies at 90." *The New York Times,* November 3, 2013. https://www.nytimes.com/2013/11/03/nyregion/allan-block-whose-sandal-shop-was-folk-music-hub-dies-at-90.html.

Rory Block (official website). https://www.roryblock.com.

— BARBARA LYNN —

"The Story of Barbara Lynn." *Mental Itch.* Accessed April 29, 2020. https://mentalitch.com/the-story-of-barbara-lynn/.

Foley, Sue. "'I Just Knew I Was Born to Play That Guitar': Barbara Lynn Recalls Her Pioneering Days as a Guitarist." *GuitarPlayer.com,* January 27, 2023. https://www.guitarplayer.com/players/i-just-knew-i-was-born-to-play-that-guitar-barbara-lynn-recalls-her-pioneering-days-as-guitarist.

— JUNE MILLINGTON —

Dykstra, Natalie. *Fanny: The Pioneering All-Female Rock Band* (New York: Beacon Press, 2021).

Millington, June. *Land of a Thousand Bridges: Island Girl in a Rock & Roll World* (Amherst: Institute for the Musical Arts, 2015).

Foley, Sue. "'You Couldn't Get the Information Because People Were Making It Up on the Spot': June Millington of Fanny Recalls Life in the Late-'60s Rock Scene." *GuitarPlayer.com,* March 17, 2023. https://www.guitarplayer.com/players/you-couldnt-get-the-information-because-people-were-making-it-up-on-the-spot-june-millington-of-fanny-recalls-life-in-the-late-60s-rock-scene.

Robinson, Lisa. "The Female Rock Trailblazers You've Never Heard Of: Fanny." *Vanity Fair,* October 2019.

Varga, George. "June Millington Reflects on Rock History and Mentorship." *San Diego Union-Tribune,* July 3, 2020.

Wilde, Jon. "David Bowie and His Admiration for Fanny: Rock's Forgotten Trailblazers." *The Guardian,* November 12, 2015.

June Millington (official website). https://www.junemillington.net.

— ALICE STUART —

Blecha, Peter. "Stuart, Alice (1942–2023)." *HistoryLink.org,* June 20, 2019. https://www.historylink.org/file/20799.

Foley, Sue. "He Picked Me Up Off the Floor and Said, 'Honey, You Play Good Guitar!': Alice Stuart Talks Playing with Albert King and Frank

Zappa." *GuitarPlayer.com*, January 24, 2023. https://www.guitarplayer.com/players/he-picked-me-up-off-the-floor-and-said-honey-you-play-good-guitar-alice-stuart-talks-playing-with-albert-king-and-frank-zappa.

Kening, Dan. "Alice Stuart Returns to the Blues with Gusto." *Chicago Tribune,* May 20, 1994.

McCarthy, Paul. "Alice Stuart: A Pioneer in Blues and Rock." *Blues Matters,* December 2024.

Schudel, Matt. "Alice Stuart, Pioneering Guitarist, Dies at 81." *The Washington Post,* March 5, 2023.

— DEL REY —

"Del Rey." *Contemporary Acoustic Roots and Country Blues,* July 18, 2017. https://www.thecountryblues.com/artist-reviews/del-rey.

"Del Rey Oral History Interview." *NAMM Oral History Library,* August 29, 2021. https://www.namm.org/library/oral-history/del-rey.

Foley, Sue. "'How Can You Make a Cult Figure of Robert Johnson, Who Recorded 30 Sides, and Ignore Memphis Minnie, Who Recorded 200?' Del Rey Speaks Up About Female Guitar History." *GuitarPlayer.com,* March 3, 2023. https://www.guitarplayer.com/players/how-can-you-make-a-cult-figure-of-robert-johnson-who-recorded-30-sides-and-ignore-memphis-minnie-who-recorded-200-del-rey-speaks-up-about-female-guitar-history.

Del Rey (official website). https://www.delreyplays.com.

— SHARON ISBIN —

"Grammy Winner Sharon Isbin Honored with 2020 Musical America Instrumentalist of the Year Award." *Guitar Girl Magazine,* October 15, 2019. https://guitargirlmag.com/news/music-news/grammy-winner-sharon-isbin-honored-with-2020-musical-america-instrumentalist-of-the-year-award/.

Foley, Sue. "Sharon Isbin on Classical Music's Guitar Problem, Self-Expression and Seeing Her Guitar as a Troubadour." *GuitarPlayer.com*, May 28, 2020. https://www.guitarplayer.com/players/sharon-isbin-on-classical-musics-guitar-problem-self-expression-and-seeing-her-guitar-as-a-troubadour.

Isbin, Sharon. "Biography." *SharonIsbin.com*. Accessed February 5, 2025. https://www.sharonisbin.com/biography.html.

Sharon Isbin (official website). https://www.sharonisbin.com.

— ALICE ARTZT —

Bellow, Alexandre. "Presti–Lagoya Duo." *Classical Guitar Magazine*, June 1987.

Cornwell, Tony. "In Praise of Classical Guitarists Alexandre Lagoya and Ida Presti." *World Socialist Web Site*, February 17, 2001. https://www.wsws.org/en/articles/2001/02/guit-f17.html.

Foley, Sue. "'She Could Do Anything at Any Speed': Classical Guitarist Alice Artzt Recalls the Unearthly Talent That Was Ida Presti." *GuitarPlayer.com*, January 6, 2023. https://www.guitarplayer.com/players/she-could-do-anything-at-any-speed-classical-guitarist-alice-artzt-recalls-the-unearthly-talent-that-was-ida-presti.

Jeffery, Brian. *Guitar: From the Renaissance to the Present Day* (London: J.M. Dent & Sons, 1977), 145.

Marillia, Anne, and Elizabeth Presti. *Ida Presti: Her Life, Her Art* (Bèrben: SRL Publishing House, 2005).

Moore, Robert. "The Legends: Ida Presti." *She Shreds*, August 2, 2017. https://sheshredsmag.com/the-legends-ida-presti/.

Wade, Graham. "Tradition and Modernity: The Legacy of Ida Presti." *Classical Guitar*, April 1994.

Wade, Graham. *A Concise History of the Classic Guitar* (Pacific, MO: Mel Bay Publications, 2001), 103.

— CAROL KAYE —

Ballard, Toni. "Berklee Welcomes Legendary Studio Bassist Carol Kaye." *Berklee College of Music,* October 18, 2000. https://college.berklee.edu/news/4554/berklee-welcomes-carol-kaye-for-bassdayze.

Farber, Jim. "The Wrecking Crew Documentary Profiles the Secret Players Behind Many 1960s and '70s Rock Hits." *New York Daily News,* March 9, 2015. https://www.nydailynews.com/entertainment/music/meet-secret-musicians-made-1960s-great-article-1.2143270.

Foley, Sue. "'If You Know Your Chords, You Can Pick Up Anything Onstage': Carol Kaye Talks Jazz Guitar." *GuitarPlayer.com,* January 26, 2023. https://www.guitarplayer.com/players/if-you-know-your-chords-you-can-pick-up-anything-onstage-carol-kaye-talks-jazz-guitar.

Reilly, Phoebe. "The Beach Girl Behind the Beach Boys." *Vulture,* April 19, 2016. https://www.vulture.com/2016/04/carol-kaye-sets-record-straight.html.

Willman, Chris. "Wrecking Crew Bassist Carol Kaye Slams 'Mrs. Maisel' Homage: 'I Am Not a Cartoon.'" *Variety,* January 3, 2020. https://variety.com/2020/music/news/wrecking-crew-bassist-carol-kaye-slams-marvelous-mrs-maisel-homage-1203455483/.

Carol Kaye (official website). https://www.carolkaye.com.

— SUSAN TEDESCHI —

Hudak, Joseph. "Tedeschi Trucks Band on Reinvention, Tragedy, and Perseverance." *Rolling Stone,* August 22, 2022.

Herzhaft, Gérard. *Encyclopedia of the Blues* (Fayetteville: University of Arkansas Press, 1992).

Susan Tedeschi (official website). https://www.susantedeschi.com.

— MIMI FOX —

"Biography." MimiFox.com. Accessed April 7, 2025. https://www.mimifoxguitar.com/bio.

"Mimi Fox: Finding Freedom in Jazz." *Guitar Player*, March 2016.

Mimi Fox (official website). https://www.mimifoxguitar.com.

— CINDY CASHDOLLAR —

Cobb, Michael. "Cindy Cashdollar: A Slide Guitarist Legend and Woodstock Native." *Inside + Out Upstate NY*, March 12, 2022. https://insideandoutupstateny.com/cindy-cashdollar-slide-guitarist-legend-and-woodstock-native/.

Foley, Sue. "Cindy Cashdollar Explains the Evolution of the Steel Guitar." *GuitarPlayer.com*, October 1, 2021. https://www.guitarplayer.com/players/cindy-cashdollar-explains-the-evolution-of-the-steel-guitar.

Cindy Cashdollar (official website). https://www.cindycashdollar.com.

— MARIAN HALL —

Arnold, Richard E. *Country Style, USA: The History of Radio Transcriptions in American Country Music* (Nashville: Country Music Hall of Fame, 1997).

Bird, Larry. "The Golden Era of Steel Guitar." *Vintage Guitar*, January 2006.

Cashdollar, Cindy. "Marian Hall: First Lady of the Steel Guitar." *Vintage Guitar*, September 2004. https://www.vintageguitar.com/2993/marian-hall/.

Foley, Sue. "'You Gotta Really Want to Do This Thing and Do It for the Love of It': Steel-Guitar Pioneer Marian Hall Shares Some Age-Old Wisdom for Musicians." *GuitarPlayer.com*, March 10, 2023. https://www.guitarplayer.com/players/you-gotta-really-want-to-do-this-thing-and-do-it-for-the-love-of-it-steel-guitar-pioneer-marian-hall-offers-some-sound-advice-for-musicians.

— ETTA BAKER —

Duffy, Timothy. *A Soulful Sound: Music Makers of the Carolinas* (Chapel Hill: Music Maker Relief Foundation, 2005).

"Etta Baker: National Heritage Fellow, 1991." *National Endowment for the Arts*. Accessed January 12, 2025. https://www.arts.gov/honors/heritage/etta-baker.

North Carolina Arts Council. "Folk Heritage Award Recipients." Accessed January 12, 2025. https://www.ncarts.org.

Simone, Susan. "Etta Baker." *Music Maker Relief Foundation*. Accessed October 26, 2020. https://musicmaker.org/artists/etta-baker/.

Photo Credits

Every effort has been made to identify and credit copyright holders. Unless otherwise indicated, image credits were provided by the artists. Some images are believed to be in the public domain.

Charo, courtesy of Alamy Stock Photo
Liona Boyd, photo by Henry Grossman
Nancy Wilson, photo by Janet Macoska
Suzi Quatro, courtesy of Alamy Stock Photo
Kathy Valentine, photo by Christopher Durst
Vicki Peterson, courtesy of Alamy Stock Photo
Jennifer Batten, photo by Sam Emerson
Rory Block, photo by Sergio Kurhajec
Sharon Isbin, photo by Darnell Renee
Ida Presti, courtesy of Alamy Stock Photo
Carol Kaye, courtesy of David Zaworski
Susan Tedeschi, courtesy of Alamy Stock Photo
Cindy Cashdollar, photo by Rob Buck